ELECTION OBSERVATION AND DEMOCRATIZATION IN AFRICA

Also by Jon Abbink

HISTORY AND CULTURE: Essays on the Work of Eric R. Wolf
(*co-editor*)

MYTHO-LÉGENDES ET HISTOIRE: l'énigme de l'ethnogenèse des
Beta Esra'el

ERITREO–ETHIOPIAN STUDIES IN SOCIETY AND HISTORY
A Supplementary Bibliography 1960–1995

Election Observation and Democratization in Africa

Edited by

Jon Abbink
Senior Researcher
African Studies Centre
Leiden
The Netherlands

and

Gerti Hesseling
Director
African Studies Centre
Leiden
The Netherlands

First published in Great Britain 2000 by
MACMILLAN PRESS LTD
Houndmills, Basingstoke, Hampshire RG21 6XS and London
Companies and representatives throughout the world

A catalogue record for this book is available from the British Library.

ISBN 0–333–76308–4

 First published in the United States of America 2000 by
ST. MARTIN'S PRESS, INC.,
Scholarly and Reference Division,
175 Fifth Avenue, New York, N.Y. 10010

ISBN 0–312–22394–3

Library of Congress Cataloging-in-Publication Data
Election observation and democratization in Africa / edited by Jon
Abbink and Gerti Hesseling.
p.   cm.
Includes bibliographical references and index.
ISBN 0–312–22394–3
1. Election monitoring—Africa, Sub-Saharan.   2. Elections–
–Africa, Sub-Saharan.   3. Democratization—Africa, Sub-Saharan.
I. Abbink, J.   II. Hesseling, Gerti.
JQ1879.A5E42   1999
324.967'0329—dc21   99–15593
                                                         CIP

10   9   8   7   6   5   4   3   2   1
09   08   07   06   05   04   03   02   01   00

Printed and bound in Great Britain by
Antony Rowe Ltd, Chippenham, Wiltshire

Contents

Contributors

Jon Abbink is an anthropologist and a senior researcher at the Afrika-Studiecentrum at Leiden University. He previously worked at the Universities of Amsterdam and Nijmegen. His Ph.D. research in the 1980s was on Ethiopian immigrants in Israel. His recent research is on culture, violence and ethnicity, and on socio-political developments and democratization in North-east Africa, especially Ethiopia. He has written on Ethiopian Jews in Israel, Ethiopian ethnology, material culture, and on the epistemology of anthropology. Among his publications are *Mytho-légendes et Histoire: l'énigme de l'ethnogenèse des Beta Esra'el* (1991) and *History and Culture: Essays on the Work of Eric R. Wolf* (co-edited, 1992).

Wim van Binsbergen is Professor of Intercultural Philosophy at Erasmus University, Rotterdam, and senior researcher at the African Studies Centre, Leiden, since 1977, where in the 1980s he headed the Department of Political-Historical Studies. Until 1998 he was Professor of Anthropology at the Free University (Amsterdam). He has done extensive fieldwork in various African countries, among them Tunisia, Guinea-Bissau, Zambia and Botswana. Among his major publications are: *Religious Change in Zambia* (1981), *Old Modes of Production and Capitalist Encroachment* (edited with P. Geschiere, 1985), *Theoretical Explorations in African Religion* (edited with M. Schoffeleers, 1985), and *Tears of Rain: Ethnicity and History in Central Western Zambia* (1992). His most recent edited book is *Black Athena: Ten Years After* (1997). He worked as lecturer at the University of Lusaka, Zambia, and was a visiting professor at the universities of Manchester, Berlin and Durban-Westville (South Africa). He has also written poetry and novels.

Robert Buijtenhuijs is a political scientist (Ph.D. 1971, Paris) and a senior researcher at the African Studies Centre, Leiden. His main research interests are African revolutionary movements and revolts, political developments in Chad, and democratization processes in Africa. Some of his main publications on these subjects are: *Le Mouvement Mau-Mau: une Révolte*

Paysanne et Anti-Coloniale en Afrique Noire (1971), _La Conférence Nationale Souveraine de Tchad: un Essai d'Histoire Immédiate_ (1993), and (with C. Thiriot) _Démocratisation en Afrique du Sud du Sahara, 1992–1995: un Bilan de la Literature_ (1995, also in English version). His book on the elections and the democratization process in Chad is forthcoming (Karthala, Paris, 1999).

Oda van Cranenburgh is a political scientist and lecturer at the Department of Political Science at the University of Leiden. Her Ph.D. thesis was on Tanzania (_The Widening Gyre: the Tanzanian One-party State and Policy towards Rural Cooperatives_, 1990). She has published on the African one-party state, democratization in Africa, and Dutch policies for development cooperation. She is also a member of the Advisory Council on International Affairs to the Netherlands Government.

Martin Doornbos is Professor of Political Science at the Institute of Social Studies, The Hague, and associated with UNRISD, Geneva, on the the 'War-torn Societies Project'. His research interests have been in the dynamics of state–society relations in Africa and India, institutional dimensions of conflict and collaboration, and the politics of resource allocation in various fields. His many publications on Africa include _Beyond Conflict in the Horn: the Prospects for Peace, Recovery and Development in Ethiopia, Somalia, Eritrea and Sudan_ (co-edited, 1991); _Not All the King's Men: Inequality as a Political Instrument in Ankole, Uganda_ (1978); and _Developing Winners and Losers: Institutionalizing Development Policies and Resource Strategies in Eastern Africa and India_ (in press). He is Editor of the journal _Development and Change_ and Contributing Editor of the _Review of African Political Economy_.

Ton Dietz is Professor of Political Environmental Geography at the University of Amsterdam (Amsterdam Research Institute for Global Issues and Development Studies, a member institute of the CERES Research School). His Ph.D. thesis was on the Pokot of northern Kenya (_Pastoralists in Dire Straits_, 1992). He has extensive research experience in Kenya and published about a large variety of development issues in that country, particularly development interventions and pastoralism. With

D. Foeken he recently wrote about democratization, elections and ethnicity in the Dutch journal *Geografie*.

Rijk van Dijk is an anthropologist and affiliated to the Afrika-Studiecentrum, Leiden, as a member of the research-group on Globalization and the WOTRO research programme *Globalization and the Construction of Communal Identities*. He has done fieldwork in Malawi on the rise of charismatic Pentecostalism in urban areas *(Young Malawian Puritans: Young Born-Again Preachers in a Present-day African Urban Environment*, Utrecht 1992). He has also been involved in UNDP election observation during the first free Malawian elections of 1994. He has published articles on Pentecostalism, globalization and the anthropology of religion in many professional journals. Among his recent publications are a chapter in J. Haynes' edited volume on *Religion, Globalization and Political Culture in the Third World* (1998). His current research focuses on charismatic Pentecostal churches in Accra and Kumasi and their relations with Ghanaian diaspora communities in The Hague (the Netherlands).

Stephen Ellis is a senior researcher at the Afrika-Studiecentrum, Leiden. He has done research on history and politics in a number of African countries including Madagascar, South Africa and Liberia. Among his recent works are *The Criminalization of the State in Africa* (co-authored with Jean-François Bayart and Béatrice Hibou) and *The Mask of Anarchy: the Roots of Liberia's War*, which will be published in 1999. He is currently a co-editor of the journal *African Affairs* and one of the joint editors of the *African Issues* series published by the International African Institute. From 1986 to 1991 he edited the newsletter *Africa Confidential*.

Dick Foeken studied human geography at the University of Amsterdam. His Ph.D. thesis was on *The Partition of Central Africa: a Politico-Geographical Analysis* (1994). Presently he is a senior researcher at the Afrika-Studicentrum, Leiden. Since the mid-1980s he has been involved in several research projects in Kenya, notably in the fields of food and nutrition, rural employment, small-scale enterprises, and urban agriculture. Major recent publications include *Tied to the Land: Living Conditions of*

Labourers on Large Farms in Trans Nzoia District, Kenya (co-authored, 1994), *Seasons and Nutrition at the Kenya Coast* (1995), and *The Kenya Coast: Problems and Perspectives* (edited, 1998).

Bas de Gaay Fortman holds MAs in Economics and Law. His Ph.D. dissertation was on *Theory of Competition Policy: a Confrontation of Economic, Political and Legal Principles* (1966). He taught at the Free University in Amsterdam and was Acting Head of Economics at the University of Zambia in Lusaka (1967–71). From 1971 to 1977 he was a member of the Second Chamber of Dutch Parliament as Leader of the Radical Party (PPR), at that time participating in a coalition government. In 1971 he became Professor of Economic Development at the Institute of Social Studies (The Hague). In 1977 he was appointed to the Chair of Political Economy there. Until 1991 he also served as a member of the First Chamber of the Dutch States-General. His publications are in the fields of economic order, the political economy of government and jurisprudence, and of security and conflict. With the economist J. Tinbergen he founded the Association of Economists for Peace. His current research interests are state formation and disintegration, and projects on economic, social and cultural rights. His latest book (with B. Klein Goldewijk) is *God and the Goods: Global Economy in a Civilizational Perspective* (1998).

Gerti Hesseling is a legal scholar and did her Ph.D. on constitutional law and political history in Senegal, which was published as *Histoire Politique du Sénégal – Institutions, Droit et Société* (Paris 1985). She has a long research experience in West Africa, particularly concerning land tenure, decentralization processes and constitutionalism. She carried out many consultancies for international organizations, such as the World Bank. She was also a member of the *Club du Sahel*. Since 1978 Dr Hesseling has been attached to the Afrika-Studiecentrum, Leiden, and has been its Director since 1996.

Ineke van Kessel is a historian and a researcher at the Afrika-Studiecentrum, Leiden, specializing in the recent history of South Africa. Her doctoral thesis on internal anti-apartheid resistance in South Africa in the 1980s was published in 1998 under the title *'Beyond our Wildest Dreams': the United Democratic*

Front and the Transformation of South Africa. She also writes as a journalist on current affairs in Africa and has been engaged as a media consultant. During the 1994 general elections in South Africa, she served as a United Nations observer.

Marie-France Lange has a doctorate in sociology and is a specialist on educational systems in Africa. She is currently Chargée de Recherche at ORSTOM (the French Institute for Scientific Research on Development and International Cooperation). Since 1984 she has worked in Togo (six years) and in Mali (four years), and has done missions in a number of other African countries. She has written articles on education in Africa and published two monographs (*Cent-Cinquante Ans de Scolarisation au Togo* (1991), and *L'Ecole au Togo* (1998)). She recently also edited *L'École et les Filles en Afrique – Scolarisation sous Conditions* (1998). At present she is engaged in sociological and political-science research on the evolution of educational systems in Africa and conditions of supply and demand as well as on the relations between knowledge and power in Africa.

Marcel Rutten is a human geographer and senior researcher at the Afrika-Studiecentrum, Leiden. He has done extensive and long-term research on development issues, water and soil management and land tenure in Kenya, especially in the Maasai districts. Among his major publications are: *Selling Wealth to Buy Poverty: the Process of the Individualization of Landownership among the Maasai Pastoralists of Kajiado District, Kenya, 1890–1990* (1992), and *The Diversity of Development: Essays in Honor of Jan Kleinpenning* (1997, co-edited). In 1997 he was a staff coordinator of the Election Observation Centre in Kenya, a group of local and external observers from Western and donor-country embassies monitoring the presidential and parliamentary elections.

Preface
Gerti Hesseling

Since the early nineties the presence of international election observers has become a familiar sight at elections in Africa. Many Western donor-countries are of the opinion that elections in Africa are an essential contribution to the establishment of a democratic political order and therefore deserve support. The Netherlands Minister for Development Cooperation noted in a recent memo to Parliament that the purpose of election observation was threefold: to express solidarity with emerging democracies, to strengthen public confidence in the electoral process, and to contribute to the free and fair conduct of elections. Between 1992 and 1996 the Netherlands has sent election observers to ten African countries, and in early 1997 requests for other missions from at least an equal number of countries were under consideration to be carried out in that same year.

In view of the growing demand for observer or monitoring missions and the relatively limited expertise in this field, it is not surprising that there is an increasing need felt on the part of policy-makers and international organizations to develop new approaches and guidelines as well as exchange views with scholars and researchers on the issues involved in election monitoring in non-Western settings, with less economic means and less secure institutional structures. The founding of the Stockholm-based IDEA (Institute for the Development of Electoral Assistance) as well as the UN Electoral Assistance Unit are witness to this trend.

This book emanates from a day-long seminar held at the Dutch Ministry of Foreign Affairs in February 1997, organized to exchange views between academic researchers, observers, and policy-makers on elections and democratization in Africa in general. Apart from the general aim of stimulating synergy between the various parties involved, the idea was to promote insights into the recurrent problems and eventual solutions to matters of election monitoring in Africa. On the basis of this meeting, researchers were invited to write a chapter reflecting on their own research findings, and/or place their experiences as election observers, either officially or unofficially, in a wider perspective.

Next to offering new academic perspectives on the highly topical issue of democratization and election observation in Africa, the aim of this book is to stimulate dialogue between research, policy and practice on this subject. In recent years, the idea has gained ground that academic research can be a strategic instrument for development cooperation, not only in its preparatory stages but also in its implementation and evaluation. The Dutch Ministry of Development Cooperation, for instance, has asked the African Studies Centre (Leiden) to carry out an extensive critical study of the literature on democratization in Africa (see R. Buijtenhuijs and E. Rijnierse, *Democratization in Sub-Saharan Africa 1989–1992*, Leiden: African Studies Centre, 1993; and R. Buijtenhuijs and C. Thiriot, *Démocratisation en Afrique au Sud du Sahara 1992–1995*, Leiden: African Studies Centre, 1995). These studies, led by Dr R. Buijtenhuijs, have shown, among other things, that election studies in Africa are on the increase, but that most of the work consists of case studies, dealing with election procedures, electoral fraud, corruption, and problems of neo-patrimonialism.

Recent surveys of election studies in Africa have been offered in special issues of the journals *African Journal of Political Science* 2(1) 1997, *Afrika Spectrum* 31(1) 1996, and very recently *Politique Africaine* 69 (1998). However, as R. Otayek noted in his introduction to the latter journal, the field of 'election sociology' is not yet well-developed. When studying the many scientific publications of the last decade on democratization in general and elections in particular, it is striking that few specifically address the phenomenon of election observation or monitoring. Most works, apart from manuals, deal again with case studies. (Interestingly, much of the literature is coming from German scholars: see for instance U. Engel *et al.*, *Deutsche Wahlbeobachtung in Afrika*, Hamburg: Institut für Afrikakunde, 1996; and the journal *Afrika Spectrum*, which has a regular series of articles on monitoring missions in Africa.)

The case studies in this book, presented in Part II, are placed within an historical-political context of elections in Africa (Part I). The Introduction is aimed at discussing some more theoretical issues in the study of elections and their observation in Africa, while Part III contains a retrospective analysis of the recent policy of the Netherlands, followed by an evaluation of a new model of donor-country observation tried out in the Kenyan general elections of December 1997.

The breadth and detail of the studies in this book may contribute to a more informed reflection on the phenomenon of election observation, and to a further elucidation of its historical, cultural and political contexts. In addition, the study of elections and their observation is relevant for the development and evaluation of policies in this field. We realize that the use of research findings in policy and political practice is often a diffuse and unpredictable process, but are confident that this book can stimulate dialogue between researchers, observers and policy-makers. We finally express the sincere hope that new insights will be translated into policies which will benefit the citizens of the African countries struggling to establish and sustain democracy.

As a final note, the editors would like to express their thanks to the Ministry of Foreign Affairs of the Netherlands, especially to Ms Kanta Adhin and Mr Jan Gijs Schouten, for their assistance in the organization of the 1997 Seminar and for supporting the idea of this book.

Introduction: Rethinking Democratization and Election Observation
J. Abbink

This book brings together studies of the broad theme of elections and democratization in Africa since roughly 1989. In this year, the so-called 'Third Wave' of global democratization, which is held to have started in the 1970s (see Huntington 1991), entered a new stage in Africa. A movement of mass protests and demonstrations then emerged against the authoritarian regimes (Engel *et al.* 1996: 1) that had installed themselves after an initial period of multi-party or single-party politics in the post-independence era. While this tide of popular unrest partly coincided with the end of the Cold War – after the fall of the Berlin Wall in 1989 – its origins predate it, and are rooted in socio-economic and political problems of African societies.

In 1989 also, the World Bank published its report on 'good governance', claiming that much of the African crisis was due to incompetent or irresponsible state leadership and administration (*Sub-Saharan Africa: from Crisis to Sustainable Growth*). This report was important because of the vital role that the Bank and its sister institution the IMF – for better or for worse – played in the developing countries, *and* because of its message: nobody would doubt the idea itself that good governance is of great significance to commonly accepted goals like economic growth, poverty reduction, sustainable development, and social justice. Still, the concept of good governance has been elusive, as have the World Bank policies to durably enhance it. Its programmes to encourage transparent government, institutional capacity or efficient administration have often been drawn up with only marginal attention to the wider socio-political context.[1] The approach is not one inspired primarily by democratic principles as such, but by a global economic and administrative logic

1

defined in the developed world. In general then, the processes of economic liberalization and administrative reform in Africa in the past decade have been hesitant and show many setbacks.

The tide of political change and democratization efforts in Africa as initiated by citizens' mass protests and the critical opposition has equally yielded inconclusive results.[2] New political openings occurred, but more salient are the continuities with earlier trends of autocratic governance and monopolization instead of sharing of power (cf. Ottaway 1997). Certainly when compared with the high aspirations voiced by the masses and the critical opposition in the late 1980s, it seems that no real irreversible breakthroughs toward democracy have been achieved (see Bratton and Van de Walle 1997, Ihonvbere 1996, Daloz and Quantin 1997, Ottaway 1997). However, there have been gains: many autocrats have gone, most Cold War-related civil wars and regional conflicts have ended, there is more press freedom and freedom of association, more economic opportunity, and, to stay within the orbit of this book, many more elections were held, introducing at least some amount of challenge and competitiveness in the political process. Nevertheless, this does not necessarily imply that 'democracy' is closer now than it was twenty years ago. Indeed, critical observers like the Cameroonian scholar A. Mbembe speak of democracy as only a domain of the 'imaginary', not of reality (Mbembe 1996: 69). New-style autocratic rulers often use electoral procedures as rituals to divide and rule or stay in power, and general social and legal conditions for a consolidation of democratization remain weak. Perhaps the most that can be said is that a broad discourse of democratization and liberalization has been opened up, both within the various African countries and between them and the 'donor-countries' from the industrialized world. This discourse – though it has the danger of being assimilated to a predominantly economic idiom of 'liberalizing markets', reduction of state spending and influence, and so on – has not yet led to the institutionalization of sustainable democratic structures and rule of law regimes. But a new awareness may have been created to deal with issues not only of good governance, but also of meeting the aspirations for democratic decision-making, participation and economic opportunities for the population at large.

In discussing these issues, the perennial question comes up of what 'democracy' is: both for African populations, and in general, as a global ideal. Is the argument that in African conditions of resource scarcity (see Mbembe 1996), economic unpredictability and a weak or arbitrary legal system, democratic ideals must be 'adapted' or cannot work? This is, in our view, only true in the sense that establishing institutional democracy in African conditions will be a long-term process, dependent on the reduction of elite competition at the national level, on broadening the social basis for effective political communication, on economic stability and on international relations with encouraging donor-countries and trade partners. But the evidence on attitudes and opinions of the common African public as well as the middle classes and intellectuals seems to substantiate the existence of underlying ideals of democratic culture, despite the adverse economic conditions which may perpetually put it at risk. On this point it is necessary for both academics, policy-makers and donors to pay more attention to the views and ideals of the wider population. I cite here one example of anthropological research on conceptions of 'democracy' in Uganda by M. Karlström (1996). This author noted that for the average Ugandan the concept of 'democracy', which is strongly related to 'civility' (Karlström 1996: 486), consisted of at least the following elements: a) freedom from oppression, b) freedom of speech and expressing opinions without being sanctioned for it, c) fair and impartial judgement in judgement of dispute and court cases, d) standards of civility, proper conduct and manners, and respect for legitimate authority. Such ideas and values have also been registered by other authors doing local-level research in African settings. They often existed *prior* to the emergence of modern ideas and practices of formal political democracy in the Western sense.

While it is difficult for donor-countries, international organizations or academics to take note of local perspectives on power, legitimacy and governance and to directly base policy on them, the fact nevertheless remains that policies to enhance democracy should take into account such views and not only focus on the ideas and schemes presented by the African elites, who usually have their own agenda.

In assessing democratization there are also other issues to consider, such as the meaning of self-determination (in African plural societies), and the relation between individual rights, group rights and socio-cultural rights. In addition, what is especially striking in the conceptions of most ordinary Africans is the frequent emphasis they put on a fair, reasonably independent, non-corrupt and non-politicized *legal system*: the *sense of justice*, which most African regimes have tried so hard to undermine and destroy in the past decades, is a core value which defines the amount of public *trust* that people have in their government, or in government in general. In its turn, trust is of course a core value of any democratic society. On this issue, social research, especially by historians and anthropologists, could still contribute much to a better understanding of processes of social reconstruction and democratization, and will yield insights which could be taken into account by policymakers and international organizations.

The topic of elections and their observation or monitoring is one important element in the efforts to stimulate political liberalization and democratization in Africa (although the latter process also depends on, among other things, patterns of economic assistance and cooperation, the role of the military, and issues of ethno-regional pluralism). Elections are not new in Africa: since the late colonial period and especially after the Second World War many countries saw an extension of electoral processes.[3] Neither is election observation a new thing developed only recently in Africa: in Latin America is has been practised for decades (for instance, by the OAS), and the UN has been monitoring and observing elections and referendums across the world since its founding in 1945. But election observation has definitely gained new relevance in conditions of political liberalization in Africa. Furthermore, in 1991 the UN established a new agency called the Electoral Assistance Unit, which has also been active in Africa.

The original scope of 'election observation' was limited: it was an attempt to ensure 'free and fair elections' (Pastor 1995: 407). It has inherent structural constraints, and cannot in itself decisively contribute to the building of a democratic culture. Many observer missions have also failed, by not fulfilling their mandate of observing in a *critical* fashion. However, the signal function of observation in Africa has been significant, and much

– probably too much – was expected of it both by donor-countries and by local voters.

There has been a spate of literature on this subject, largely in the form of field reports and of articles by observers (some of the more valuable are Bjornlund et al. 1992; Geisler 1993; Pilon 1994; Meyns 1995; Fengler and Mair 1996; Nevitte and Canton 1997; Carothers 1997; Elklit and Svensson 1997). The only significant book-length study of election observation is the one edited by Engel *et al.* (1996), a valuable in-depth evaluation of the German experience.[4] There are also manual-like monographs on election observation. These have a more limited scope and are prescriptive more than evaluative and analytic (for some of the most interesting, see Garber 1984; Mair 1997; Tostensen *et al.* 1997; to a lesser extent, Goodwin-Gill 1994). All these studies are essential, but in many of them one notes a tendency of repetitiveness, or at least of identifying common problems and suggesting fairly similar solutions. Really new or striking insights are getting scarce, although the new factual information of the cases studies is important. Indeed, the issues identified by, for instance, Geisler in her path-breaking article (1993) still hold relevance and are widely discussed until this day.

Perhaps this indicates an emerging consensus on the nature and value of election observation. We might think here of the following points which keep coming up in the discussions: a) the need to seriously take into account the *legal* and *political conditions* under which elections are organized and actually take place; hence, more long-term observation would be advisable; b) cooperation between foreign observers and resident diplomats, who know conditions in the country better, should be developed; c) the role of domestic observers should be taken more seriously, and if need be they should be supported with training, materials and funding; d) a 'code of conduct' should be developed for foreign observers; e) in connection with the foregoing, some professionalization of foreign observers should perhaps be aimed at, for example in recruitment, training and actual observation activities; f) the nature of the post-election statements by foreign observers should be constructively critical, enumerating positive and negative aspects, and should not *a priori* take the form of a watered-down overall consensus judgement.

This book includes studies on both electoral processes (and especially of the role of foreign observers therein) as well as on general issues of the historical and socio-cultural backgrounds or contexts of democratization, elections and political legitimacy. Within this broad range, one can discern two main lines: a) the line of political scientists and political geographers, which focuses more on the actual procedures of elections and their observation and contains rich and essential empirical material, and b) that of sociologists, anthropologists or contemporary historians, more concerned with the contextual factors which tell us more about the underlying representations and habits related to local political culture, regime formation,[5] and legitimacy in African countries, as they interact with the actual organization and conduct of elections. The nature of political power, authority and the central state are homogenous but subject to different cultural interpretations and practices (cf. Schatzberg 1993; Tall 1995). Also, the democratic process itself may initially lend itself to confusion and fear (see Van Dijk's chapter below). An unmediated imposition of the logic of democracy in its late twentieth-century Western form is impossible, and by implication the practice of election observation is not unproblematic even if the legal procedures put in place have been followed. This does not necessarily mean that democracy has to be 'adapted to conditions in Africa' (a somewhat paternalistic argument), and that one has to favour relativism. But in order to gauge whether democratization – in the sense of the general aim of enhancing political communication, political freedoms and equitable social justice – has really been served, an analysis of political culture and social context is necessary as well, because of a) the need to identify conditions of inequality that inhibit that aim, and b) the fact that people's ideals and cultural commitments vary significantly across socio-cultural settings.

It is our view that advances in the study of elections and their international observation – both in the academic, comparative sense, and in the more political sense of enhancing democracy and the rule of law state (*Rechtstaat*),[6] ideals upheld not only by donor countries but also, at least rhetorically, by most authoritarian regimes – can only come about by an analytic broadening of the view on elections and democratization and by a fruitful *combination* of the two approaches mentioned above: the political science and the historical-anthropological perspective.

On the one hand, it seems obvious that yet another series of election observation reports from the field and articles by political scientists and observers will not generate many new structural insights, apart from up-to-date advice on how to improve procedures and practices for the next occasion. There also seems to be an emerging consensus on what meaningful elections, *ceteris paribus*, really are. A reasonably complete list of criteria and issues could now be drawn up which allows us, as people concerned to see the causes of democracy, equality and justice advanced in Africa, to organize reasonable and meaningful elections (not only 'free and fair' – a qualification which is more and more difficult as the crucial indicator of democratic process) and further the growth of a democratic, civic culture. Such a list could be of use in improving current practices of election observation. Some good examples exist (Goodwin-Gill 1994; Mair 1997; Von Meijenfeldt 1995), and lists will also be presented in this book (see for example Van Cranenburgh and Rutten).

But, also for political scientists, this alone is not sufficient. Sustainable democracy needs the consolidation of institutional, social and legal frameworks which make the process of open political communication *independent* of the persons who happen to be in power. The analysis of elections and their observation should hence be seen as a stepping stone to exploring underlying and related issues of democratization *beyond* these occasional election happenings.

On the other hand, sociological-anthropological and historical analysis of these issues of democratization and elections cannot do without drawing upon the latest information from political science, and must continuously test its assumptions and generalities on the context and constitution of power and politics against field realities. Especially the application of specific political science theories (see Hyden 1996 for a brief survey) in these approaches would be very useful. Hence, an integrative view is necessary, with the ultimate aim to come to a long-term evaluation of the past ten-year episode of election observation in Africa in historical and cultural terms. Such a perspective could also stimulate reflection on issues of democracy as a 'trans-cultural' ideal, on the concepts of human rights and rule of law, and on the discourse of diplomacy as the political buffer in international relations occasionally subverting the lofty and easily proclaimed ideals. Multi-party democracy, elections for a national state parliament, and the *Rechtstaat* are undoubtedly 'Western' in their first formulation, having taken a long time to mature there. And even in the West the gains are not irreversible, witnessing the recent elections in Austria and France, and seeing the steady erosion of the legislative power in favour of the executive. Europe is perhaps still haunted by the ghost of the Nazi rise to power after general elections in Germany in 1933.[7] Election observation – like development aid – in its post-Second World War form, is also in large part a Western invention and should be looked upon as such: the result of a historical and cultural conjuncture and which is not beyond scrutiny and criticism.

Recognizing the fact that election observation has been seen as a means to enhance democratization, several chapters in this book pay attention to shortcomings and controversial aspects of observation (cf. also Carothers 1997: 21–6). In recent years, these have been brought out for a variety of reasons: the meaning of elections and their observation in countries with a notoriously difficult and undemocratic political system is unclear, the mandates of the observers are often not clear enough, their standards and methodology are elusive, the presence of observers and their often hesitant reports can be easily misappropriated by African governments and bent in their favour, donor countries may have other interests or 'hidden agendas' and in the end may even not care much about long-term democratization when economic perspectives of the country in question seem to improve.

As the cultural and political-philosophical underpinnings of both African democratization and election observation are often not fully realized either, we also intend, at least, to put such more fundamental matters on the agenda of scientific debate and stimulate the debates to rise above the empiricist dimension of only describing elections and observation in Africa as a technical exercise. This literature of course has other aims marked by a prescriptive and also repetitive tone, and often tends not to take into account long-term developments in political regime formation and mutation and their effect on democratization efforts in African countries. Such studies should be valued for their full and critical reporting as well as for their offering many valuable suggestions for policy improvements, but they cannot be the last word on the *meaning* and *future course* of election observation and democratization in Africa.

But we also feel a measure of scepticism: toward the pace and depth of democratization in Africa, but also toward the all too pragmatic and sometimes compromising attitude of those observers and donor agencies purporting to stand for democracy and rule of law, but putting the rules and principles on hold in view of certain economic and political gains they expect. While this may not be the general rule and the dilemmas of observation should not be underestimated (Kumar 1998: 11–12), this attitude subverts the idea of election observation as a serious signalling device for autocratic regimes in Africa. A weak or ambiguous statement will not encourage the culture of democracy. A long-term view on African politics and its international relations context also cautions us as to the transformative potential and the durability of elections, election observation and Western (and other donor-countries') declared support for processes of democratization. The example of Zambia is a case in point: the euphoria of certain observers and analysts on the peaceful transfer of power from Kaunda to Chiluba (Anglin 1992: 33; Bjornlund *et al.* 1992: 431) seems naive and premature in retrospect, considering the discomfiture of a new regime in many respects worse than its predecessor. So despite a seemingly democratic transition things can go wrong. More than just poll watching is needed to make meaningful statements about democratization (Carothers 1997: 22), and democratization, in Africa as elsewhere, will obviously take time (cf. Bratton and Van de Walle 1997: 268). In a sense, the study of foreign election observation is *also* a study of democracy and political culture in Western (and other) donor-countries where the democratic polity has to face new challenges both of a social and technological nature. A comparative perspective on the global varieties of 'democracy' would highlight the nature of similarities and differences in the experience of establishing and sustaining democratic institutions and of the upholding of democratic discourse and values.

This book concentrates on democratization and election observation in Africa because some of the most interesting and chal-
lenging material to study this topic comes from there. It
contains studies on many aspects of the subject: on the actual
vote-casting process, the role of parties and mass media,
the actual observation practices of foreign and domestic teams,
the role of international organizations and NGOs, and on
background issues of political culture, regime formation and
legitimation, the role of (armed) force, and attempts at peace-
making and reconciliation.

The various contributions here may also have relevance in
that prospective observers can, during their preparation and
training for observation periods, not only reflect further on the
practical and moral issues involved, but also may take into
account the wider political and cultural context of elections and
their observation as foreigners. Without considering the historical, social and political conditions before and after the actual
feat of observation itself, no reliable or credible evaluation
can be made on what role the elections play in a process of
democratization.

Electoral observation is, in a sense, only the first layer of the
policy of promoting good governance and democratic institutions in formerly autocratic countries. The second layer, in
which it is embedded, is that of the *conditions* of politics, regime
formation, political communication between elites and broad
masses of the population, and the nature of the judicial system
in the country concerned. On this account Africa is still in deep
problems as far as democratic institution-building and elite
mentality is concerned (see Bratton and Van de Walle's
qualified pessimistic assessment, 1997: 268; compare also the
studies in Daloz and Quantin 1997). This is mainly because of
ingrained 'neo-patrimonial' political systems[8] – that is, political systems of governance dominated by personalized authority,
patronage and clientelism, private appropriation of public
funds, selective resource distribution, nepotism and ethnic or
other favouritism (cf. Bratton and Van de Walle 1997: 61f). The
fact of regimes being neo-patrimonial is related to the issue of
resource scarcity and the idea of zero-sum competition and
access to state funds at the expense of others (Mbembe 1996).
Another, related, development is the growing 'criminalization'
of states in Africa (cf. Bayart *et al.* 1997). This is not an

exclusively African phenomenon, but prominent nevertheless. It goes without saying that criminalization – while tuned very well into the global economy – subverts democratic ideals and practices of political accountability, transparency and control, legal impartiality, or resource access and allocation.

For a proper perspective on democratization processes beyond elections it seems inescapable to examine their connection to other social preconditions of politics and governance in Africa, such as:

- the ideology of power as indivisible, entailing a view of opposition and freedom of opinion and organization as 'illegitimate' or 'divisive';
- enduring material scarcity: the state is then a machine for resource distribution to capture and a prize that cannot just be given up;
- entrenched neo-patrimonialism (see above), with personalized power and clientelism;
- legal insecurity and arbitrariness, suggesting a lack of an independent judiciary and a systematic subversion of rule of law ideals;
- the constitution and reproduction of (elite) power in non-formal, non-institutionalized domains and networks. This is the 'invisible' aspect of African politics and regime maintenance.[9]

Statements by observers as to whether elections have been conducive to the establishment of democracy in a country cannot be made while neglecting the impact of such conditions on the political process and on the attitudes of the common people. Certainly a *theoretical* explanation of why elections that seem to be reasonably free and fair do not lead to more democracy and rule of law must draw upon a close analysis of such conditions, as they determine the electoral process and the politics of regime survival.

Elections organized and more or less successfully held in a country with an entrenched autocratic regime not respecting basic rights of its citizens and not according any legitimate role to opposition parties, civic society and an independent judiciary, *have no real meaning*, not even in the widest stretch of the imagination. The attempt of foreign observer units to see the best aspects of the process, declaring the faulty elections a 'step in the right direction' (one of the most worn-out metaphors in this field), and thus come to a joint statement of 'qualified support' or the like, is then an effort in self-delusion and of justifying the effort of funding and observing itself: a form of damage control (if not of downright cynicism in the eyes of the voters in those countries). When this is becoming the habitual practice of foreign observers (as the 1997 Kenyan case again seems to demonstrate), then the critics of foreign election observation are right.

The issues discussed in this volume cover a broad range of phenomena related to election observation and its connection with processes of democratization:

- the historical and ideological context of elections as element in African politics and political liberalization (Van Cranenburgh, Ellis);
- the hopes, promises and possibilities of elections in situations of conflict resolution and establishing civic peace (Van Kessel, De Gaay Fortman). This is a sensitive subject which has not yet been receiving much study, and the two contributions here break new ground;
- wider historical and socio-cultural conditions of politics and elections (Van Dijk, Abbink). These studies relate to cultural representations and historical specificities of a country's 'political culture' and to what could be called the 'imaginary' in politics;
- the fragile texture of election preparation and execution in African countries with a heritage of autocracy and neo-patrimonialism (Doornbos, Dietz and Foeken, Buijtenhuijs, Abbink, Lange);
- 'retrieving' election observation: countering the dangers of its sliding into irrelevance or meaninglessness and thinking about new policies and models to improve election observation (Rutten, Van Cranenburgh).

Most chapters are based on first-hand field experiences of the authors either as official observers or as Africanist scholars carrying out observational field studies in the countries described. They thus can offer not only new factual insights on recent developments in a number of key African countries, but also provide material for reflection on more theoretical and comparative issues related to elections and democratization.

We hope therefore that this book will demonstrate the continued need to study the experiences with election observation in depth, in order to deepen both theoretical and practical knowledge of its potential and meaning, and also to help to adjust over-confident plans and optimistic scenarios.

If we look at things from the political science angle, a crucial point in our view is that the international discourse on 'democratization' should be re-erected on the bedrock of ideas of political and human rights (as indicated by, for instance, Goodwin-Gill 1994, clearly setting out the links between existing international treaties and agreements relating to democratization, elections and humans rights) and of (re)building of state institutions. As we have suggested above, such an approach might be attempted in order to *reconnect* with the views and aspirations of the common people in Africa, who are struggling in the 'informal economies', who are the victims of corruption, nepotism and ethnic discrimination, but are trying to survive and improve their lives. They are yearning for economic breathing space, honesty or at least some legal predictability in business dealings, legal guarantees, and political and media freedoms. We think it is not unfair to say that the diplomats and international organizations have only a rather limited idea of what these views, aspirations and daily struggles of the common people are, and often they are not much interested in them.

It can also be noted that foreigners in Africa, be they diplomats, tourists, businessmen or advisers, suffer from what might be called 'structural amnesia' in their dealings with the country they live in or visit: they do not always take into account recent historical developments, do not remember the peculiarities of local political culture and the impact of crucial events, and 'forget' the long-term political manoeuvres or games played by the power-holders, who are often masters in appropriating the discourse and symbolism of democratization (this subject in itself would be worth a separate study, also to improve the institutional memory on matters such as election observation and policy formulation *vis-à-vis* the developing countries). Among most African elites the conception of many foreigners and donor-country officials as basically gullible and naive is unchanged. Structural amnesia is one of the problems which hinder the faulty democratization process in Africa, next to more commonly identified points such as resource scarcity, economic vulnerability, political instability, zero-sum game thinking, lack of public trust and lack of a dependable and fair legal system. In the context of international assistance and co-operation toward Africa, there is reason to rethink current approaches, perhaps giving attention more than before to legal and judicial matters and enhancing the structure and spirit of a rule of law. In recent policy approaches and experiences of donor-country election observation in Africa, more critical assessments are heard. In this respect, election observation as a political instrumentality to express commitment to democratization has advanced beyond its beginnings in the 1990s. Principled commitment to democratization and rule-of-law thinking is not contradictory to efficient economic assistance programmes and the opening of markets. Pragmatic or over-cautious *Realpolitik* fueled by business interests and political competition for influence by donors in some places remains – or can become – predominant. But then there should of course be no surprise if politics in Africa – and towards Africa, as buttressed by the conventions of international diplomatic discourse – will continue to be one of the major bottlenecks of realizing stated goals like socio-economic development, legal accountability, growth of public trust or political stability. Democratization should not only be seen as an affair of the elites but should be 'given back' to the African populations who courageously started to press for it more than ten years ago.

NOTES

1. This is evident from the internal *Country Assistance Strategy* (CAS) documents that outline World Bank–IDA support for certain developing countries. These reports have a fairly short-term perspective, and ignore or bypass issues like national consensus, the role of the opposition and of civil society organizations, freedom of the press and other media, and the abuse of human rights. These issues are not seen by the Bank as being linked in any way with the exercise of governance, power and elite rule in these countries.
2. For a critical survey of research on democratization, see Buijtenhuijs and Rijnierse 1993, and Buijtenhuijs and Thiriot 1996.
3. An important overview, with a discussion of the main theoretical trends in this literature, is Cowen and Laakso 1997.
4. While editing this Introduction, the recent volume edited by Kumar (1998) on post-conflict elections and international assistance (with four chapters on African countries) came to our notice.

5. *Regime* defined as the body of operative rules and practices of governance and of the constitution of power (based on Sandbrook 1996: 85). These 'rules' are partly non-institutionalized and often based on arbitrary, uncontrollable use of force, intimidation and the like.
6. See on the relation between these two concepts the excellent discussion by Sejersted 1988.
7. Although it is often forgotten that the NSDAP, in its best national result in July 1932, only received 37 per cent of the national vote, and *not* an absolute majority. The position of political party stalemate, presidential authoritarianism and manipulation of faulty constitutional clauses then led to Hitler's assumption of power.
8. Which at most essential historical junctures were supported by foreign powers (for example, Mobutu's Zaire, Eyadema's Togo, Mengistu's Ethiopia). This incidentally also holds for most of the so-called 'new leaders' in Africa.
9. An example would be the dismissal of people from jobs in the state sector because of lack of political loyalty but by accusing them of 'corruption' or 'incompetence': the standards and procedures to determine the latter are often fictitious and the accusations can rarely be upheld in a court of law (where the plaintiff would often have no chance of a reasonable and speedy trial either). Furthermore, the people replacing them are usually equally corrupt and incompetent (foreign observers cannot check such cases in detail and often go by rhetoric and appearances).

REFERENCES

Anglin, D., 1992. 'International Monitoring as a Mechanism of Conflict Resolution Southern Africa' (Bellville: University of the Western Cape, Working Paper, Centre for Southern African Studies).

Bayart, J.-F., S. Ellis and B. Hibou, 1997. *La Criminalisation de l'Etat en Afrique* (Brussels: Editions Complexe).

Bjornlund, E., M. Bratton and C. Gibson, 1992. 'Observing Multiparty Elections in Africa: Lessons from Zambia', *African Affairs* 91: 405–31.

Bratton, M. and N. van de Walle, 1997. *Democratic Experiments in Africa: Regime Transitions in Comparative Perspective* (Cambridge: Cambridge University Press).

Buijtenhuijs, R. and E. Rijnierse, 1993. *Democratization in Sub-Saharan Africa 1989–1992: an Overview of the Literature* (Leiden: African Studies Centre).

Buijtenhuijs, R. and C. Thiriot, 1995. *Démocratisation en Afrique au Sud du Sahara 1992–1995* (Leiden: African Studies Centre; also in English version).

Carothers, T., 1997. 'The Observers Observed: the Rise of Election Monitoring', *Journal of Democracy* 8(3): 17–31.

Cowen, M. and L. Laakso, 1997. 'An Overview of Election Studies in Africa', *Journal of Modern African Studies* 35(4): 717–44.

Daloz, J.-P. and P. Quantin (eds), 1997. *Transitions Démocratiques Africaines* (Paris: Karthala).

Elklit, J. and P. Svensson, 1997. 'What Makes Elections Free and Fair?', *Journal of Democracy* 8(3): 32–46.

Engel, U., R. Hofmeier, D. Kohnert and A. Mehler, 1996. 'The Second Wind of Change: Demokratisierung in Afrika, 1989–95', in U. Engel *et al.*, *Deutsche Wahlbeobachtung in Afrika* (Hamburg: Institut für Afrika-Kunde), pp. 1–29.

Fengler, W. and S. Mair, 1996. 'Zur Wahlbeobachtung der Präsidentschafts- und Parlamentswahlen in Tansania vom Oktober 1995', *Afrika Spectrum* 31(1): 93–100.

Garber, L., 1984. *Guidelines for International Election Observation* (Washington, DC: International Human Rights Law Group).

Geisler, G., 1993. 'Fair? What has Fairness Got to Do with it? Vagaries of Election Observations and Democratic Standards', *Journal of Modern African Studies* 31(4): 613–37.

Goodwin-Gill, G.S., 1994. *Free and Fair Elections: International Law and Practice* (Geneva: Inter-Parliamentary Union).

Huntington, S.P., 1991. *The Third Wave: Democratization in the Late Twentieth Century* (Norman–London: University of Oklahoma Press).

Hyden, G. 1996. 'Rethinking Theories of the State: an Africanist Perspective', *Africa Insight* 26(1): 26–35.

Ihonvbere, J., 1996. 'Where is the Third Wave? Critical Evaluation of Africa's Non-Transition to Democracy', *Africa Today* 43(3): 343–68.

Karlström, M., 1996. 'Imagining Democracy: Political Culture and Democratisation in Buganda', *Africa* 66(4): 485–504.

Kumar, K., ed., 1998. *Postconflict Elections, Democratization and International Assistance*. Boulder–London: Lynne Rienner.

Mair, S., 1997. *Election Observation: Roles and Responsibilities of Long-Term Observers*. Maastricht: ECDPM (Working paper no. 22).

Mbembe, A. 1996. 'Une Economie de Prédation: les Rapports entre la Rareté Matérielle et la Démocratie en Afrique Subsaharienne', *Afrique 2000* 24: 67–81.

Von Meijenfeldt, R., 1995. *Election Observation: Report of an ECDPM Workshop.* (Maastricht: ECDPM).

Meyns, P., 1995. 'Grenzen der Internationalen Wahlbeobachtung: Anmerkungen eines Wahlbeobachters in Mosambik', *Afrika Spectrum* 30(1): 35–47.

Nevitte, N. and S.A. Canton, 1997. 'The Role of Domestic Observers', *Journal of Democracy* 8(3): 47–61.

Ottaway, M., 1997. 'From Political Opening to Democratization?', in M. Ottaway (ed.), *Democracy in Africa: the Hard Road Ahead* (Boulder–London: Lynne Rienner), pp. 1–14.

Pastor, R.A., 1995. 'Elections, Monitoring', in *Encyclopedia of Democracy* (Washington, DC: Congressional Quarterly, Inc.), vol. 2, pp. 407–9.

Pilon, M., 1994. 'L'Observation des Processus Électoraux: Enseignements de l'Élection Présidentielle du Togo', *Politique Africaine* 56: 137–43

Sandbrook, R., 1996. 'Transitions without Consolidation: Democratization in Six African Countries', *Third World Quarterly* 17(1): 69–87.

Schatzberg, M.G., 1993. 'Power, Legitimacy and "Democratisation" in Africa', *Africa* 63 (4): 445–61.

Sejersted, F., 1988. 'Democracy and the Rule of Law: Some Historical Experiences of Contradictions in the Striving for Good Government', in

J. Elster and R. Slagstad (eds), *Constitutionalism and Democracy* (Cambridge: Cambridge University Press), pp. 131–52.

Tall, E.K., 1995. 'De la Démocratie et des Cultes Voduns au Bénin', *Cahiers d'Etudes Africaines* 35(137): 195–208.

Tostensen, A., D. Faber and K. de Jong, 1997. *Towards an Integrated Approach to Election Observation? Professionalising European Long-Term Election Observation Missions* (Maastricht: ECDPM).

Part I
The Context of Elections in Africa

1 Democratization in Africa: the Role of Election Observation

O. van Cranenburgh

INTRODUCTION

In the 1990s international observation of multi-party elections emerged as a booming industry. Since the end of the bipolar world system, a universal consensus has appeared on the desirability of pluralist democracy. In Africa, many one-party or military regimes were replaced by governments deriving their mandate from multi-party elections. In countries which had suffered decades of civil war, a peace process was to be started with multi-party elections. New armies of international election observers were sent to these countries by donor governments, international organizations and NGOs. The new international consensus on democracy in practice implied a heavy emphasis on multi-party elections in international policies to promote democracy.

Support for democracy and democratization has received ample attention in policy documents of bilateral donors and international organizations in the framework of stimulating 'good governance' (see also Ellis, this volume). The language used in these documents often shows how complex and multi-faceted the problem of democratization is: to varying degrees these documents pay attention to historical, cultural and institutional factors enabling democracy to flourish. For example, in the Dutch memorandum with the budget for the Netherlands Ministry of Foreign Affairs for the year 1997, there is a warning that democracy is more than the outward appearance of elections. However, in practice, policy measures are strongly focused on elections. In the context of aid conditionality (also known as 'negative linkage') aid is increased or decreased as governments of developing countries agree to hold elections.

These policies imply considerable pressure on sometimes unwilling governments. In the context of policies to support the process of democratization itself (known as 'positive linkage' policies), most resources are spent on financial and/or technical support for elections and the sending of observers.

Implicit in this emphasis on multi-party elections is the assumption that elections are the pivot around which democracy and democratization revolve. I will examine the validity of this assumption by reviewing some perspectives on the role of elections in democratization. Next I will examine the role of election observation. Is international observation of elections indeed helpful as suggested by the emphasis it receives in international policies? Some seven years of international election observation provide sufficient experience to pose some critical questions about the contribution of observation in processes of democratization.

ELECTIONS AND DEMOCRATIZATION

What is the place of multi-party elections in democracy and democratization? The answer to this question varies according to different schools of thought on democracy. For the purpose of this review I will group perspectives on democracy into four 'schools of thought'.

a. The Procedural Approach to Democracy

Joseph Schumpeter wrote in 1943 that democracy does not entail 'rule by the people' as assumed in what he terms the classical approach to democracy. In his view, democracy, both empirically and normatively, should be defined as a method by which decision-making is transferred to individuals who have gained power in a competitive struggle for the votes of citizens. His ideas were to inspire a whole school of thought on democracy. In his work on the so-called 'Third Wave of Democratization', the American political scientist Huntington (1991) adopts this 'minimal approach' equating democracy with multi-party elections. This approach is relevant in the analysis of African politics, because increased pressures for multi-party elections coming from both domestic and international actors, explicitly or implicitly, rely on the ideas of this school.

In an extreme version this approach becomes highly reductionist: multi-party elections are then seen as a necessary and
sufficient condition for democracy. This 'perversion' of the procedural approach is not very often espoused by political scientists, but one could argue that the heavy emphasis on
multi-party elections in international policy is an expression of
this reductionist view. The assumption that multi-party elections are a sufficient condition for democracy may be countered
by the argument that competitive elections have contributed to
violations of civil and political rights (applicable to, for
example, Kenya, Tanzania, Ethiopia and Zanzibar); and that
competitive elections exacerbate ethnic conflict (Kenya,
Rwanda, Burundi), both situations being rather incongruous
with what we normally associate with democracy.

The well-known criticism of the procedural approach to
democracy is that this type of democracy may be elitist and un-
dervalues the importance of participation of citizens in decisions that affect their lives. However, critics of the procedural
approach, which in the context of Africa speak of the inade-
quacy of the 'Western model', are often unaware of the full implications of the approach of this school. While it has been
described as 'minimal', most authors in this school list a
number of procedural/formal requirements necessary for elections to be free and fair (see for example Dahl 1971). These requirements, including at least equal political rights, freedom of
expression, freedom of organization and the presence of plural-
istic media, are in effect not so minimal at all. It is clear that
this school implies an important potential role for election observation in assessing the free and fair nature of elections. I will
argue later that one of the shortcomings of election observation
is that the full range of these requirements is not covered.

b. Participatory Democracy

Participatory democracy, which of course goes back to the classics, and is evident in the views of Rousseau, received a new
impulse in the West with the growing criticism of 'elitist democracy' during the 1960s. One of the values receiving a central
place in this school is participation of citizens beyond the vote
in four- or five-yearly elections. Referenda and other forms of
more direct participation in decision-making are thought to be

essential. In this school of thought, the meaning of democracy extends beyond the formal political sphere, and values like socio-economic equality may receive an important place.

This school too knows an extreme version where the claim to represent a form of political democracy becomes highly contested. Out of disappointment with elections and the formal trappings of 'elitist' democracy, some will discard the notion that multi-party elections constitute a necessary condition for democracy at all. The definition of democracy is stretched far beyond the political realm to include social and economic equality. It becomes maximalist: in a perverted form other normative goals come to supersede the value of political democracy.

In the African context this school has exerted considerable influence. It has inspired justifications of the one-party system in the post-independence period (van Cranenburgh 1990). In a more recent version, strands of this school of thought reappear in the arguments to install a 'no-party system' such as the Ugandan 'movement system', built on 'resistance councils' from the local level up (a model which also appears to have been adopted by Laurent Kabila's AFDL in Democratic Republic of Congo (ex-Zaire)).

In this school of thought the value of election observation may be to assess to what extent no-party elections may still be considered 'fair' though they cannot be entirely 'free' (cf. Doornbos, this volume). The implication of these views and real-world political experiments for election observation is that observers must further define and refine the criteria to be used for assessing elections (see below).

c. The Substantive/Material Approach to Democracy

Robert Dahl listed one further condition for 'polyarchy', next to the procedural one it shared with our first school: the presence of institutions through which government policy is dependent on votes and other means of voicing preferences by citizens (Dahl 1971: 3). This prerequisite points at what I call material/substantive conditions for democracy. For electoral competition to be meaningful, it must have some connection with alternative preferences of citizens with regard to government policies.

This approach requires an examination of the actual functioning of political parties. Political parties must then be analysed as linkage mechanisms between state and civil society. In the structural functional approach to comparative politics the functions of political parties have been defined as communication and socialization, recruitment and selection of leaders, and the articulation and aggregation of interests (Almond and Powell 1966: 114–27). Do political parties in democratizing countries function as mechanisms to articulate societal preferences? A multi-party system based on personal factions does not perform the linkage function Dahl implied in his concern that policies reflect preferences of citizens.

This indicates that the functioning of political parties is highly dependent upon their societal context, in particular the political culture. Defined as 'the pattern of individual attitudes and orientations toward politics among the members of a political system' (Almond and Powell 1966: 50), the political culture approach was recently revived in the study of democracy in developing countries. In an influential study, R. Putnam showed that in the absence of a civic community, democratic institutions do not work. Only when citizens are informed and organized into social, economic and cultural organizations and enter into relationships based on norms of equality, can democracy work (Putnam 1993). The analysis was applied to democracy in developing countries (see for example Diamond 1994).

In this view, multi-party politics based on clientelism and corruption cannot substantially further democracy. Where clientelism and localism prevail, formal political reforms will do little to promote democracy. In many African countries, politics is still highly personal and clientelistic; these features are strengthened both by political institutions (see below) and political culture. Where these circumstances prevail, formal political changes will mask substantive continuity in politics (for the case of Tanzania, see van Cranenburgh 1996). From this school of thought it is apparent that international policies to support democracy should address the issue of strengthening civil society, and the capacity of political parties to formulate alternative policies.

d. The Institutional Models Approach

This school of thought looks at the different institutional and constitutional forms democracy may take. In this contribution,

I only mention two models which are prevalent to deal with governing heterogeneous political communities, both revolving around dividing and limiting power: *federalism* and *consociationalism*. While both models may be combined and share some characteristics, the one is based on the division of power on a territorial basis, while the other does so for groups in society. Arend Lijphart has written extensive comparative studies about this phenomenon. He explained how stability was (and can be) maintained in divided societies using proportional representation, power sharing in the executive and veto power for constituent groups. Refining earlier work he introduced the fundamental distinction between 'majoritarian' and 'consensus democracies' (the latter term replacing 'consociational democracy') (see Lijphart 1977 and 1984).

In the African context, the consociational or consensus model of democracy is increasingly relevant. Populations are heterogeneous based on ethnic, religious and language criteria. At the same time the highly centralized model of governance as imposed shortly after independence has served to limit the representation of particular ethnic groups or to create a bias in the allocation of resources.

Numerous questions remain as to how democracy can take account of the existence of ethnic loyalties, but it is evident that the combination of centralism with strongly majoritarian forms of government introduced with independence have contributed to the alienation of ethnic, religious or political minorities. The single-member district system, with a relative majority enough to represent a whole district, has increased the zero-sum nature of politics in Africa, while at the same time reinforcing localism and personalism in politics (see Hyden 1994). In the transition to multi-party politics, the fear that ethnic loyalties might threaten the unity of the state has inspired an attempt to prohibit the formation of political parties on an ethnic, religious or regional basis. We may question the prudence of this approach, which may turn out to be counterproductive. While it must be the choice of Africans to decide which system best suits their needs, it is necessary for international policies to put on the agenda the question how political institutions may be designed to accommodate ethnic, religious or regional differences, rather than attempt to repress them.

SYNTHESIS

All schools of thought imply that there is much more to democracy than voting in a multi-party election. To lay a foundation
for international policies to support democracy, including election observation, I wish to formulate a synthesis from the different schools outlined above. The effort is meant to arrive at a
workable set of requirements for democracy which may help to
clarify the role of election observation.

I put forward that competitive elections are a necessary,
through not a sufficient condition for democracy. The 'necessary' is taken from the procedural school, and must be taken to
include the full range of formal/procedural requirements as
outlined by several authors in the school. This implies a conver-
gence with the human rights agenda in so far as it concerns the
fundamental civil and political rights. This approach is based
on the conviction, as evidenced in several elections in Africa,
that without these procedural requirements as in the protection of civil rights and freedoms, elections will not contribute to
anything we may call democracy. Put more generally, the rule of
law must provide the context for democratic institutions. In the
absence of these conditions, elections may become an instrument for manipulation and sometimes even violence.

By using the word 'competitive' rather than 'multi-party' I
wish to allow for the theoretical possibility that competition is
present in the framework of a one-party or no-party system.
With respect to competitiveness, in the case of a no-party
system, elections must allow for individual candidates to
express their own views and appeal to voters with (different)
policy proposals (cf. Doornbos's chapter on Uganda, below).
The necessary competitiveness is perhaps more easily granted
within a multi-party context, although even in that case it is
possible that the elections offer no meaningful choice to citizens (see Abbink's chapter below).

Therefore, my thesis states that competitive elections are a
'not sufficient' condition. While sticking to the minimal requirement of the procedural school, we also need to go beyond
formal/procedural requirements and add those factors emphasized in both the substantive and institutional model schools.
Do the parties or representative organs constitute a mechanism

to link the preferences of citizens to the government? Is the organization in civil society able to give meaning to the process? Finally, the institutional requirements school stipulates that in the case of plural societies, we need to assess whether mechanisms are built in to guarantee the rights of minorities and ensure fair representation.

INTERNATIONAL OBSERVATION OF ELECTIONS

International observation has played a significant role in first-time competitive elections in countries undergoing a process of transition to democracy. The idea is that given the transition situation, both institutions and the culture supporting free and fair elections are weak. Newly emerging opposition parties are often suspicious *vis-à-vis* the government or the ruling party, and the population insecure. International observation may help to build confidence and have a certain preventive effect in deterring fraud. But to what extent is observation also adequate to assess the democratic nature of elections?

The various perspectives on the relation between elections and democracy all have implications for election observation. It is quite clear from each of the perspectives described above that for an assessment of the democratic nature of elections a rather broad range of factors must be covered, ranging from the basic civil and political rights and the fairness of electoral rules and their implementation, the consequences of the electoral system itself given a particular social context, to, finally, even the nature of parties involved in a competitive election.

In practice, election observation is insufficiently geared to an assessment of these broader factors influencing the democratic nature of elections. Observation has been criticized by political actors in the countries receiving them, by some of the observers, by academics and by some officials who have been closely involved in observation. Horacio Boneo, who headed the UN division for electoral support, wrote:

> Observation is done in a costly manner without much improvement in methods, and without the development of standards and criteria based on the acquired experience.
>
> (IDEA 1996: 16)

Not only are some faults apparent in the way observation is done, there is little evidence of learning from mistakes. In a later chapter, the question is addressed to what extent these faults exist due to, or perhaps in spite of, policies of governments and organizations sending observers.

Here, the following weaknesses of international observation deserve attention.

1. Despite a broadly shared consensus that democracy is more than voting on election day, international observation is heavily focused on procedures on polling day. Most international observers arrive in the country a few days before polling day; they are insufficiently informed about the local political situation and the national electoral system and the specific problems experienced in the period running up to the election. Neither do observers stay long enough to cover the period after polling day, some even leaving before final results are announced. It is obvious, however, that on polling day only a small part of the electoral process may be covered. It is precisely in the preparation of elections that many opportunities for irregularities and abuse occur, such as in the delineation of constituencies; registration of parties, candidates and voters; guaranteeing access to the media and fair campaigning. The period of field presence is too short to cover the entire process. This implies that many observer missions' conclusions are not founded on sufficient factual data. Realization of these shortcomings have led to the use of a small group of longer-term observers, but in practice they are not very effective in covering the broader factors, lacking clear guidelines or adequate preparation or being forced to spend much time in preparing the work of short-term observers. The strong bias toward polling day presence remains.

2. International observers often lack expertise. On the one hand this has to do with methods of recruitment: political factors, such as ensuring support, often appear to weigh more heavily than expertise. It is a supply-driven process, whereby influential politicians, such as parliamentarians, or people involved in Third World solidarity groups, are drawn in. On the other hand, the lack of expertise is related to inadequate training of observers, both by the responsible Ministry in the sending country and by the responsible agency within the recipient country. Both factors reinforce each other. For example, the use

of volunteers in the Netherlands strongly contrasts with the use of highly professional civil servants by Sweden and Australia.

3. There is a lack of criteria and operational guidelines to assess the democratic nature of elections. International observers are dealing with inherently difficult cases: in countries where democracy is consolidated and free and fair elections are the rule, international observers are not necessary; in countries which do not meet certain minimal conditions for free and fair elections, observers are not sent. Observers are sent to countries which have limited experience with free elections, which undergo a transition from authoritarian rule or a peace process. In those situations, the rules of the game are often being debated and therefore fluid; democratic values are not yet strongly rooted in the political culture. The norms for free and fair elections cannot be as strict as for those countries where democracy is consolidated, but this grey zone does not imply that observation can be done adequately without any operational set of criteria for assessing the free and fair nature of elections. These norms should be made explicit and operational, taking into account the specific local conditions.

4. There is no adequate procedure for the formulation of a common 'statement' by observers about the elections. Normally, observers fill out checklists when visiting polling stations and a summary regional report is compiled. A coordinating secretariat (often a UN bureau) will draw up a statement, but is entirely free to decide if, and if so which, observers play a role in formulating the statement. Often there is pressure to produce a consensus statement, resulting in rather vague formulations; in recent years, there is even a tendency to refrain from using the words 'free and fair' (the lack of operationalization of these concepts leaves room for many different conclusions!). In some cases donor-governments, through their ambassadors, are directly involved in formulating the statement; the UN headquarters may be involved in actually editing the text. It is clear that these actors may have direct interests to steer the statement in a certain direction: often donor-governments are eager to find a legitimation for continued aid; while the UN must always be careful not to anger governments. Political motives often undermine the objectivity of the statement.

Due to these weaknesses international observation has lost credibility. Around 1990, opposition parties were the primary actors urging for international observation to ensure a free and fair process; from 1995 on, many opposition groups have become disenchanted with election observation because often elections which were the subject of intense domestic criticism have been unduly legitimized. It is my impression that African governments are now in the forefront of inviting international observers, as they have become convinced that observation does not threaten the legitimacy of their actions. This turning point in the assessment of international observation is the result of the weaknesses of election observation as described above. Some of these weaknesses are being addressed through the policies of governments and international organizations involved in election observation; others seem resistant to change. If policy-makers fail to address each of these weaknesses, the legitimating function of international observation may well lead to undermining its own aims, and the presence of observers will become purely symbolic.

IMPROVEMENTS

The future of election observation clearly depends on regaining the respect and legitimacy of the exercise through feeding back into the observation process the lessons learnt in the past. Constructive learning from experience will lead to an improvement in methods. Here I will focus on five points which need immediate attention: (1) operationalization of the criteria for free and fair elections; (2) lengthening the period of observation to include the entire election cycle; (3) changing the recruitment and improving the training of observers, while also enhancing their cooperation with local monitors; (4) designing a clear procedure for the formulation of a statement; and (5) adherence to a code of conduct for international observers.

1. Criteria for Free and Fair Elections

It is necessary to arrive at a clear operationalization of the concept of 'free and fair elections'. A distinction should be made between criteria derived from internationally agreed norms and criteria derived from the national electoral laws. It should be made explicit at the outset when national legislation presents conflict with certain internationally agreed minimal norms.

Freedom should be covered by examining the presence of fundamental civil rights, the right to vote and to be elected, freedom of organization and of the press, and freedom to campaign. Here it is necessary for the government to refrain from actions infringing upon these rights.

Fairness is much more difficult to monitor, because apart from the absence of fraud, it also refers to equal opportunities for the political actors. Equal opportunities may have to be created and thus often require action by the government, such as providing for campaigning or granting subsidies and ensuring access to the media. In transitions from a one-party regime it may be particularly difficult to 'level the playing ground'. The ruling party has superior resources, financial, personnel and symbolic, and may use the advantage of incumbency (implementing long overdue road repairs in a particular district) in an attempt to bolster the party in power.

To be fully able to assess the 'free and fair' nature of elections, international observers must cover much more than the voting procedures on election day. At least he following issues must be covered.

Before the elections:

- the formulation of electoral laws and regulation regarding political parties and party finance;
- the Election Commission: neutrality of officers or balanced representation of parties;
- in the single-member district system: the delineation of constituencies to check for 'gerrymandering' (drawing boundaries of district to ensure victory for a particular party) or unacceptable imbalances in size;
- the registration of political parties;
- the procedures for the registration of candidates;
- registration of voters (were all parties allowed to canvass for voter registration?);
- voter education (is it done sufficiently and in a balanced manner?);
- subsidies for parties or candidates (were they allocated fairly and actually issued?)
- campaigns (were all parties allowed to campaign? did all have access to the media?);

- a free and responsible press;
- procedures to guarantee secrecy of the vote.

After the elections, attention should be paid to:

- the counting process up to the final announcement of the results;
- maintenance of secrecy of the vote;
- freedom from harassment for supporters of opposition parties;
- adjustment of rules and procedures in parliament to allow participation of opposition parties;
- continued protection of civil and political rights, including freedom of the press;
- procedures for complaints.

2. Period of Observation

Coverage of all these aspects of elections implies a significant lengthening of the period of observation in the field. A redirection of resources away from massive deployment of observers on election day is necessary to enable a smaller group of well-trained observers to be present in the field during the preparations for the elections up to the trajectory after polling day, including the final count, announcement of results and the immediate aftermath. Recently, so-called 'long-term' observers have been stationed in the field in an attempt to cover a part of these aspects; in practice, however, their activities tend to be directed to preparing the ground (logistically more than substantially) for the observers to cover polling day (see Foeken and Dietz, Rutten, and Van Cranenburgh in this volume, for changes in Dutch policy in this respect). Shifting the emphasis away from polling day toward the entire election cycle means that we might speak of 'democracy observation' instead of election observation. It also implies that a much greater role must be played by domestic observers and that more opportunities must be created to exchange information with them.

3. Recruitment and Training of International Observers

A longer period of observation has implications for the recruitment of international observers. It means professionalization of election observation. Professionals are better able to remain in the field for a longer period; moreover, they will build up experience. Observers must receive adequate training to assess institutions, regulations and practices using internationally agreed criteria for free and fair elections. Long-term democracy observation by professionals also allows more room for them to cooperate with domestic observers, with the aim of ultimately building up domestic capacity for election observation (see other chapters in this book).

4. Statement

A statement on the elections should be formulated by or at least supported by the observers who were involved in the exercise. While coordination by the UN is useful, the tendency to produce a consensus statement is unnecessarily burdensome for this process. It may lead to a vague statement watered down by the need to accommodate conflicting views. If necessary, a minority opinion could be added to the statement, making explicit on what grounds different conclusions are reached. Pluralism is a good thing in election observation, as in elections!

5. Code of Conduct

Who controls election observers? The guidelines issued to observers are insufficient on the points of ethical norms and the substantive foundation of their work. Existing guidelines emphasize the distinction between 'observation' and 'involvement': observers watch and report only. However, the mere presence of observers creates many grey zones. Doing nothing may not be a neutral act; the presence of observers tends to have a legitimizing function. In the newly founded Institute for Democracy and Electoral Assistance (IDEA) in Stockholm, a first attempt has been made to formulate a code of conduct. International acceptance and adherence to a code of conduct must be ensured.

CONCLUSION

In countries undergoing a transition to democracy, international observation may have important functions. However, the role of international observation will only contribute meaningfully to it if the process of observation is improved and expanded in the direction suggested above: it must cover a much broader range of factors so that it can actually claim to observe democracy rather than merely voting technicalities on polling day. I have argued that this implies longer-term professional observers. The argument presented here does not necessarily imply a complete withdrawal of international observers on polling day: as long as their role is to assist longer-term observers in moments of high activity, such as during voter registration, campaigns or on polling day, they may perform a useful function. The message conveyed in the above critique is that a judgement about the free and fair nature of an election may never be based exclusively or even primarily upon activities and reports of short-term observers.

Recognizing that democracy observation is primarily called for in situations of transition, it must be emphasized that it will be a temporary phenomenon. The exercise, if it is to go beyond polling observation, must simultaneously aim to create or stimulate the domestic capacity to observe elections and follow critically the consolidation of democracy.

Finally, it must be emphasized that international policies to support democracy imply a range of other instruments besides observation. Such policies must aim at the broader factors conducive to democracy listed in the schools of thought reviewed above. Decisions to devote resources to massive observation missions may do so at the cost of other instruments, such as technical support for elections, support to journalists, the media, training of the judiciary or police, and NGOs active in fields which indirectly help to create conditions for democracy and the rule of law. In the end, the promotion of an open political debate between actors in civil society, whether they be professionals, NGOs, political parties or parliamentarians, may help to shape both a culture and institutions to sustain democracy.

REFERENCES

Almond, G.A. and Bingham Powell, G., 1966. *Comparative Politics: a Developmental Approach* (Boston and Toronto: Little, Brown).

Cranenburgh, O. van, 1990. *The Widening Gyre: the Tanzanian One-Party State and Policy towards Rural Cooperatives* (Delft: Eburon).

——, 1996. 'Tanzania's 1995 Multi-party Elections: the Emerging Party System'. *Party Politics* 2(4): 535–47.

Dahl, R.A., 1971. *Polyarchy: Participation and Opposition* (New Haven–London: Yale University Press).

Diamond, L., ed., 1994. *Political Culture and Democracy in Developing Countries* (Boulder: Lynne Rienner).

Goodwin-Gill, G.S., 1994. *Free and Fair Elections: International Law and Practice* (Geneva: Inter-Parliamentary Union).

Huntington, S.P., 1991. *The Third Wave: Democratization in the Late Twentieth Century* (Norman–London: University of Oklahoma Press).

Hyden, G., 1983. *No Shortcuts to Progress: African Development Management in Perspective* (London: Heinemann).

——, 1994. 'Political representation and the future of Uganda', in H.B. Hansen and M. Twaddle (eds), *From Chaos to Order: the Politics of Constitution-Making in Uganda*, pp. 180–91. London: James Currey/Kampala: Fountain Publishers.

IDEA, 1996. *Democracy Forum – Report of the Democracy Forum in Stockholm, June 12–14, 1996.* Stockholm: Institute for Democracy and Electoral Assistance.

Lijphart, A., 1977. *Democracy in Plural Societies: a Comparative Exploration.* New Haven–London: Yale University Press.

——, 1984. *Democracies: Patterns of Majoritarian and Consensus Government in Twenty-one Countries.* New Haven–London: Yale University Press.

Putnam, R. et al., 1993. *Making Democracy Work: Civic Traditions in Modern Italy.* Princeton: Princeton University Press.

Schumpeter, J., 1976. *Capitalism, Socialism and Democracy.* Boston: Beacon Press (first edn 1943).

2 Elections in Africa in Historical Context
S. Ellis

INTRODUCTION

An outstanding feature of the international order established in the aftermath of the Second World War, now undergoing such profound change, was its reflection of certain underlying suppositions about the nature of states and the origins of the power they wield. Every member of the United Nations accepts the proposition that the world is divided into sovereign states which have jurisdiction over a specific territory, and that these states have the right and duty to govern. This was the community of nations which African countries joined, a few as founder-members in 1945, many more as newcomers admitted after they had attained independence from colonial rule, mostly in the 1960s.

Every African member of the United Nations, with South Africa in the period of apartheid constituting the only significant exception, bases its right to govern on the principle that the tenants of power are representatives of the popular will, no matter how diverse are the precise methods which politicians, generals and kings actually use in becoming heads of state. A few African heads of state have been literally born to power (like Morocco's Hassan II or, to a lesser extent, Ethiopia's Emperor Haile Sellassie I), but far more have seized it by force, notably the numerous ambitious soldiers who have carried out *coups d'état*. Some have conquered power after long guerrilla campaigns carried out either against colonists and settlers reluctant to cede power to representatives of African populations, or, more recently, against an incumbent independent government. The first to achieve power in Africa through a guerrilla campaign against a post-colonial government was Hissein Habré in Chad in 1981. This path to power was followed by many others who also made it to head of state, such as in Ethiopia and Eritrea. In the first generation after independence, many African leaders had actually been voted into power in elections supervised by the departing colonialists, and thereafter retained it until their death (like Presidents Houphouët-Boigny and Kenyatta) or until their overthrow (like President Nkrumah and many others). A few of the first generation of heads of state, elected to power in colonial times, eventually resigned and handed power to chosen successors, like Presidents Senghor of Senegal, Nyerere of Tanzania and Ahidjo of Cameroon. But from the end of the colonial period until the late 1980s, only in Mauritius was one party actually voted out of office and replaced by another in constitutional fashion.

Despite this wide variety of techniques for acquiring power, every African country has experienced fairly regular elections of some sort or another (see the survey by Cowen and Laakso 1997), usually ones in which the whole adult population has, in theory, been allowed to participate. In South Africa, in the days of apartheid, national elections were restricted to white citizens only, since blacks were increasingly deemed to be citizens of the homelands designated by the South African government, and they were expected to cast their votes there. Although white South Africans were free to vote for opposition parties or candidates, in practice a victory by the National Party was always a foregone conclusion. In many other countries, the absence of opposition parties and a stifling political control of every aspect of elections often made such contests useless as means of removing an incumbent government or head of state. In the great majority of cases, the main function of elections was less to choose a government than to serve as a form of legitimation of political choices which had already been made by other means, of confirming political facts. Elections symbolized that the people had an opportunity to express themselves, and thus they made an important contribution to maintaining the principle that the ultimate source of sovereignty was the people's will, any appearance to the contrary notwithstanding. Since 1945, this notion of popular sovereignty has generally been the accepted international standard for the legitimacy of any state, challenged only in recent decades by the emergence of new bases of political legitimacy, notably in those Islamic states[1] which claim that sovereignty is based on the will of God as it is expressed in holy writ.

The formal view that legitimate government can be based only on the 'will of the people', symbolized by elections, is a relatively recent one even in Europe and North America, where the roots of the contemporary notion can be traced back to the eighteenth century, when democratic theory emerged (Locke, Spinoza, Montesquieu). General suffrage, however, was also in Europe only achieved in the course of the twentieth century. In Africa, the idea of popular sovereignty expressed through elections is in most cases newer still. Before the colonial period, Africa had a great variety of polities – thousands in the later nineteenth century – with widely differing forms of government. They varied from powerful centralized monarchies or empires to the so-called stateless societies particularly common in parts of West and Central Africa, in which some form of public order was maintained without any centralized institutions of the type which Western observers were able to classify as constituting a state (see Horton 1985). Inasmuch as this great variety of systems can be said to have had any principle of legitimation in common it was a religious one: namely, the notion that all power has its ultimate origin in the supernatural or invisible world, and that humans can acquire or lose power only with the acquiesence of the denizens of this invisible world, God or gods and spirits. Hence the institutions by which Africans in pre-colonial times actually regulated access to power were often based on the specific arrangements they made to identify and influence the forces of the invisible world, such as the so-called secret societies which played such a prominent role in the government of many West African communities, or the priests, clerics and diviners who played a role as king-makers in the monarchies of Dahomey, Ashanti or Imerina.[2]

A great error made by political scientists imbued with theories of modernization, and the various officials, technocrats and planners who shared their basic suppositions, was to believe that the principle of the sovereignty of the popular will, to be tested most obviously through general elections, was replacing all other principles of sovereignty throughout the world, and moreover that this was necessary for any country which wished to develop.[3] There is now increasing evidence that the adoption throughout Africa of constitutions based on notions stemming from the European Enlightenment tradition that power emanates from popular sovereignty, and from the separation of politics and religion, has not displaced other notions of political legitimacy but, in time-honoured fashion, has instead simply been assimilated into a broader range of thought (Ellis and Ter Haar 1998). Thus, while there is abundant evidence that elections, at least until the 1990s, rarely served as effective instruments for the regulation of supreme power in sub-Saharan Africa, they have at the same time become widely established as one technique among others to express the legitimation of power.

Perhaps the oldest example of an African territory having the right to vote in national elections on the European model is the four communes of Senegal, French colonial settlements whose inhabitants had voting rights from the mid-nineteenth century. This was an example of a colonial institution being introduced into African politics, an effect of colonial rule in general. For while colonial governments were notable for their authoritarianism, and based their claim to legitimacy not on any appeal to the will of the people they governed but rather to a mixture of an alleged racial superiority and a supposedly greater skill in public administration, they did gradually introduce elections, among other trappings of popular representation. Some colonial jurisdictions gave rights to certain Africans based on a property qualification, as in Cape Colony in the earlier twentieth century, or allowed individual Africans to acquire the right to vote through assimilation into the European political ambit, as in the French and Portuguese traditions. But generally speaking the introduction of elections in which the mass of the African adult population could participate occurred only after 1945, and in conformity with the new views of international order which we have referred to as forming a central part of the worldwide system of international relations emerging from that period. Generally speaking, British colonial authorities in West Africa realized by about 1950 the necessity of formulating new policies for the accommodation of social forces which had emerged during and after the Second World War, and the last years of the colonial period saw an attempt to build unified, integrated parliamentary political systems that would form the bases for political independence (post-1970). Similar developments occurred rather later in the British colonies of Central, Eastern and Southern Africa, where the presence of a significant settler population complicated the political strategies of colonial administrations but also assured the early development of administrative and legal structures able to accommodate the aspirations of at least a part of the population to vote regularly for the choice of their political representatives. In the French empire too, ordinances issued in August and September 1945 established electoral colleges which included provision for Africans to elect representatives to the Constituent Assembly which was to plan a new constitutional future for France and its colonies. This was to lead directly to the rights of French-speaking Africans to vote for candidates to the French national assembly and to the holding of regular elections and of multi-party political activity throughout French-speaking Africa. In this sense it could be said that the tradition of regular elections in which the adult population has the right to vote dates in most of sub-Saharan Africa from the late 1940s or early 1950s. These developments occurred later in the Belgian Congo and in Portuguese colonies.

MULTIPARTY POLITICS AND THE REVIVAL OF ELECTIONS

To reread now some of the early classics of Africanist political science, written in the 1950s and 1960s, is to enter a world of hopes for the most part unrealized (cf. Cowen and Laakso 1997 for an overview of theoretical perspectives). The euphoria which many Africans and many non-Africans felt at independence, and the general optimism that a new world was being created from the best mix of African and European traditions, was soon tempered by the realities of political life. Among the most obvious signs of this was the move towards single-party states in which elections were affairs of mind-numbing predictability, in which diverse Fathers of the Nation, Great Teachers, *présidents-fondateurs* and Great Helmsmen received 99 per cent and more of the vote, as did their parties. Nevertheless, it is sometimes forgotten that there were many examples of African countries which did not become single-party or no-party states: Mauritius and Botswana never did,

Senegal adopted a single-party constitution only for some 10 years, and Ghana, Nigeria and Sudan all oscillated between military rule and multi-party politics in the 1970s and 1980s. With the exception of Mauritius, however, none succeeded in achieving the acid test of multi-party effectiveness, namely the transfer of national power as the result of victory at the ballot box.

Moreover, by the late 1970s, with the rise in world oil prices and profound shifts on world commodity markets, there was also evidence that many African countries were in deep economic and financial difficulties. Senegal was the first to undertake a structural adjustment programme, in 1980, as the condition for receiving loans from the International Monetary Fund and the World Bank without which the government risked insolvency. A clear pattern emerged throughout the decade of the 1980s: one after another, African governments on the verge of bankruptcy requested emergency loans from the international financial institutions, which reacted by first inspecting their economic policies and making recommendations which were, in effect, conditions for the receipt of loans. The experience of intervention in the financial and economic policies of African states soon led the World Bank to the more profound conclusion that the root cause of poor economic performance in sub-Saharan Africa was not merely ill-advised policies, but 'a crisis of governance'. A study published by the World Bank in 1989 was explicit in stating that 'History suggests that political legitimacy and consensus are a precondition for sustainable development' (World Bank 1989: 60), and this was soon to be translated into a demand that African governments which wished to be eligible for aid from the international financial institutions and from the donor community generally should undertake reforms of their systems of politics and government as well as of their detailed economic policies. Occurring as it did at a time when many Africans, particularly in urban areas, were openly demonstrating their dissatisfaction with the people and the institutions which had governed them since independence, this was to lead to a wave of political reform which most often took the form of the adoption of multi-party constitutions and competitive elections. In effect, African states which had for decades used elections as symbols of their legitimacy, even when these were single-party states, now subscribed to the principle that multi-party elections which might be considered free and fair were the standard norm for legitimacy.

DEMOCRATIZATION AND ELECTIONS IN THE 1990s

It now appears that the wave of democratization which was such a pronounced feature of African politics in the early 1990s has produced sufficient results to be subject to a provisional evaluation (Bratton and Van de Walle 1997). A significant number of African states have witnessed changes in government through elections, including Cape Verde, Benin, Zambia, Mali, Madagascar, Namibia and South Africa. However, there is also a significant number in which incumbent heads of state and political parties steeped in the traditions of single-party rule have managed to retain power in multi-party elections, including Côte d'Ivoire, Gabon, Cameroon, Kenya, Togo and others. In two cases – Benin and Madagascar – dictators voted out of office in democratic elections later regained power through subsequent elections in a surprising reversal of fortunes.

The mere fact of an incumbent party or head of state retaining power under a new constitutional dispensation cannot, in itself, be taken as evidence of any failure of democratization, but there is abundant evidence that in many cases this has been achieved through techniques, sometimes verging on illegality, which cannot be considered free and fair. These vary from the use by incumbents of state-controlled media to acquire advantage in campaigning, and gerrymandering of electoral districts and regulations, to the bribing of rival candidates, the manipulation of ethnic loyalties, the intimidation of voters and the rigging of elections, recorded not only by the press but also by international observers.[4]

Even where there have been examples of successful political change through the ballot box, such as in Benin, Zambia, Mali and – most important of all – South Africa, this has not generally produced the changes which advocates of political liberalization had hoped to see, either in terms of increased power-sharing or of greater economic prosperity. A popularly elected government in Zambia has not only reproduced many of the less commendable habits of its predecessor (which it strongly resembles not least because of the number of ex-ministers who have managed to regain power by switching parties at the appropriate moment), but has also managed to be more deeply immersed in the culture of smuggling and corruption than its predecessor. The democratic government of Mali appears too feeble to have a major effect on its country's fortunes, and has also experienced difficulties in the management of elections (see the chapter by Lange, this volume). While South Africa's transition from apartheid to full-scale democracy clearly marks a major change, it is too early to regard the transition as being complete. There are still many changes taking place in South Africa which can legitimately be regarded as an integral part of the move away from apartheid and which are far from being played out. South Africa is a democracy, but of what type exactly remains to be seen.

We may also make some further observations concerning the role of elections in regime changes. Of prime importance is the fact that elections themselves, while of undeniable importance, may clearly be seen in many cases to be the symbolic recognition by the electorate of political bargains already reached by elite actors. The most significant example of this is undoubtedly the South African general elections of April 1994 which brought to power a government of national unity dominated by the African National Congress and headed by President Mandela. This was the crowning achievement of a new political dispensation reached by a complex mixture of negotiation and violence during previous years, and most notably in the period since 1990 (see Van Kessel, this volume). A similar point could be made in regard to the Liberian election of July 1997, the fairest in the country's history of one and a half centuries, which, however, brought to power the country's leading warlord, Charles Taylor, principally because he was seen as the victor in the preceding seven years of war. One might observe that all elections contain an element of ritual performance inasmuch as the opinions of the voters are formed not only on polling day but in the period of political debate and action which precedes the election. Nevertheless, in situations where political conflict has all too often taken the form of armed struggle, it is a point which should not be overlooked. The Angolan elections of 1992, in which the losing party, UNITA, rejected the results and reverted to armed struggle, serves to illustrate the dangers inherent in placing too much faith in elections alone as an instrument of political change. This has become still more evident to judge from the number of occasions, such as in Burundi and Niger, on which governments democratically elected in the period of reform since 1990 have been subsequently overthrown by military coups. In Congo-Brazzaville, the events of late 1997, in which a former head of state – though decisively assisted by the armed intervention of Angolan government troops – led a major military campaign to overthrow a democratically elected president, set a still more ominous precedent. It suggests that the *coup d'état*, which many had hoped had lost its primacy as an instrument of political change in Africa, is now undergoing a revival.

One of the most penetrating analysts of politics in Africa, the late Claude Ake, in illustrating his contention that multi-party activity had failed to produce genuine democracy in most of Africa, asserts that the reason is that democratization in itself is 'totally *indifferent to the character of the state*' (Ake 1996: 6). He continues:

> Democratic elections are being held to determine who will exercise the powers of the state with no questions asked about the character of the state as if it had no implications for democracy. But its implications are so serious that elections in Africa give the voter only a choice between oppressors. This is hardly surprising since Africa largely retains the colonial state structure which is inherently anti-democratic, being the repressive apparatus of an occupying power. Uncannily, this structure has survived, reproduced and rejuvenated by the legacy of military and single-party rule. By all indications, it is also surviving democratization, helped by the reduction of democracy to multi-party elections. So what is happening now by way of democratization is that *self-appointed military or civilian dictators are being replaced by elected dictators.* (Ake, ibid.)

In short, elections, albeit an important institutional aspect of national politics, do not determine the manner in which a state operates and are not even the most important elements of factional political competition. The real stuff of politics, that is, arrangements made for the resolution of conflicts and the distribution of resources within society, is situated in other sites, and uses other techniques. These are increasingly informal in nature.

Since the late 1970s, sub-Saharan Africa has undergone two great movements of reform, connected to one another. These are in the fields of economics (where they most obviously take the form of liberalization programmes known as stuctural adjustment) and politics (where they take the form of democratization and the strengthening of civil society and campaigns for good governance). There is evidence that social groups in pursuit of their particular or factional interests create political fields which make incidental use of the institutional forms of a liberal state, but include other forms of mobilization and communication which have no official existence.

Some writers consider that the existence of such parallel or informal networks amounts to a 'shadow state', that is to say, a political system in which political struggle turns upon the control of 'elements of society associated with the production and reproduction of capital' (see Reno 1995: 12). In such a system, despite the collapse of public administration, tenure of state power remains of vital political importance since it is a privileged position for reaching those bargains with elements of society which constitute the shadow state. Such a state is one in which the official apparatus of government is shadowed at every level by an unofficial apparatus consisting of networks of interest within which political and economic bargains are constantly being negotiated. It is the existence of a so-called shadow state which explains why in countries like Sierra Leone and Liberia, despite the terrible tribulations they have suffered in recent years, the state – and especially a normative idea of the state – has not disappeared nor has it entirely collapsed.

ELECTIONS AND STATES

Perhaps the main problem facing analysts of African affairs in these circumstances – and, even more, confronting political actors who aspire to encourage African societies in the direction of peace, power-sharing and economic prosperity – is to distinguish the real workings of political systems from the institutional forms which states and societies have adopted in an effort to display the trappings of legitimacy, very often under

pressure from the international donors on which they are financially dependent. Some formal institutions of state and government, including elections in some cases, are best considered as
façades, institutions of little real substance which nevertheless
function to attract attention or to represent principles whose
connection to reality is more complex.

Perhaps a key notion in analysing the actual ways in which
transactions are made is that of 'informality', originally developed by economists and anthropologists seeking to understand
the high degree of economic activity which, in many parts of
Africa, has always taken place outside the scope of formal institutions and formal regulation.[5] International proponents of
economic reform have made the mistake, basing themselves
particularly on influential studies of other continents (De Soto
1989), of assuming that informal economic activity in Africa
represented a potential private sector of the economy frustrated only by the heavy hand of state regulation. That this is
an inaccurate analysis may be demonstrated by the fact that
the widespread introduction of liberal economic reforms
throughout Africa has led not to the erosion of the informal
sector, but in many cases to its growth. Above all, informal
economic activities may be seen not to exist in isolation from a
putative formal sector, but above all to be closely combined with
it in an integrated whole (Hibou 1996).

If indeed the operations of informal economies can be regarded as a useful analogy for those of informal *political* systems
– the exercise of power outside established institutional and
legal, and therefore in some way accountable, frameworks – it
seems important to emphasize that these should not be regarded as divorced from such formal institutions as electoral
laws and regulations, but to see formal and informal political
structures as part of a seamless whole.

Subsequent chapters in this book will analyse in detail the
social and political context of elections, individual elections,
and technical questions arising from their observation. This is a
subject in need of further study because elections, even in circumstances when they may often appear to be inadequate as
instruments of political change, are certainly not without
significance. The history of Africa over the past half century
suggests that elections are firmly established as a means by
which rulers try to establish or demonstrate their claims to

legitimacy. There is little reason to believe that elections will cease to fulfil this role in the foreseeable future, if only in a rhetorical sense in many cases. How they relate to other systems of legitimation, to the constitution of power, and how these together are connected to the struggles of political and economic life, will be a matter for on-going consideration, especially in assessing the nature and substance of good governance, political liberalization and democratization on the African continent.

NOTES

1. In Africa, perhaps only Sudan might be qualified as such.
2. On secret societies, see Little 1965–6. For a wider-ranging collection, see Ranger and Kimambo 1972.
3. The literature on this subject is enormous. A good summary is Leys 1996.
4. One example among many is *An Assessment of the October 11, 1992 Election in Cameroon* (National Democratic Institute for International Affairs, Washington DC, 1993).
5. A pioneering article in the study of this field is Hart 1973.

REFERENCES

Ake, C., 1996. *Is Africa Democratizing?* (Ikeja: Malthouse Press/Centre for Advanced Social Science Monograph no. 5).

Bratton, M. and N. van de Walle, 1997. *Democratic Experiments in Africa: Regime Transitions in Comparative Perspective* (Cambridge: Cambridge University Press).

Cowen, M. and L. Laakso, 1997. 'An Overview of Election Studies in Africa', *Journal of Modern African Studies* 35(4): 717–44.

De Soto, H., 1989. *The Other Path: the Invisible Revolution in the Third World* (New York: Harper and Row) (English edn).

Ellis, S. and G. ter Haar, 1998. 'Religion and Politics in Sub-Saharan Africa', *Journal of Modern African Studies* 35(2): 175–201.

Hart, K., 1973. 'Informal Income Opportunities in Urban Government in Ghana', *Journal of Modern African Studies* 11(1): 61–89.

Hibou, B., 1996. *L'Afrique est-elle Protectionniste? Les Chemins Buissonniers de la Libéralisation Extérieure* (Paris: Karthala).

Horton, R., 1985. 'Stateless Societies in the History of West Africa', in J.F. Ade Ajayi and Michael Crowder, (eds), *History of West Africa* (Harlow: Longman), vol. 1, pp. 87–128.

Leys, C., 1996. *The Rise and Fall of Development Theory* (London, Bloomington and Nairobi: James Currey, Indiana University Press, and East African Educational Publishers).

Little, K., 1965–6. 'The Political Function of the Poro', part I, *Africa* 35(4): 349–65; part II, 36(1): 62–72.

Post, K.W.J. , 1970. 'British Policy and Representative Government in West Africa, 1920 to 1951', in L.H. Gann and P. Duignan (eds), *Colonialism in Africa 1870–1960*, vol. 2, pp. 31–57 (London: Cambridge University Press).

Ranger, T.O. and I.N. Kimambo (eds), 1972. *The Historical Study of African Religion* (London: Heinemann).

Reno, W., 1995. *Corruption and State Politics in Sierra Leone* (Cambridge: Cambridge University Press).

World Bank, 1989. *Sub-Saharan Africa: from Crisis to Sustainable Growth* (Washington, DC: The World Bank).

3 Stability or Democracy: on the Role of Monitors, Media and Miracles

I. van Kessel

INTRODUCTION[1]

The interventionist mood of the 1990s has spawned new breeds of development-funded travellers to Africa. Aid workers and development consultants have been joined by peace-keeping armies, police trainers, officials of political parties, peace monitors, election observers – to name just of few of the new agents sent out to assist African states in transition processes towards a more democratic mode of governance. This is by and large a new type of involvement in political processes in Africa. There are as yet few rules: the new roles are not clearly defined. These new types of role-players often have only a vague notion of what they are supposed to achieve. They are sometimes deployed in several capacities which may shift over time, thus adding to a blurring of their responsibilities. Nor is it always clear who sets the agenda for various types of international involvement.

In this chapter, I will argue that a clear demarcation of the role and responsibility of peace monitors and election observers is in the interest of both stability and democracy and that some duties, notably the monitoring of democratization as a long-term process, are best left to local actors. The last part of this chapter will therefore focus on the role of independent media as monitors of democracy and, in a broader sense, as agents of democratization.

What is the role of international election monitors? To monitor the elections, report irregularities and deliver a considered judgement on the 'free and fair'-ness of the elections? And – by their presence – inspire confidence in the democratic

50

process? Or do election monitors have a wider responsibility? Is the monitor also the guardian of stability? What if the requirements of truthful reporting on the elections are at odds with the perceived need for political stability? From a basically technical exercise meant to check on correct procedures and to promote a 'levelling of the playing field', election monitoring has evolved towards a political signal, involving a nod of approval or disapproval from donor-countries. What if prioritization of stability undermines the credibility of election monitoring? Does election monitoring serve its purpose if the reports of monitoring missions are inspired by the political agenda of donor-countries?

On the other hand, democratization involves much more than the regular ritual of multiparty elections.[2] Recent African history is littered with flawed and often deliberately manipulated elections. We don't need the 1933 elections in Germany to remind us that multiparty elections do not necessarily signal a democratic process. If other conditions – notably the rule of law – are absent, elections may not result in democratic governance but in a consolidation of authoritarian rule, under which the losers of the electoral contest remain excluded from the political process. A verdict on the technical correctness of the elections has no bearing on the democratic content of the political process.

In the first part of this chapter, I will argue that the duties of election observers should not be compounded with the responsibilities of peace monitors. If there is a role for international monitoring of African elections, it should be with a clear and limited mandate. To illustrate my argument, I will use the 1994 South African elections as an example of diffuse and overlapping patterns of responsibility of international actors.

On the eve of the elections, South Africa was in the grip of fear of violent conflagration. But during the long days of a momentous but extremely chaotic election, the voting exercise was transformed into a 'small miracle', to quote president Nelson Mandela. Both in popular memory and in diplomatic discourse, the South African elections and the transitional arrangements on power-sharing have become a model which is held up as an example for other African countries. But a model of what, exactly?

SOUTH AFRICA: FROM NIGHTMARE SCENARIO TO MODEL

International observers in South Africa have served in the role of peace monitor, election observer and 'monitor of democracy' with a long-term engagement. By all accounts, South Africa's first democratic election in 1994 was the most monitored election ever. From the second half of 1992, substantial numbers of observers from the United Nations, the European Community and the Organization of African Unity, and later from the Commonwealth as well, began arriving in South Africa. Over a period of one and a half years, these organizations deployed 2,513 observers in South Africa, in addition to domestic observers and observers from foreign NGOs (Anglin 1995: 525). Their initial task was to assist in bringing an end to the violence and to create conditions for negotiations, as a preliminary to the ultimate purpose of promoting conditions conducive to free and fair elections. Subsequently, their mandate was expanded to include the observation of the election itself. The rationale for having international observers was that by their mere presence they contribute to a climate conducive to free political participation. Anglin argues that in the case of South Africa, observers sometimes played a useful role as mediators during marches or mass gatherings with a potential for violence. Peace-keeping activities were indeed within the expanded mandate of the United Nations Observer Mission to South Africa (UNOMSA), as established by Security Council resolution 894 in 1994, which referred to 'activities relating to peace promotion and the reduction of violence'.

But the dramatic decline in violence in the final week of the campaign had little to do with the huge influx of observers (Anglin 1995: 535). That the election itself took place in an atmosphere of relative peace was due to the fact that the Freedom Front and the Inkatha Freedom Party, two political parties with the most potential for violent disruption, had at the last minute decided to participate in the polls. As the election date drew nearer, new contingents of observers kept streaming in. Their mandate was not only to assess the elections, but also to determine whether the rules of the game were conducive to the holding of free and fair elections. Among their many responsibilities was the monitoring of domestic monitors, notably the Election Monitoring Directorate of the Independent Electoral Commission, the Independent Media Commission and the police. In briefing sessions, a strong message was hammered into the observers: so much was at stake in South Africa's first democratic elections that this exercise could not be allowed to fail. The consequences of failure would be too ghastly to contemplate.

During this period, the international missions worked closely with the South African Independent Electoral Commission (IEC). The IEC was installed only in December 1993 and was thus left with precious little time to organize this vast operation. In the preparatory phase, the international observers pointed out inadequacies and offered advice on more adequate procedures. In their final reports after the elections, they differed on some important points with the IEC. While the IEC declared the elections 'substantially free and fair', these words were conspicuously lacking from the joint statement of the international missions. They concluded that the people of South Africa had indeed been able to participate freely in the voting and that 'the outcome of the elections reflects the will of the people of South Africa' (United Nations 1994: 22–5).

Both UNOMSA and the European Union Election Unit noted some glaring deficiencies. These ranged from a shortage of ballot papers in the polling stations to unofficial transport of ballot boxes to the never explained tampering with the computer program used to accumulate the results in the central results unit of the IEC's head office. Results now had to be totalled with a manual system, leading to even more delays in a week characterized by excruciatingly long waits. The final reports of the EU mission and UNOMSA are in broad agreement in their praise for the spirit of compromise manifested by the parties in the aftermath of the election, although they differ on not insignificant matters such as the scale of irregularities. While the EU declared that procedures were impeccable in some 90 per cent of the voting stations (European Union Election Unit 1994: ii), the UN reported that only '81.13 per cent of voting stations [were] observed to be applying procedures correctly' (United Nations 1994: 81). It is not clear whether this substantial discrepancy was caused by more vigilance on the part of the UN observers or by a more lenient interpretation of the rules in the EU camp.

The EU report regretted the inadequate logistics and the 'non-transparent process of dispute settling', which was done by party officials without the presence of any international observers. But it went on to state that 'nevertheless, the parties agreed without major reservations to accept the election results as they were proclaimed, and all political quarters seem to be content with it' (European Union Election Unit 1994: 81). The EU mission did, however, not evade the crucial question: acceptance by all parties is not necessarily the same as free and fair elections. 'Whilst the final results may be plausible, sheer plausibility is not satisfactory for observers. Since the election results have not yet been presented in sufficient detail it is not possible to assess to what extent the result is not only plausible but correct and thus fair '(European Union Election Unit 1994: 81).

The UN report equally acknowledged that the elections were far from perfect. It expressed severe criticism of the inadequate planning in the pre-election phase. But in spite of these 'systemic problems' (United Nations 1994: 23) and 'evidence of irregularities' in the counting process (ibid.: 29), the report concluded with praise for the consensus which was maintained throughout the process. 'Fortunately, the perseverance and spirit of compromise that prevailed in the negotiations was sustained. The political parties demonstrated remarkable maturity and responsibility, thus helping to achieve an overall acceptable, credible result. This is one of the great lessons to be drawn from the whole South African process of change' (ibid.: 39). From this phrase, it is not quite clear what the lesson entails exactly: in case the electorate produces an 'unacceptable' result, would it then be up to the parties to help achieve an overall acceptable outcome? Did the outcome of the elections reflect 'the will of the people' or 'the will of the parties'?

In view of the broad mandate of the observer missions, which included peace-keeping as well as election monitoring, it is understandable that the reports address both the issue of political stability and the fairness of the election. But this broad mandate results in a blurring of responsibilities. An unhealthy confusion reigns between the acceptability of party deals in the interest of stability and the basic meaning of elections, which are after all held to establish the preferences of the citizens by counting their votes. As peace monitors, international agents can support an arrangement between parties which is likely to maintain the peace. As election observers, they are supposed to monitor that the 'will of the people' is identified by counting their votes, rather than by non-transparent deals between party bosses. If the international missions have sent a signal to South Africa that the outcome of elections can be settled in a deal between parties, then they have left a legacy which does not augur well for future elections.

In evaluating the largest exercise of its kind in UN history, the UN report is rather self-congratulatory on the impact of the peace-keeping role by the observers deployed by the international community. 'As an exercise in preventive diplomacy, drawing on the strengths of several organizations to support indigenous efforts towards peace and national reconciliation, the international community's efforts in South Africa since 1992 offer a unique and positive demonstration of the benefits of such cooperation' (United Nations 1994: 38). It could have worked out less beneficially. During the instruction sessions for UN observers on short-term assignment for the election week, more attention was given to safety precautions and evacuation procedures than to the technicalities of the election and the fine points of the political contest. This resulted in an atmosphere of heightened anxiety among the observers, many of whom came ill-prepared and already feeling insecure in an unfamiliar environment. One shudders to think what the effects of a stampede of election observers towards their designated evacuation points would have been on the stability of South Africa.

Anglin equally believes that the international observers were most effective in their role as peace monitors. He stipulates that the role of election observers was modest: the major contribution of the international observers was, in fact, as peace monitors during the preceding year and a half (Anglin 1995: 541). The outcome was accepted because the political parties agreed to acquiesce in the published results, not because of the verdict of the observers on the validity of the elections.

A MODEL OF WHAT?

This account raises some interesting questions. Are the roles of peace monitor and election observer mutually interchangeable? And why and how did the political parties in South Africa, in spite of glaring flaws, come to accept the published results? The South African transition was based on a series of compromises between political elites. While the political culture of the confrontational phase of anti-apartheid resistance in the 1980s had celebrated the importance of popular participation, the reality of the 1990s dictated that parties in the long negotiation process became skilled in damage control and conflict containment. This is perfectly understandable and acceptable. As Steven Friedman noted: 'Whatever the costs of the secret deal-making, manipulation and manoeuvring which lay at the centre of the negotiation process, it yielded benefits whose merits would not have to be explained to the inhabitants of Bosnia, Rwanda or Northern Ireland' (Friedman 1994: 336).

So far, so good. But in the euphoria following Nelson Mandela's inauguration, a flawed election was transformed into a model. A model of what? Of democracy or of consensus, compromise and conciliation?

I share the relief and the joy about the miracle which launched South Africa towards a common future of freedom and equal opportunities. My only concern is that we should be clear about what happened. I do not dispute that in certain situations peace and stability are more important considerations than the proper conduct of multi-party elections – as long as we do not confuse these notions, because that is doing democracy a disservice. If stability is the supreme concern, the international community should limit itself to sending peace monitors rather than election observers. The South African experience with negotiated power-sharing might hold interesting lessons for other countries. But the negotiated election should rather remain a unique miracle, and not be advertised as a model to be emulated.

The questions addressed above are of course not unique to the South African situation, as demonstrated in various other chapters of this book, notably those on Ethiopia and Chad. Is election monitoring predominantly a technical exercise to check whether the rules have been applied consistently? Or is it a political gesture, meant to bestow legitimacy on the government which emerges from these elections? Do observers have other responsibilities beyond their mandate as election observers? Two contending positions emerge from the body of policy papers and articles on the subject. The pragmatic view, often held by policy-makers and officials of foreign governments and embassies, emphasizes the observers' responsibility for political stability in the host country. What would happen if they declared the elections invalid? Even if conditions do not fully satisfy elementary requirements of democracy, election observation can still contribute to the political stability which is vital for the further development of the democratization process. This process requires dynamic criteria rather than absolute standards. Even imperfect elections, it is argued, have been useful as a mechanism to bestow legitimacy on new rulers who at least move in the right direction, as in Tanzania.

The other view, prevalent among journalists and academics in the West, argues that the application of double standards would make the whole exercise of questionable validity. Moreover, Africans themselves time and again insist on strict criteria and feel cheated when told that their democracy ought to be measured against a special set of rules. Third World countries apparently deserve Third World democracies. If the verdict 'unfree and unfair' is excluded from the very beginning of the monitoring mission, then what is the point of the exercise? If stability is the primary concern, then why bother with election observers? Election observers should not be confused with peace monitors: that will put the credibility of the whole institution of election monitoring at stake. Limiting the damage should not amount to legitimizing a government (Buijtenhuijs 1997).

The South African case differs, however, in some respects from other questionable elections. No party felt cheated out of victory. On the contrary, the phase of negotiations had produced an inclusive formula for the transition period up to the next elections in 1999. Any party with at least 20 per cent of the vote was entitled to have a vice-president; all parties with at least 10 per cent were entitled to ministerial posts in the Government of National Unity. These 'sunset' clauses meant that the National Party was spared a total eclipse: with 20.3 per cent of the vote, the National Party was entitled to one of the two vice-presidential posts. With 10.5 per cent of the vote, Inkatha entered the cabinet with three ministers. In the post-election euphoria, president Nelson Mandela became ever more generous, offering ministerial posts even to parties which had not made the 10 per cent mark. However, the true miracle was not the elections, but the spirit of compromise and conciliation, which all of a sudden had descended on this polarized, violence-ridden country. Stability in South Africa was preserved not because of the carefully worded verdict of the international observers, who to their credit have not glossed over the irregularities, but because the parties had decided not to contest the results. A negotiated election result seemed the logical conclusion to the negotiated revolution which rested on consensus arrangements between the major players.

Even in official documents, it became fashionable to hail the South African elections as a miracle. The EU report stated that 'given South Africa's history of racial discrimination and oppression, its massive problems of poverty and unemployment, and the tragically high levels of violence, the success of the election is little less than miraculous' (European Union Election Unit 1994: vi). Once the miracle was proclaimed, few doubting Thomases were willing to express their doubts publicly for fear of being branded spoilers of a singular success story. While the observers flew back home to spread the legend of the miracle, newspaper verdicts on the outcome remained more down to earth.

MEDIA COVERAGE OF THE MIRACLE

'No one will ever know if the result is an accurate reflection of the will of the South African people; indeed, if it is so, it is probably by accident', commented the *Financial Times* on the 'designer outcome' which bore such a conspicuous resemblance to the ideal outcome (*Financial Times*, 7–8 May 1994). The chairman of the IEC, justice Johann Kriegler, had set the tone when he cancelled the required procedure of conciliating the inventory of the ballot boxes with the records of the electoral officers, with the commandment that the election was 'about national reconciliation, not ballot reconciliation' (the *Guardian*, 3 May 1994). Like everybody else, *Guardian* correspondent David Beresford was duly impressed with the wave of goodwill which had suddenly swamped the country, but he did not confuse the miracle with a democratic election. 'C'est magnifique, mais ce n'est pas la démocratie' was his paraphrase borrowed from a French general in the Crimean war, to describe the miracle which had taken on a truly religious dimension. The reports and the editorials in the *Weekly Mail and Guardian* provided a clearer picture of the South African elections than the official reports of the observer missions. This fiercely independent left-liberal South African weekly told the stories of the stuffing of ballot boxes, the setting up of 'pirate' polling stations and the issuing of voter cards to under age youths. When complaints from all parties kept piling up, the whole exercise threatened to end in disaster. In a series of local deals, party officials decided to cut a deal rather than challenge the outcome. The IEC gave its blessing 'in the national interest'. Challenged on the legality of the horse-trading, chairman Kriegler said: 'Come now, come now, let's not get purist, let's not be overly squeamish. They are in a power game with one another and if they want to settle by withdrawing objections, that's fine. There is nothing wrong ethically or legally' (*Weekly Mail and Guardian*, 6–12 May 1994). The *Weekly Mail* concluded that the manipulated election result reflected what the major parties agreed they should have achieved at the polls in some regions. Most controversial were the results in KwaZulu-Natal, where Inkatha emerged victorious with a majority of one seat in the provincial assembly and a national percentage poll of 10.5 per cent.

While the media were digging into the less savoury aspects of the miraculous elections, the international observers returned home to find that the miracle had created a worldwide community of believers who longed to join in the celebration rather than be disturbed by questions about behind-the-scene deals.

In their debriefing session with the Foreign Ministry, Dutch observers with the various missions manifested both pride with the happy ending and a certain uneasiness with the horse deals. Observers who had served in KwaZulu-Natal found it particularly galling that people had gone to great lengths and had sometimes demonstrated great courage in the exercise of their vote, only to find that the bosses had made a deal behind their backs. Mr Job de Ruijter, a former Dutch minister who headed the observer delegation of the European Union, admitted that there had been a non-transparent network of decision-making and that backroom deals had influenced the results, but stated that all of this was well within the IEC mandate. However, in his public statements he was less outspoken, which is perhaps indicative of a certain uneasiness with the shady sides of the miracle. In a public lecture some weeks later, he backtracked on his earlier statement, denying that some outcomes had been fixed in backroom deals and painting a picture of a more or less model election. He now offered a new and simple explanation for Inkatha's felicitous results: 'You must remember, there are a tremendous lot of Zulus in Natal.'[3] Such a reference to the irrational tribal nature of African politics is usually sufficient to satisfy an unsuspecting audience. While assuming that Zulus have some primordial predisposition to vote for Inkatha, this 'explanation' conveniently skips the basic fact that the contest in Natal was not between Zulus and other ethnic groups, but between Inkatha loyalists and ANC loyalists, nearly all of whom were Zulus.

The *Weekly Mail* had a more plausible explanation: faced with the choice between 'Bloodshed or Buthelezi', the ANC decided not to push its allegations of fraud beyond a point of no return. After a personal plea by Nelson Mandela, ANC leaders in KwaZulu-Natal dropped their plans to challenge the election results in court. Acknowledging the temptation to join in the celebrations and to 'go along with a cover up of the Independent Electoral Commission's performance', the *Weekly Mail* pronounced nevertheless a harsh verdict: 'By last weekend, Judge Kriegler had to admit that he had to throw aside the rules, the safeguards and what few systems he had in place just to get out some sort of result. By Wednesday afternoon, he had to acknowledge that counting accuracy and care had given way to horse-trading among the parties. He had ceased to be a judge, ruling on the accuracy and validity of the result, but ... a mediator, desperately negotiating a result that all parties would accept' (*Weekly Mail and Guardian*, 6–12 May 1994).

Both in journalistic and academic writing on the elections, different views have been expressed on the role of the IEC and its chairman. While some believe that the IEC was part of the deal, the predominant view was that it acquiesced in a series of deals concluded by the parties. The IEC then went along with their 'consensus results'. Kriegler argued that his mandate was not to ensure that the results were accurate, but that the process was free and fair. If the political parties wanted to horse-trade over disputed ballots, that was their business (*Africa Confidential*, 20 May 1994). Summarizing the election experience in KwaZulu-Natal, Hamilton and Maré concluded:

It is not clear how far the votes attributed to parties in this region are removed from the actual preferences and voices of those who were treated so badly by the election machinery and political parties, and who had borne the brunt of more than a decade of violent confrontation. The published results were a product of a trade-off between the competing parties. Despite all attempts at creating transparency in the voting process, the trade-off that characterized the final moments of vote-counting in KwaZulu-Natal remains opaque. It is widely assumed that the ANC's reluctant acceptance of the results had to do with averting further violence in the region. The electorate is being asked to accept that disputes about irregular ballot boxes and allegations concerning the lack of security in the transporting of boxes and the issuing of temporary voter cards to under-age voters have been shelved, perhaps only temporarily, by both the ANC and the IFP in an attempt to normalize politics in the region. (Hamilton and Maré 1994: 86)

Neither the international observers nor the media have fully exposed the inside story of the South African election. But the media were at least more discerning in distinguishing between the requirements of stability and the demands of democracy. The massive numbers of international observers performed a useful service as guardians of stability, although this credit is more due to long-term monitors than to the troops of observers which arrived shortly before the election. But the media did a better job as watchdogs of democracy.

Peace monitors or election observers: these hordes of international watchdogs are in any case likely to be a passing phenomenon. More sustainable is of course the building of local capacity. Independent media – for all their faults – are most suitable for the long-term role of watchdogs of democracy. In the last part of this chapter, I therefore turn to the role of media as monitors of democracy.

MEDIA AS MONITORS OF DEMOCRACY

Media play a variety of roles as informers, educators and entertainers of the public. Mass media provide information on public policy issues and provide a platform for discussion. Media help empower their audience by making them aware of their civil and political rights and by explaining how and why these rights should be exercised.

With regard to elections, their role is to provide a platform for political discussion in which the main issues are discussed from various points of views, to enable political parties to present their programmes to the electorate, to provide voter education in a more technical sense, and to monitor the conduct of electoral campaigns and the elections themselves. In the case of the South African elections, the media have been praised for their constructive role, in spite of initial suspicions. Much of the mainstream media in South Africa were widely regarded as representing either the vested interests of the National Party or of English-speaking big business. Suspicion was particularly strong with regard to the South African Broadcasting Corporation, long regarded as the mouthpiece of the National Party. The transitional authority in South Africa set up an Independent Media Commission (IMC) to ensure equitable treatment of all political parties by broadcasting services and to ensure that state-financed publications and state information services were not used to advance the interests of any political party. The IMC found that the treatment of political parties had been broadly equitable on radio and television. Monitoring the press did not fall under the mandate of the IMC, but international observers and NGOs did monitor the performance of the print media. UNOMSA stated that 'it is safe to conclude that the print media contributed positively to creating an atmosphere conducive to free and fair elections' (United Nations 1994: 27). Significantly, a survey conducted by the Independent Forum for Electoral Education found that some 75 per cent of respondents depended on the print and broadcast media for voter education (United Nations 1994: 27). The EU mission had an equally positive judgement on the role of the media.

This is an interesting verdict, because it contradicts the widespread notion that media necessarily function as their masters' voice. At first sight, the ANC was at a disadvantage in media coverage, because the liberation movement did not figure among the newspaper tycoons. English-language newspapers were traditionally supportive of big business and the Democratic

Party, while the Afrikaans language dailies and weeklies were vociferous supporters of the National Party. Only some weekly papers with a fairly limited circulation, such as *New Nation* and the *Weekly Mail and Guardian*, favoured the ANC. Nevertheless, in all the main newspapers the ANC received by far the most coverage, although not all coverage was sympathetic to the movement. Editorial endorsements of the Democratic Party in most of the English language papers had no visible effect on voting patterns: the DP came out with a dismal 1.7 per cent of the vote. News coverage largely ignored the Democratic Party and focused on the main contenders, the ANC and the National Party (Silke and Schrire 1994). Editorial criteria on news value were apparently established in the relative autonomy of the newsroom and not dictated in the boardrooms of the media conglomerates. Predictably, the white-owned but black circulation *Sowetan* told its readers that 'the ANC and the PAC are the only parties for whom our choice should be made' (*Sowetan*, 25 April 1994). This even-handed treatment of both liberation movements could not stop the downfall of the Panafricanist Congress, which ended up with 1.25 per cent of total votes.

At the time of the elections, broadcasting remained largely a state monopoly. But to everybody's surprise, radio and television coverage of the election period was remarkably balanced and fair. In the case of the SABC, the growth to mature reporting was no doubt helped by the guidelines and the monitoring by the IMC (Silke and Schrire 1994: 128–9). The interesting lesson of this experience remains that media can play a constructive role both as educators of the public and as watchdogs on behalf of the public, even if they are not regarded as unpartisan.

These favourable verdicts only indicate that the South African media were well behaved in the election period and that they contributed to levelling the playing field without giving undue advantage to one party. However, their role went beyond fair reporting. As monitors of the elections they were as vigilant as the international observer missions and certainly more outspoken.

The verdict on the role of the press in African elections in general is of course not universally favourable. Media coverage of the 1995 general elections in Tanzania has come up for some severe criticism. The Election Media Bulletin published by the Association of Journalists and Media Workers described newspaper coverage as 'appalling', noting 'violation of professional ethics, malicious and outright lies, open bias, deliberate misrepresentation and the failure to distinguish between government function and campaign' (Richey and Ponte 1996: 83).

In Zimbabwe, which functions *de facto* as a one-party state, independent media, along with an independent judiciary, provide some kind of countervailing power. Human rights organizations have praised the role of the independent press in election coverage. In a report on the 1995 parliamentary elections, the human rights organization ZimRights found that 'the independent media, such as the *Financial Gazette*, the *Sunday Gazette* and *Horizon Magazine*, generally related fair, unbiased and informative coverage to the public'. The government-owned media, on the other hand, were 'demonstrably propagandistic, partisanly belligerent, and lacked objectivity in their reporting and subject matter. Since these are the only daily newspapers, this level of propaganda was very damaging' (ZimRights 1995: 6).

Unlike international observers, media are continuously on the spot as watchdogs of democracy, although – like international observers – they are often ill equipped for their role. The South African example of responsible reporting in the transition period is not easily duplicated elsewhere in Africa. South Africa's media infrastructure and its relatively well-established tradition of editorial autonomy is probably unrivalled in Africa. In other countries, such as Rwanda and Burundi in the 1990s, the media did not serve as monitors of democracy but as spoilers, propagating ethnic hate speech which contributed to the general atmosphere of heightened polarization. Journalists are of course not all brave Davids, locked in a courageous battle with the power-holding Goliaths. Although they like to portray themselves as watchdogs of the public interest, they can be as selfish and irresponsible as the much-maligned politicians. But if African countries are to embark on processes of democratization, African media will have to come into their own, moving beyond the familiar stereotypes of praise singer of the ruler or unashamed propagandist for the opposition.

PHASES OF DEMOCRATIZATION

Literature on democratization typically distinguishes three phases in the process: origins, transition and consolidation.

The first multi-party elections are then seen as the crucial part of the transition phase. The role of international observers is usually limited to this phase. Media do not only follow the process throughout, they are also an intrinsic part of it: the watchdog doubles as an actor. In the first part of this chapter, we have examined the role of media as monitors of elections. Here we turn to the media as actors in the fray: how have the media fared in their broader role as agents of democratization?

Literature on the role of the media in democratization processes is scarce. As Buijtenhuijs and Thiriot note in their survey of the literature, most publications focus on obstacles encountered by the independent media rather than on their role in opening up the political arena (1995: 47).[4] In the few exceptions to this rule, the authors generally believe that the role of the media has been underestimated (Randall 1993; Sandbrook 1996).

Although media rarely had a triggering role in the start of the democratization process, they caused an indispensable snowballing effect. In some countries, as in Kenya, Malawi and Tanzania, media were also instrumental in the first phase, formulating demands for an opening up of the one-party state before the political opposition had regrouped into political parties. In Malawi, where no independent press had survived Banda's dictatorship, public debate was fuelled by newspapers which were faxed from Zambia in order to circumvent the censors. In Zimbabwe, which so far has not made the transition towards genuine multi-party elections, independent media – and in a few exceptional instances even the state-controlled media – have exposed corruption by state and party officials, land grabbing and tampering with the electoral rules. In some cases, exposures in the press resulted in the dismissals of government ministers or the restitution of farms or other assets. As in Malawi, new technology makes life easier for journalists and more difficult for censors. A report compiled by the Catholic Commission for Justice and Peace on the massacres perpetrated by the Zimbabwean army in Matabeleland in the mid-1980s was not published in Zimbabwe, because of its sensitive nature. It was, however, leaked to the *Mail and Guardian* in Johannesburg, which not only published abstracts from the report, but put the full text of the report on Internet. Via the *MandG*'s Internet site, the report found its way to the media in

Zimbabwe. In Benin, outgoing president Mathieu Kérékou even blamed the press for his election defeat.

Referring more to Latin America than to Africa, Randall notes:

> Though the national media themselves rarely played a 'triggering' role, in a situation in which popular protest or opposition demands were already beginning to mount, they could widen awareness of issues and help put some kind of frame on events. They could mobilize and orchestrate popular protest. By deepening and accelerating political communication in this way they significantly added to the pressures on the authorities. (Randall 1993: 636)

Even if they were not instrumental in the first phase, media played an indispensable role in the next phase. In the African context, few – if any – countries can be said to have progressed to the third phase: consolidation.

Both Sandbrook and Randall distinguish between the role of domestic media and the impact of international media. Domestic media did not play a vital role in the political openings of the early 1990s. In the nascent phase of political liberalization, it was actually the international mass media that helped crystallize opposition to authoritarian and often inept governments. Images of the fall of dictators – and their statues – in Eastern Europe had a powerful impact on African audiences. The message was that military coups and civil war were not the only methods available to get rid of autocrats: they could be removed relatively peacefully by popular mobilization. In several countries, including Zaire, the government prohibited the transmission of television pictures of the execution of Nicolae Ceaucescu, the much-feared Rumanian dictator. The growth of short-wave radio, satellite television and fax machines undermined government control over information. Media in Africa did not initiate the democratic opening, but the idea caught on by contagion, in which media played a crucial role (Sandbrook 1996: 83).

After decades of one-party rule, repression and harassment, the indigenous media were not in a fit state to take the lead as champions of democracy. Moreover, a sizeable part of the print media and almost all the audio-visual media were controlled by editors who faithfully implemented the role of transmission belt of the ruling elite. But in several African countries the press was never fully reduced to the role of praise singer of the president and his party, or of the military dictatorship. Among the remarkable features of the political thaw in many African countries is the impressive number of independent publications which sprang up almost overnight and the eagerness of a news-starved readership which devoured the new titles. In Cameroon, the number of newspapers and magazines increased from about 15 prior to January 1990, to nearly 100 in 1993. In the same period, the circulation of the government-owned *Cameroon Tribune* dropped from about 30,000 to 5,000 (Takougang 1994).

Some of this boom was just transient. Many titles collapsed within one or two years because their owners concentrated solely on the editorial message of the paper and neglected to look into economic viability. After the first outburst of enthusiasm, circulations declined because the readership lost interest. Nevertheless, the present media landscape in Africa shows much more diversity than ever before.

BEYOND PRAISE SINGERS AND RABBLE-ROUSERS

Like political parties, independent media have a hard time in defining their role in the process of political democratization. The 'all or nothing' nature of African politics results either in docility or extreme polarization. Ruling parties are inclined to marginalize the opposition. Opposition parties are not geared to the role of loyal opposition: rather than formulating an alternative political programme, they set out to subvert parliamentary procedures.

The news media are caught up in much the same game: they tend to be either docile mouthpieces of the government or scandal-mongering rabble-rousers who are not overly concerned about the accuracy of their stories as long as they expose the outrageous deeds of the rulers. Freed from the strait-jacket of developmental journalism, in which media were relegated to the role of tools in the hands of the ruling elite which supposedly carried the heavy responsibility of architects of nation-building, newspapers plunged enthusiastically in the political arena. Like the political parties, they were ill prepared for their new freedom. The flaws of the African news media have come up for much criticism: they are branded as unprofessional, irresponsible, sensationalist, partisan and venal. One Cameroonian journalist likened the role of the independent press to that of a house-fly: 'It has a habit of being around when things start stinking. So, what better then can one expect from the press in a Cameroon where almost everything has been stinking for over forty years' (Takougang 1994: 14).

There are obvious limitations to the role of the media as agents of democratization. In a predominantly rural continent afflicted by poverty and illiteracy, many citizens do not have access to mass media. As Kwame Karikari has noted, the press in Africa is urban-centred and has an elite orientation. Very few newspapers target an audience of workers and peasants. The re-emerging press in Africa remains an elite institution. The use of colonial languages excludes the majority of the population. Language is the most obvious limitation on the press as an effective medium for popular involvement in mass communication (Karikari 1993). Radio of course has more potential as a medium well suited to reach both the urban poor and rural peasants. It is cheaper and more accessible than print media, but remains state controlled in many African countries. Where the airwaves are opened up for other broadcasters, it is often only for commercial stations where popular participation is limited to phoning in with requests for the listeners' favourite music.

Whatever their shortcomings, media are indispensable to the democratic process. Will the media in Africa be able to fulfil the role of monitors of democracy and agents of democratization, in view of the domestic political and economic situation, the international setting and wavering donor support?

Mass media in Africa are confronted with an impressive range of constraints, ranging from government restrictions, extra-institutional harassment, small readership markets, a limited economic base, and the poor state of the media industry itself. Although the 1990s saw an unprecedented blossoming of new publications, the revival of the independent press is fraught with dangers. While most authors point to a relaxation of controls on the media, the picture is by no means rosy. Kenneth Best, the former publisher of the *Daily Observer* which appeared first in Monrovia and then in Banjul, and who was subsequently forced to leave the Gambia, even stated that 'media practitioners and media organisations in Africa have never known more repression and brutality than what we are facing today'. Lawsuits and licensing of media publications or journalists have become more widespread than before, while another old weapon against journalists – murder – took more victims than at any other time in history. In 1994 alone, Africa lost some 80 journalists, more than all the media people killed in the Second World War (Best 1997: 31).

In an eloquent plea for press freedom as a core condition for sustainable democratization, Peter Takirambudde gives an overview of the legal obstacles facing the press in various African countries. In his view, democratization cannot survive in circumstances wherein the press remains largely unfree. 'Sustained democratization would require a supportive environment in which a critical tradition and freedom of expression predominate. These elements are conspicuously lacking in most of the emerging "democracies"' (Takirambudde 1995: 20). Media freedom can only be revived if African states make the transition from patrimonialism to constitutionalism: the arbitrary powers of the rulers need to be replaced by the rule of law, an impersonal, impartial and predictable rule that protects the rights of all citizens. In a democratic society, media are indispensable as a counterbalancing institution. Takirambudde deals with both formal and informal repression, censorship and self-censorship.

Much of the current discussion on the role of the media focuses on the relationship between the state and the media. The state is singled out as the main obstacle for a free press, both because of repressive practices and because the state is the owner of the majority of daily newspapers and the vast majority of radio and television stations. Rather neglected in the current debate are the constraints of the market. Political liberalization has created more space for independent media. But what have been the effects of economic liberalization? Takirambudde believes that, in the long run, the restructuring of African economies towards market systems may hatch a large and powerful entrepreneurial middle class that would believe strongly in individual liberty and would increasingly assert their rights against the state. Thus, in the long term, economic liberalization would contribute significantly to the creation of self-sustaining environment for media freedom.

In the short run, the impact of Structural Adjustment Programmes (SAPs) and economic liberalization is more ambivalent. Liberalization of imports and abolition of exchange controls has enabled media to import their own newsprint and equipment, thus robbing the government of one instrument of control. But the consequences of SAPs for the purchasing power of urban residents have impacted negatively on their ability to buy newspapers as well as on advertising budgets. As a rule of thumb, advertising accounts for at least two-thirds of newspaper revenue. One intended effect of SAPs is a redistribution of income from the cities to the rural areas: this is potentially harmful for newspapers. The bulk of their readership is urban based. Advertisers are only interested in a readership with purchasing power. Therefore, if independent media are totally at the mercy of market forces, it is difficult to sustain media diversity and to reach audiences which hold little attraction for advertisers.

The inherent risk of the free-market system is that media become hooked on the consumer market rather than on the needs of citizens. For this reason, several European countries, including Sweden and the Netherlands, have instituted various methods of subsidizing the media, ranging from low tax tariffs to straightforward (temporary) subsidies. Particularly devastating for the press in Africa has been the steep rise in the price of newsprint on the world market, which has increased by some 30 to 40 per cent over the past years. Newsprint is the single biggest expenditure for African newspapers. Many newspapers have been forced to peg their circulation at a fixed number, not because of lack of demand but because of the prohibitive costs of newsprint. In the past, various organizations – such as UNESCO and Canadian NGOs – used to subsidize paper purchases for educational and news media purposes. But in the present market-oriented environment, subsidies are out of fashion.

What part can the international community play in enabling independent media to fulfil their role as monitors of democracy? Support can be given in various ways: advocacy, material assistance (both to individual media and to help create an enabling environment for a free press), training, and political conditionality.

Organizations for human rights, press freedom and journalists' organizations have been active in the sphere of advocacy, but their activities are largely limited to supporting individual journalists who have run foul of the authorities. Conceivably, there is also a role for international solidarity in supporting campaigns for legal reforms conducted by African media organizations. One clear example is the current battle in many African countries between the state that wants to maintain its monopoly over broadcasting, and media organizations that demand the opening of the airwaves to independent broadcasters. Assistance to individual media projects is channelled through various NGOs, such as the Communication Assistance Foundation in the Netherlands. But with less than 1 per cent of the total budget of the Dutch Minister for Development Cooperation allocated to media in the Third World, there is scope for improvement.

Assistance can be given to individual newspapers or radio stations, but can also be used to create an environment in which newspapers can survive and thrive. Subsidy schemes for newsprint could be a temporary measure to facilitate the take-off of newspapers. Publishers can also pool resources and set up a joint import scheme which will enable them to buy newsprint at a discount, as the Senegalese publishers are doing with the help of the Canadian embassy (Best 1997: 33). In countries where the only printing press is controlled by the government or the ruling party, the provision of printing presses would make a huge difference. There is a massive need for training. Journalists are often poorly trained, ill paid, have a low social status and therefore often feel insecure in their battles with authorities. If independent media are to fulfil their watchdog role in emerging democracies, they will have to become more professional. Only media with a reputation of reliability and accuracy will be taken seriously by the ruling elites. Among the journalistic profession in Africa, it is widely and emphatically recognized that journalism and newspaper management are in need of more professionalism. Training needs are diverse, ranging from training in journalistic skills and ethics to newspaper management, advertising, marketing, technical expertise with regard to printing equipment, computer technology, desk top publishing.

More contentious is the case for political conditionality. Takirambudde notes that political conditionality has been employed as a tool to promote democracy, but that this tool has not been very effective because of insufficient down-to-earth links between political conditionality and the achievement of 'real' human rights, such as press freedom. Rather than on global and imprecise demands, political conditionality should be more surgically targeted on rigorous respect for freedom of the media (Takirambudde 1995: 53).

Professional journalism does not mean unpartisan journalism. Like the media in Europe, media in Africa will have their own socio-political profile and their own political preferences. There is nothing wrong with that, as long as it does not result in distortion of the news. Media are partisan; but so are observers. The report of the European Union mission to the South African elections freely recognizes that it is always difficult to find neutral observers. Explaining why 'monitoring' was preferred above the more interventionist mode of election 'observing', the report states: 'The many national and international observer groups that were present, brought together people from a wide variety of backgrounds: with a range of political commitments and often patchy knowledge of the electoral regulations. It is preferable to have them play the unobtrusive role of observing rather than intervening in the process' (European Union Election Unit 1994: 44).

CONCLUSION

International advisers and monitors can play a useful role in countries emerging from a past of authoritarian rule. Their duties and responsibilities ought to be clearly defined. Their reports should not be inspired by the political agenda of their country of origin. A clear distinction between peace monitors and election observers is crucial in order to avoid an unhealthy confusion between the interests of political stability and the requirements of democracy. In any case, the role of international observers is limited to the transition phase and to a limited sphere of activities, such as elections. The broader democratic process requires 'monitors of democracy', but this role is best left to local actors, notably independent media. This is therefore not a plea for either/or monitors or media: both have a role to play. But while much attention has recently been given to various forms of international involvement and intervention, the role of the media in Africa is much neglected.

The donor community is narrowly focused on multi-party elections as the litmus test of democratization. A political conditionality which singles out multi-party elections as the crucial element, without taking account of the wider environment, risks being counter-productive. Indispensable for sustainable democratization are independent media. Governments – not only in Africa – have a tendency to dismiss media as 'irresponsible' and therefore not very relevant to the democratic process. Tension between governments and media is however a normal condition in democracies. As Lord Jacobson once said when opening a debate in the House of Lords on the state of the press (cited in Grant and Egner 1989: 263): 'Relations between politicians and the press have deteriorated, are deteriorating … and should on no account be allowed to improve.'

NOTES

1.   In this article, the terms 'observer' and 'monitor' are used interchangeably.
2.   Van Cranenburgh 1997; Sandbrook 1996; Ellis 1996; Hyden 1996; Shaw and Maclean 1996; Young 1997; Abbink 1995. For an extensive survey of the literature on democratization up to 1995, see Buijtenhuijs and Rijnierse 1993 and Buijtenhuijs and Thiriot 1995.
3.   Lecture by Mr J. de Ruyter for the Nederlands Genootschap voor Internationale Zaken (Netherlands Society for International Relations), The Hague, 14 June 1994.
4.   Some recent books on the subject are: Bourgault 1995; Hachten 1993; Tudesq 1995.

REFERENCES

Abbink, J. 1995. 'Breaking and Making the State: the Dynamics of Ethnic Democracy in Ethiopia', *Journal of Contemporary African Studies* 13(2): 149–63.
Anglin, D.G. 1995. 'International Monitoring of the Transition to Democracy in South Africa, 1992–1994', *African Affairs* 94(377): 519–43.
Best, K. 1997. 'Journalists under Fire', *West Africa* (special issue, *West Africa at 80*, July 1997): 31–3.

Bourgault, L. 1995. *Mass Media in Sub-Saharan Africa* (Bloomington: Indiana University Press).

Buijtenhuijs, R. 1997. 'Limiter les Dégâts ou Cautionner des Abus? L'Observation Internationale du Référendum Constitutionnel et des Elections Présidentielles au Tchad (mars–juillet 1996)', in: *Observatoire Permanent de la Coopération Française* (Paris: Karthala).

Buijtenhuijs, R. and E. Rijnierse, 1993. *Democratization in Sub-Saharan Africa 1989–1992* (Leiden: African Studies Centre).

Buijtenhuijs, R. and C. Thiriot, 1995. *Démocratisation en Afrique au Sud du Sahara 1992–1995* (Leiden: African Studies Centre).

Ellis, S. 1996. 'Africa after the Cold War: New Patterns of Government and Politics', *Development and Change* 27(1): 1–28.

European Union Election Unit, 1994. *Observing South Africa's 1994 National and Provincial Elections: Final Report to the European Commission from the European Union Election Unit* (Johannesburg).

Friedman, S. 1994. 'The Brief Miracle?', in S. Friedman and D. Atkinson (eds), *The Small Miracle: South Africa's Negotiated Settlement.* Special issue, *South African Review* 7: 331–7 (Johannesburg: Ravan Press).

Grant S. and B. Egner, 1989. 'The Private Press and Democracy', in J. Holm and P. Molutsi (eds), *Democracy in Botswana* (Gaborone: Macmillan), pp. 247–63.

Hachten, W.A. 1993. *The Growth of Media in the Third World: African Failures, Asian Successes* (Ames: Iowa State University Press).

Hamilton G. and M. Maré, 1994. 'The Inkatha Freedom Party', in A. Reynolds (ed.), *Election '94 South Africa: the Campaigns, Results and Future Prospects* (London: James Currey), pp. 73–88.

Karikari, K. 1993. 'Africa: the Press and Democracy', *Race and Class* 34(3): 55–66.

Lodge, T. 1995. 'The South African General Election, April 1994: Results, Analysis and Implications', *African Affairs* 94: 471–500.

Hyden, G. 1996. 'Rethinking Theories of the State: an Africanist Perspective', *Africa Insight* 26(1): 26–35.

Keene-Young, B. 1994. *Media Coverage and the Electoral Process. International Briefing on South Africa's First Democratic and Non-racial Election: Presentation Six* (Brussels: EU).

Randall, V. 1993. 'The Media and Democratisation in the Third World', *Third World Quarterly* 14 (3): 625–46.

Richey L. and S. Ponte, 1996. 'The 1995 Tanzania Union Elections'. *Review of African Political Economy* 23(67): 80–7.

Sandbrook, R. 1996. 'Transitions without Consolidation: Democratization in Six African Cases', *Third World Quarterly* 17(1): 69–87.

Shaw, T. and S. Maclean, 1996. 'Civil Society and Political Economy in Contemporary Africa: what Prospects for Sustainable Democracy?', *Journal of Contemporary African Studies* 14(2): 247–64.

Silke, D. and R. Schrire, 1994. 'The Mass Media and the South African Election', in A. Reynolds (ed.), *Election '94 South Africa: the Campaigns, Results and Future Prospects* (London: James Currey), pp. 121–43.

Takirambudde, P.N. 1995. 'Media Freedom and the Transition to Democracy in Africa', *African Journal of International and Comparative Law* 7(1): 18–53.

Takougang, J. 1994. 'The Press and the Democratization Process in Africa: the Case of the Republic of Cameroon' (Paper presented at the Annual Meetings, Toronto, African Studies Association).

Tudesq, J. 1995. *Feuilles d'Afrique, Etude de la Presse de l'Afrique Subsaharienne* (Bordeaux: Maison des Sciences de l'Homme).

United Nations, 1994. *Report of the Secretary-General on the Question of South Africa*. Security Council (S/1994/717) (New York: UN).

Van Cranenburgh, O. 1997. 'Meerpartijenverkiezingen in Afrika: de Averechtse Effecten van Politieke Aanpassing'. *Internationale Spectator* 51(4): 214–17.

Young, C. 1997. 'Democracy and the Ethnic Question in Africa'. *Africa Insight* 27(1): 4–14.

ZimRights 1995. *Election Monitoring Report; Parliamentary Elections 1995* (Harare: ZimRights).

4 Elections and Civil Strife: Some Implications for International Election Observation

B. de Gaay Fortman

INTRODUCTION

In Africa elections tend to be organized in a setting of rather high degrees of civil strife. In many cases political violence has become an integral part of the political struggle. Electoral violence erupts particularly in situations in which elections offer a genuine possibility of changing existing power relations. As a result of the poor state of the economies the stakes in politics have become extremely high. Often, political power has become the dominant social good in the sense that those who have it, 'can command a wide range of other goods' (Walzer 1983: 10). Consequently, any threat to a position of political power may result in suppressive violence.

In this chapter elections and civil strife will be analysed against the background of four factors which tend to affect the role of elections in processes of democratization: a malfunctioning party system, the lack of adequate checks and balances, authoritarian leadership, and the problem of legitimate government under adverse economic conditions. Although they arrive on the scene only after the stage has been set, monitors should be aware of the state of affairs in regard to each of these institutional elements. Most problematic, in my view, is the state of the economy. In the preparation of monitors it is particularly that fourth factor which tends to be overlooked. This might seem to be understandable, since they can do nothing to remedy adverse economic conditions. However, a proper understanding of the political economy of elections may well contribute to more effective monitoring. Naturally, monitors cannot operate as if they were Martians. Though not in any way identifying with one of the parties, they may be expected to relate to the country as such, certainly in regard to its development.

In the following section democratization will be discussed in a contemporary African setting. It is in this context that political violence has to be understood. Next, each of the four coordinates within which elections tend to take place – a malfunctioning party system, lack of democratic checks and balances, a culture of authoritarianism and adverse economic conditions – will be discussed. Finally, some conclusions will be drawn in regard to elections and democratization in general and the role of international observation in particular.

DEMOCRATIZATION AND VIOLENCE

After the fall of the Berlin Wall and the end of the Cold War, sub-Saharan Africa, too, came under great pressure to democratize. The background, as we know, is economic as well as political. It was, particularly, the lack of democracy that had made real existing socialism rigid, non-reformable and appallingly inefficient (De Gaay Fortman 1994a). Politically, dictatorship is not merely seen as structural and systematic suppression of fundamental freedoms but also as being conducive to inter- and intra-state collective violence. In an analysis of *Democracy, Power, Genocide, and Mass Murder*, Rummel, for example, found only one political indicator of *democide* (genocide, massacres, extrajudicial executions and so on): totalitarian power. Democracy, he concludes, is inversely related to democide:

> That power kills is the primary and, for domestic democide, singular general explanation of democide ... and the more democratic the less domestic collective violence.
>
> (Rummel 1995: 25).

Behind the non-violent character of democracies is not merely a system of government but a certain relationship between polity and economy based upon the necessity of *legitimacy*. This becomes clear when synthesizing the two major branches of social theory on collective intra-state violence: resource mobilization theory (Tilly) and relative deprivation theory (Gurr). At the roots of civil strife, then, is not just collective action through political mobilization (Tilly 1975), but also a breeding ground of socio-economic discontent. It is a part of the human being's constitution that 'if frustrations (discontent, dissatisfaction, grievances) are sufficiently prolonged or sharply felt, aggression is quite likely, if not certain, to occur' (Gurr 1970). This 'frustration–aggression mechanism' may, however, be mitigated by certain social conditions that affect the manifestation of latent aggression into actual collective violence (De Gaay Kortekaas and Fortman 1996). One of these is *regime legitimacy*. This factor may reduce aggression as the frustration experienced may find an outlet in political struggle of a peaceful nature. Here lies the basis of a theory behind Rummel's findings, since democracy is a process – often even regarded as the *only* process (for example Schmitter and Carl 1991) – for the creation of legitimate government.

Taking Abraham Lincoln's definition of 'government of the people, by the people, and for the people' as a starting-point, we may conceptualize democracy as representative government, participatory government and accountable government. It is particularly in relation to the former that the call for 'free and fair' elections has to be understood. Representative government implies that those who rule should not just come from the people, but there should actually be mechanisms to ensure that they represent the people in processes of decision-making. Here the focus is on the *constitution* of political power. In that connection it seems useful to quote Schumpeter, who sees democracy as simply *competition for political leadership*:

> the role of the people is to produce a government, ... and ... the democratic method is that institutional arrangement for arriving at political decisions in which individuals acquire the power to decide by means of a competitive struggle for the people's vote.

(Schumpeter 1947: 269)

Thus, representative government is not so much the people's rule but the politician's rule. What is essential, however, is the substitutability of the politician through 'the democratic method'. In an essay entitled *The Fifth Modernization* the Chinese dissident Wei Jingsheng explained the system to his countrymen in the following simple terms:

What is true democracy? It means the right of the people to choose their own representatives to work according to their will and in their interests. Only this can be called democracy. Furthermore, the people must also have the power to replace their representatives anytime so that these representatives cannot go on deceiving them in the name of the people.

(quoted in *The New York Times*, 14 Dec. 1995)

Indeed, an essential feature of representation is the *substitutability of those in power*. If the ruled are dissatisfied with their rulers they should have an opportunity of replacing them. This is usually done through elections. If regimes do not provide such mechanisms, the only way to replace those in power is through a change of the regime. This usually implies violence.

The problem is that democracies cannot be established just like that. Democracy is a process that has to start with *democratization*. In sub-Saharan Africa, however, there appear to be certain adverse conditions under which processes of democratization through the ballot box appear to be very difficult, to say the least. Where these are neglected, democratization may get completely out of hand and produce entirely reverse effects to what Rummel's findings on the relationship between democracy and non-violence would seem to point at. As Gurr has warned:

the process of democratization that is so vigorously fostered by US foreign policy is bound to increase the opportunities for communal protest and rebellion in plural societies throughout the world, with effects analogous to those we observed in the 1980s: some new democracies may be able to accommodate rising communal demands, but the odds are that most will not. And the ensuing civil wars will add to the diffusion of communal conflict and to the floods of refugees who will create future communal tensions.

(Gurr 1993)

Illustrative is what happened in Rwanda in 1994. Merely the declaration of a multi-party system and the preparation of genuine elections was enough to trigger off terrible intra-state collective violence. In Nigeria and Burundi elections did lead to a result that implied a transfer of office, but the respective armies preferred to retain power. Violence was used to reverse the outcome of democratic change. In Kenya the introduction of multi-party elections in 1992 resulted in dangerous escalations of regime-orchestrated violence rather than in Moi's removal from office.

Electoral violence could sometimes be avoided through proper preparations for a transfer of power. An example is Sierra Leone where elections appeared to be the way to transfer power from a military government that had already lost all sense of credibility, to a civilian administration. This happened in 1996. Already one year later a new military *coup d'état* had underscored the relativity of that process.

An exceptional situation occurred in Zambia in 1991. Kenneth Kaunda's personal decision to accept his election defeat and leave State House led to an unusually peaceful transfer of power to the opposition. But once that latter group – adorned with the promising name 'Movement for Multi-party Democracy' (MMD) – attained office, elections were again orchestrated towards a certain positive outcome for the ruling party.

The South African elections in 1994 came at the end of a long period of transition. The country's susceptibility to intra-state violence had already become more than manifest, and at times it had been at the brink of civil war (particularly in KwaZulu-Natal). However, responsible political as well as religious leadership played its part in the preparation for democracy. Thus, a process from civil strife on an ethnic basis towards full civil warfare could be prevented.

Let us now take a closer look at the four factors that have already been identified as elements impeding the role of elections as a process to establish legitimate government: the party system, lack of adequate checks and balances, authoritarianism and adverse economic conditions.

THE PARTY SYSTEM

African political parties were formed with one principal objective: national independence. Thus, of the three aspects of democratic government – representation, accountability and participation – the nationalists' struggle specifically embraced only the first one. Colonial rule was inherently authoritarian in all its manifestations and was to be replaced by *government of the people*, in the sense that those who rule the country should be indigenous to that country. In the case of settler rule or white minority rule, the fight was for *majority rule*. With the installation of the Mandela government in South Africa this struggle came to an end.

At the time of independence various types of parliamentary democracy and party organization were inherited from colonial powers that had done nothing to enhance the acculturation of modern democratic institutions. Now that the one-party state is in total disrepute it seems salutary to recall that the multi-party system has generally not been a success in Africa either. Within the countries that imported their parliamentary democratic models a multi-party system had developed on the basis of a 'crystallization of society into non regional and non territorial social classes, together with the structures of interclass compromise promoted by the passage of time and the hegemonic influence of capitalism' (Davidson 1992: 207). In Africa such a crystallization had not been given any chance to develop. Indeed, the party system was either based on multiple organizations of an ethnic nature, or on one dominant African party fighting for independence that could totally defeat the European settler party as soon as there were elections based on universal suffrage.

In this context 'free and fair' elections to establish representative government could play only a limited role. It is true that such elections were held to mark the transition to independence, but these lacked the element of anxiety and possible surprise that is usually connected to the electoral struggle for political power in a Western industrialized context. The new power relations had already been determined; elections were held just to legitimize the outcome of the struggle for independence.[1] Illustrations can be found in Malawi, Tanzania, Zambia and Zimbabwe. After independence, too, practical possibilities for the electorate to replace those already in power remained utterly limited, even before the transition to one-party systems. Taking Zambia as an example here, there was a real opposition to the governing United National Independence Party (UNIP), viz. the African National Congress (ANC), but outside Tongaland (Southern Province) that party enjoyed hardly any support. Within the framework of the Westminster constituency system with its 'winner takes all' rule, the outcome of the multi-party elections that were held between 1963 and 1973 was never a surprise: Congress won all the seats in Tongaland and a few others, and UNIP the rest. Thus, in practice it was the parties rather than the voters who decided who would represent the people in parliament.

Yet, elections did always lead to a certain amount of *violence*, particularly between the youth wings of the two parties. In that light Kaunda's move to incorporate the ANC in UNIP while reconstituting the system into a 'one-party democracy' could easily be explained to the electorate. The new system did provide the voters with an opportunity to get rid of their sitting members and at the same time it reduced electoral violence. In other instances of civilian transition to one-party rule, too, the 'Independence Party' had already acquired a monopolist position, initially based on popular support. Its differences with the minor parties tended to be founded on discontent of an ethnically exploited nature rather than on distinct political programmes. Although in countries within this category – Kenya is another prominent example – the transition to the single-party state was not entirely desired, it still attained a certain degree of formal legitimacy through such means as a public referendum.

In most cases, however, the one-party state was created as result of a military *coup d'état*. Between 1965 and 1975 more than half of the regimes in sub-Saharan Africa had attained power through a *coup d'état* (Chege 1995: 5). But since the military was still a rather young and, in terms of the power struggle, non-homogeneous institution, the ensuing regimes tended to be subject to new take-over attempts. Thus, ten years later the number of successful *coups* had already reached a total of 61 (ibid.) An extreme case was Benin, with six *coups* in a period of nine years.

Generally the multi-party model was interpreted as 'the majority rules' rather than 'the majority decides, the minority is respected'. There was contempt rather than respect for political adversaries. This resulted in political violence, particularly during election time. Not surprisingly, policies of transition to a single-party state often attained a certain degree of public support.

Despite certain instances of single-party elections that did result in the replacement of people's representatives at the local level, in one respect such systems failed completely in terms of the substitutability of those in political power: at the top. To oppose the incumbent president/party leader was regarded as utterly disrespectful. But this did not mean a real change from the multi-party period since incumbent leaders were not unseated anyway. Post-independence multi-party systems still meant one-(dominant)party government. Thus, an entrenched concentration and personalization of political power developed at the top. However, the failures of the one-party state should not be explained primarily from a *representation* perspective. On the contrary, it was the multi-party state in the immediate post-independence period that failed in terms of establishing proper mechanisms for representation. Hence, now that the search is for *democracy and good governance*, there is little reason to regard the reintroduction of multi-party systems as a panacea.

In sum, it is the party system as such that appears not to work very well in Africa. Political parties are not formed on the basis of distinct views on policies and the public interest, but attempts are made to unite people against others whom on the basis of cultural identity factors they are inclined to see as *enemies*. The idea is to eliminate such adversaries also beyond the ballot box. In such an environment elections may trigger off collective violence. This constitutes the background to modern trends towards 'no-party democracy' (for example Uganda). In whatever way one might assess that phenomenon, elections in such a system tend to be quite meaningful with relatively little violence. But the problem remains the substitutability of leaders at the top, even where the electorate is offered a choice. This has to do with concentration and personalization of power and the symbiosis of different institutions of the state which, for the sake of democracy, might better be segregated. Hence, in terms of governance – fighting corruption, for example – no-party systems remain troublesome.

CHECKS AND BALANCES

'Government for the people' means that those in power should be accountable. Hence they should not only be substitutable but their actions should be subject to control. Those who rule on behalf of the citizens must be accountable to them. In terms of institutional arrangements, this means more than just a parliamentary system in which ministers can be called to account for their policies and decisions. Where power is totally concentrated, control becomes highly problematic. A crucial factor is the division and separation of powers or, in other words, the existence of institutional *checks and balances* through such institutions as an independent judiciary and a free press.

Democracy requires not merely the control of political power but also a *separation* of powers. Historically the creation of democracies is connected with the rule of law which implies primarily *government by law* rather than through purely arbitrary execution of power. In this regard the function of law is to limit rather than to extend state power. Thus, politics, too, is restricted by law. The State itself should be subjected to established legal processes while the term 'law' does not mean just any Act of Parliament but includes provisions for the implementation of human rights. This is the requirement of the *Rechtstaat* (rule of law) which should not be regarded as a status that can be either acquired or not but rather as a continuous process of subjecting power to law in a normative sense. It implies a judiciary separated from the executive. Indeed, an *independent and accessible judiciary* may be seen as one of the essential institutions of a modern democracy.

Another such institution is a *free press*. Accountability is meaningless where political actions and operations cannot freely come out into the open and where public criticism is suppressed. Generally, it is the separation of institutions that may provide the necessary checks and balances. Noteworthy is the relationship between the Central Bank and the Ministry of Finance. Without making the responsibility for the value of the currency independent of the financial management by the government, there is no protection against populist inflationary policies.

At this point we may conclude that while from a *representation* perspective the single-party state was not a complete failure – certainly not in comparison with multi-party rule – it is from an *accountability* focus that one has to describe its attempts to concentrate, monopolize and homogenize power as undemocratic.

Not surprisingly, it was, particularly, the single-party rulers who responded to calls for democratization by simply narrowing down the issue to the question of multi-partyism. An example is

the late President Hastings Banda's reaction to the general call
for democracy in Malawi: announcing a referendum on the
question whether multiple parties should be admitted. Since he
made no inclination whatsoever to give up his full control of
police, judiciary and media this was seen as a shrewd way of
avoiding some of the most pressing issues in democratization.
Not surprisingly, the opposition's immediate response was to
call for press freedom and revocation of arbitrary police powers
for arrest and detention. Indeed, without institutional mechanisms for political accountability including basic democratic
freedoms, the multi-party system would not constitute a real
improvement. Donor pressure reinforced such demands with
the result that in June 1993 Banda lost his referendum despite
attempts to play upon public fear of tribal domination and
chaos.

Compared to the Malawian experience President Daniel arap
Moi's reaction to the movement for democratization in Kenya
in 1992 might be seen as more cunning. Trusting that power-
hungry politicians would immediately abuse freedom of association to restore tribal and personality-based political divisions,
he passed over the referendum stage and at once called a
general multi-party election. Also, because of haste on the part
of the donors there was insufficient time to concentrate first on
measures for the establishment of accountable government.
Thus, Moi succeeded in his attempt to retain power through his
control of the media, widespread intimidation, insufficient
checking of the electoral process by the observers sent by the
donor-countries that had insisted upon free and fair multi-party
elections, and the 'winner takes all system' which Kenya had inherited from the British. With a minority of the popular vote
Moi could continue his one-party government. 'The minority
rules, the majority is not respected' was the unfortunate result
of this 'democratization' process, together with a disturbing es-
calation of political violence.

Generally, accountability becomes rather problematic in situations of one-party government. In the African context it is not
just a multi-party system that is required but *multi-party government*, meaning the operation of checks and balances already
within the administration. In Zambia the defects of multi-
partyism in connection with one-party government are already
manifesting themselves again, as they did in the period

immediately following independence. It is particularly the Westminster model that produces single-party government as a result of multi-party elections (and, occasionally – Lesotho – even single-party parliament). The reintroduction of multi-party systems might be an appropriate occasion for establishing electoral systems that are more conducive to political coopera-tion, consensus-seeking and coalition politics. South Africa pro-vides an encouraging example here. It is noteworthy that even in Britain itself, the home of the Westminster model, there is increasing doubt as to the merits of an electoral system that tends to produce single-party government on the basis of less than half of the popular vote. The realization by a significant part of the electorate that within the political power relations of their constituency, their vote would have no significance anyway, is not very conducive to electoral participation. This brings us to an obstacle in regard to the third aspect of the concept of 'democracy'.

AUTHORITARIANISM

'Government by the people' means participatory government. Those in political power must not only be substitutable and subject to control but the people should also participate in po-litical processes. This found expression in the old Roman rule *Quod omnis tangit debet ab omnibus approbari* (What touches all has to be approved by all). As the Aragon nobility said to King Philip II of Spain: 'We, whose value as human beings is the same as yours, make you our King and Lord provided that you protect our freedoms; if not, you are no longer our King.' The phrase *basic democratic rights* refers to the conditions for popular participation: freedom of peaceful assembly and of association, freedom of thought, conscience and religion, freedom of opinion and expression, the right of all to take part in the government of their country, and of equal access to public service. In this category of rights we find guarantees against any tyranny of the majority (or of the minority for that matter, if a minority happens to be in power). In terms of collective rights, the so-called *minority rights* are included here, such as the right of ethnic, religious or linguistic minorities to follow their own ways of life.

In Africa there used to be types of participatory government based on relationships between chief, elders and people within the framework of mechanisms for *direct democracy*. Through processes of double alienation (Frantz Fanon) – taking people's customs away from them first, reformulating these for the purpose of colonial rule and then returning them to the people as if they were still their own – 'traditional' rule became autocratic (De Gaay Fortman and Mihyo 1993: 143). After independence the number of laws, orders and decrees increased tremendously, but the involvement in policy-making and implementation by those directly affected was even further reduced.

It was, particularly, *developmentalism* that continued the trend of double alienation after independence (ibid.: 156ff). Based on unjustified beliefs in the capacities of the state as an instrument of development, people were confronted with all sorts of plans to develop them from above; even, if deemed necessary, against their own will.[2]

Perhaps more than anything else, democracy is a *culture*, a culture of tolerance, of human equality, of restricted politics, of respect for different or even opposing views. Democracy goes against that historical human tendency to be connected with some absolute focus of identity, an ultimate warrant of truth. As opposed to, for example, the nationalist identity, the democratic identity is not based on natural unanimity or at least consensus but rather on relative truth and a continuous need to search for consensus.

The cultural institutional basis for democracy lies in *civil society*. This term refers to 'that segment of society that interacts with the state, influences the state, and yet is distinct from the state' (Chazan 1990: 281). It implies organizations that take an interest in the affairs of governance beyond their own group interests. There is an obvious interaction between civil society and good governance as mentioned above. As Judd has put it:

> Civil society needs government to be open, responsive, and accountable. And an active civil society, acting not only as a check and balance on government but also informing political debate is essential and indispensable to politically sustainable development.

(Judd 1992: 7)

In Africa there has always been 'an institutional landscape between the family and the state' (Chazan), although colonialism highly negatively affected traditional structures for political participation. In recent years there was a remarkable growth of voluntary associations in Africa. Conducive to this development were the relaxation of official controls over associational life (the tendency to connect every initiative with the ruling party) and the expansion of communication networks. It is particularly the churches that have significantly expanded their activities into the realm of civil society. In Zambia, Kenya and Malawi, for example, they were at the roots of a democratization process.

The basis of a well-functioning civil society is education. In this respect, the situation in Africa today is extremely worrying. Deteriorating economic conditions have particularly affected the quality of education. This brings us to the fourth obstacle to democracy in a contemporary African context: malfunctioning economies.

ADVERSE ECONOMIC CONDITIONS

As United Nations election observer in Malawi in 1993 – the referendum on multi-partyism – and in 1994 – the first free presidential and parliamentary elections – I know how impressive elections in Africa can be. In the remote district of Chikwawa West, in the middle of nowhere and forty miles inside, the voters were highly committed, patient and happy with the newly acquired opportunity. *Tafuna kusintha* – we wanted change – was the general explanation of the result the day after.

Focused group discussions by Jimmy Carter's National Democratic Institute two years later revealed a general sense of frustration among these same people. Political progress was followed by economic deterioration. Yet, the villagers made clear they did not desire a return to dictatorial rule. (What they did emphasize was that development assistance should not reach them through MPs and ministers but only through their own local leaders such as chiefs and headmen.) But they expressed major worries in regard to their reduced standard of living.

Nyanganbayaki Bazaara gives the following (African) definition of democracy:

> Democracy should not be understood in the narrow sense of elections held every four or five years. Democracy means access to resources.

In order to understand the apparent link between polity and economy we first have to go a little deeper into the meaning of legitimacy. Naturally, democracy is not just an end in itself. It is meant to result in the constitution and continuous acceptance of government by its citizens or, in other words, *legitimacy*. Fukuyama, for one, sees a regime as democratic when it is *legitimized* through the consent of the ruled (1993). Here, democracy and legitimation become synonymous. Van Gunsteren and Andeweg see legitimacy as an essential by-product of democracy. The term *by-product* means that the 'production' of legitimacy is not automatic; nevertheless it is essential for without it democracy will lose its meaning. 'Without the citizens' support, who recognize the regime as being legitimate, a political democracy cannot survive' (Van Gunsteren and Andeweg 1994: 100). A problem with 'pure by-products' is, generally, that they cannot be aimed at, even where and when their production is regarded as essential. Thus, paradoxically, politicians in power cannot just aim at legitimacy, through major efforts in public relations for example. Rather, they have to aim at the right policies and if these are successful they might produce 'people's subjective perceptions' (Fukuyama 1993: 15) that constitute the regime's legitimacy.

Thus, legitimacy is a rather complex concept with both *objective* and *subjective* aspects while relating to the *principles*, *means* as well as *outcome* of the use of power (Tarifa and De Gaay Fortman 1995: 1). In principle, there is no objective reason why the fulfilment of certain well-defined rules for the constitution and execution of government would result in an undisputed 'title to rule' (Lipset 1994). The problem is that it cannot objectively be determined what is required to create 'a propensity among the citizens generally to obey the rulers and the rules' (Frank 1990: 16). Hence we cannot escape subjective aspects in the sense that a regime is regarded as legitimate to 'the degree to which it is generally accepted by its citizens' (Lipset 1981: 22) or 'recognized as having the right to govern' (Giddens 1990: 357). A combination of objective and subjective aspects is found in Lipset's definition of legitimacy as

> the capacity of the system to engender and maintain the belief that the existing political institutions are the most appropriate ones for the society.
>
> (1981: 64)

From this perspective legitimacy becomes a matter of *justice* in the sense of 'the right outcome of the political system: the right distribution of goods, opportunities and other resources' (Dworkin 1986: 404). In Dworkin's concept of *integrity* (which he regards as the essence of law), justice is related to both fairness and due process: 'Fairness is a matter of the right structure for [the political] system, the structure that distributes influence over political decisions in the right way. Procedural due process is a matter of the right procedures for enforcing rules and regulations the system has produced' (ibid.).

The right institutions, the right procedures and the right outcome: there lies the secret of legitimate government. However, an outcome that makes government acceptable to the citizens will not be easy to achieve in case of lack of *economic performance*. If democracy does not deliver, the political system gets in trouble.

It was the British economist Dan Usher who devoted a minor opus to *The Economic Prerequisite to Democracy*. His book 'is a study of how society protects democratic government by entrusting the economy with a task that the legislature can never perform – the task of assigning the major part of income and other advantages' (1981: ix). His concern is 'conflict over assignment' in societies governed on the basis of majority rule. 'For democracy to survive,' Usher feels, 'there must be a prior agreement among citizens on a set of rules for assignment that voters and legislators will not lightly overturn.' He refers to this as a *system of equity*, defined as 'a set of rules for assigning income and other advantages independently of and prior to political decisions arrived at in the legislature' (1981: viii–ix). Douglass North would speak here of 'the institutions as rules' (North 1992), while my own terminology is based on Amartya Sen's notion of entitlement (1981).

Usher's main point is that democratic government would not be feasible if existing entitlement positions were not respected. This may be seen as part of the rule of law, and, indeed, here lies a major cause for worry in many African countries today. Not merely state arranged entitlement but state intervention in private entitlement systems, too, has become a predominant phenomenon (De Gaay Fortman 1997: 25–8). As a result the stakes connected to positions of political power have become too high, as was already observed above.

However, where Usher's analysis stops another worry begins. Suppose there exists a 'system of equity' in the sense of legally structured entitlement positions, but a growing number of citizens is dissatisfied with its operation and outcome. In a democracy they would attempt to elect leaders who corrected existing 'assignment', as well as, in an orientation towards structural change, the 'system of equity' that had produced it. If it appears, however, that no elections can make any difference to assignment and systems of equity, democratic government may lose its legitimacy in the subjective perceptions of people. This is exactly what happened in the Philippines after the Second World War when a democratically elected government appeared to be unable to effectuate the necessary land reform:

> The nice democratic government of the post-1945 Philippines lacked the power to knock landlords' heads together; the country has paid the price ever since.
>
> (*The Economist*, 29 June 1991: 18)

In such a situation citizens are likely to abstain from voting. This has quite serious consequences. While it is difficult to establish exactly in what ways votes may legitimate a political system (Held 1987: 181), non-participation definitely points to a lack of consent. Hence, a strongly reduced voters' participation in elections may be seen as an indication of a process of legitimacy erosion. Thus, a turn-out of between 5 and 10 per cent as is now customary in by-elections in Zambia, for example, may be interpreted as a sign of the impossibility of democracy in that country under the prevailing socio-economic conditions.

In the African situation donors now tend to perceive politics and economics jointly in one context of governance. The economic aspect tended to be reduced, however, to structural adjustment. Often this implied even further reductions of the standard of living of those destined to benefit from the blessings of multi-party elections. There are recent indications, however, that the International Monetary Fund is beginning to perceive the political implications of certain economic policies. If people's basic entitlement positions – that is, their structural possibilities to claim access to resources and to make legitimate claims to the goods and services they need – face constant deterioration, they get susceptible to attempts to mobilize political violence. In Mozambique the Fund has recently recognized this danger, and hence conceded that civil servants' pay should not fall below the poverty level and that credit should be directed towards rural areas hit by the war (*The Economist*, 28 June 1997).

Indeed, the state of the economy in relation to legal systems and their operation should have some effect on the time at which and the manner in which elections are being held. In conclusion, then, the African experience seems to point to the following strategic recommendation for international intervention in regard to democratization:

pacification → power-sharing → economy and
rule of law → elections

FINAL REMARKS

Of course the world is too complicated for straightforward strategies as recommended above. Elections are often necessary at an early stage, simply because the government in power is considered as being the major stumbling block in any process of democratization or because there has to be at least *a* government. However, if in countries such as Liberia, Sierra Leone, Rwanda and Burundi, elections are organized at a relatively early stage in the process of democratization, these should be very well orchestrated with an almost fully predictable outcome. The role of monitors in such elections is to ensure that this outcome is not frustrated through manipulation and rigging. That outcome may be expected to imply substantial processes of transformation. Intervention policy may already prepare for peaceful transition. Definitely, responsibilities following from international monitoring do not stop with a result declared to be the outcome of 'free and fair' elections.

A second concluding remark is that election observation itself cannot be confined to inspection of voting procedures either. NGOs, in particular, may find appropriate means to strengthen civil society. A very difficult issue is external support to political parties. In an initial stage of transition from tyranny – as was the case in Malawi, for example, in the period 1992–4 – this may, however, be necessary in order to move towards a pluralist political setting.

Thirdly, international election observation should start at the earliest possible stage, and focus primarily on the second and third aspects of democracy as outlined in this chapter: checks and balances (separation and distribution of powers), and participation. Of crucial importance is the establishment of independent media to which all parties can find access.

International election observation is part of international intervention. The analysis in this chapter shows the importance of coordination with other instruments of international intervention. Rather, worrying in my view is the lack of contact – let alone coordination – between donors on 'governance, democracy and human rights' and those who concentrate their efforts on the state of the economy. A clear but unfortunately rather unexploited link lies in the notion of economic, social and cultural rights. Indeed, the interdependence and indivisibility of human rights that is so frequently confessed in international declarations, has not as yet become a foundation stone of international development cooperation practice. Particularly in efforts towards peace-making, the economic dimension should not be overlooked. The issue here is that, in the usual African context, shifts in political power relations are likely to have immediate effects on entitlement positions. This point finds a striking illustration in the case of Rwanda (De Gaay Fortman 1994c).

In rather peaceful situations with relatively high degrees of *stability* – Malawi, for instance, and South Africa – every attention must be given to improvement of socio-economic conditions. Regular election observation without structural economic support is not likely to be conducive to genuine democratization.

NOTES

1. Notably, in Chichewa (or Chinyanja) the term for independence and for democracy is the same: *ufuru wa kudzilamulira*: the freedom to make one's own laws.
2. Notorious is the example of the Ujamaa villages in Uganda where people were forced into resettlement on the basis of an ideology – *Ujamaa* or familyhood – which, they were told, was in fact their own (De Gaay Fortman 1991).

REFERENCES

Ake, C. 1994. 'A World of Political Ethnicity', in R. van den Berg and U. Bosma (eds) *Historical Dimension of Development, Change and Conflict in the South* (The Hague: Ministry of Foreign Affairs), pp. 48–52.

Chazan, N. 1990. 'Africa's Democratic Challenge', *World Policy Journal* 9(2): 279–307.

Chege, M. 1995. *Africa's Transition to Democracy: a Preliminary Assessment* (Cambridge, Mass.: Center for International Affairs, Harvard University).

Davidson, B.G. 1992. *The Black Man's Burden: Africa and the Curse of the Nation State* (London: James Currey).

Diamond, L., J.J. Linz and S.M. Lipset (eds) 1990. *Politics in Developing Countries: Comparing Experiences with Democracies* (Boulder, Colo.: Lynne Rienner).

Dworkin, R. 1986. *Law's Empire* (London: Fontana).

Frank, T.M. 1990. *The Power of Legitimacy among Nations* (New York–Oxford: Oxford University Press).

Fukuyama, F. 1993. *The End of History and the Last Man* (New York: Avon Books).

Gaay Fortman, B. de, 1991. *A False Start: Law and Development in the Context of a Colonial Legacy* (The Hague: Institute of Social Studies, Working Paper, General Series, no. 112).

——. 1994a. *Is Socialism Possible?* Paper for Research Seminars State/Society Relations, ISS, The Hague, 29 March.

——. 1994b. 'Conceptualising Democracy in an African Context', in *Quest – Philosophical Discussions. An International African Journal of Philosophy* 7(1): 61–75.

——. 1994c. *Sitting Back in Horror: Intra-state Violence in a Global Context*, Dies natalis lecture, Institute of Social Studies, The Hague, 10 Oct.

——. 1998. 'Beyond Income Distribution: an Entitlement Systems Approach to the Acquirement Problem', in Y. Brenner et al. (eds), *Heterodox Economics and Income Distribution* (Brookfield, UK/Cheltenham, US: Edward Elgar). (Published as ISS Working Paper No. 249, The Hague.)

——. and P. Mihyo, 1993. 'A False Start: Law and Development in the Framework of a Colonial Legacy', *Verfassung und Recht im Übersee* 26(2): 136–63.

Giddens, A. 1990. *Sociology* (Cambridge: Polity Press).

Gunsteren, H. van and R. Andeweg, 1994. *Het Grote Ongenoegen. Over de Kloof tussen Burgers en Politiek* (Haarlem: Arasmith) [in Dutch].

Gurr, T.R. 1968. 'A Causal Model of Civil Strife: a Comparative Analysis Using New Indices', *American Political Science Review* 62: 1104–24.

——. 1970. *Why Men Rebel* (Princeton: Princeton University Press).

——. 1993, 'Why Minorities Rebel: a Global Analysis of Communal Mobilization and Conflict since 1945', *International Political Science Review* 14(2): 161–201.

Held, D. 1987. *Models of Democracy* (Cambridge: Polity Press).

C. Kortekaas and B. de Gaay Fortman, 1996. *Collective Violence within States: towards a Political Economy of Entitlement, Disasters, Anxiety and Human Security* (The Hague: Institute of Social Studies, research seminar paper, 96–04).

Lipset, S.M. 1981. *Political Man: the Social Bases of Politics* (expanded edition) (Baltimore: Johns Hopkins University Press).

——. 1994. 'The Social Requisites of Democracy Revisited', *American Sociological Review* 59(1): 1–22.

North, D.G. 1992. *Institutions, Institutional Change and Economic Performance* (Cambridge/New York: Cambridge University Press).

Prunier, G. 1995. *The Rwanda Crisis: History of a Genocide 1959–1994* (London: Hurst and Co.).

Rummel, R.J. 1995. 'Democracy, Power, Genocide and Mass Murder', *Journal of Conflict Resolution* 39(1): 3–26.

Schmitter, Ph.C. and T.L. Karl, 1991. 'What Democracy is ... and is Not', *Journal of Democracy* 2(3): 75–88.

Schumpeter, J.A. 1947. *Capitalism, Socialism and Democracy* (London: George Allen and Unwin, 3rd impression 1981).

Sen, A. 1981. *Poverty and Famines: an Essay on Entitlement and Deprivation* (Oxford: Oxford University Press).

Tarifa, F. and B. de Gaay Fortman, 1995. *Political Legitimacy in Communist and Post-communist States* (unpublished paper).

Tilly, C. 1975. *The Formation of National States in Western Europe* (Princeton: Princeton University Press).

——. (1978). *From Mobilization to Revolution* (Reading: Addison-Wesley).

Usher, D. 1981. *The Economic Prerequisites to Democracy* (Oxford: Blackwell).

Walzer, M. 1983. *Spheres of Justice: a Defence of Pluralism and Equality* (Oxford: Blackwell).

Wamba-dia-Wamba, E. 1992. 'Beyond Elite Politics of Democracy in Africa', *Quest – Philosophical Discussions* 6(1): 28–44.

Part II
Case Studies

5 African Multi-partyism and the Quest for Democratic Alternatives: Ugandan Elections, Past and Present

M. Doornbos

INTRODUCTION

In the post-Cold War era, donor discourses on African development have given much prominence to support for democratization processes. Laudable as these objectives are in principle, questions have often arisen as to what criteria to use and what incentives to employ when trying to translate these ideas into policy. Debates about these departures have all but ended, while praxis to date has added further queries. Specifically, high expectations among donors about multi-partyism, and the benefits of promoting its adoption, more often than not have been frustrated, reinforcing several of the questions raised (Ellis 1996).

Notwithstanding the wide breadth that democratization processes may have potentially, the actual scope for giving 'neutral' support has often appeared rather limited. This seeming paradox is in part a matter of the focus chosen, namely of a primary preoccupation with the concretely observable facts of political life, which has followed from the premise and donor consensus that Africa's current predicaments essentially revolve around issues of 'governance' (World Bank 1997). A different understanding of and policy approach to Africa's crisis, which would emphasize the primary need for economic rehabilitation and social safeguards in an era of aggressive globalization, conceivably would offer a broader (albeit more indirect) range of external policy instruments in support of democratization.

With the current focus, the scope for the kind of external support that might be given is further circumscribed due to the fact that donors generally must avoid being branded as partisan to political contests. Giving support to specific democratic currents, movements or parties thus would not do in principle, as this might be construed as constituting gross interference in domestic political processes. (None the less, several Western European political parties, some of them governing parties in their own countries, have led themselves be tempted to engage in supportive relationships with their presumed spiritual counterparts in Africa and elsewhere. Besides, NGO-routes have been used for similar kinds of support.)

Among possible supports to democratization processes, donors have often 'naturally' favoured giving material and logistic assistance to the holding of national elections. Elections are expensive and complex propositions, especially if there is no routine to their organization. Aside from potentially representing a crucial step in democratization procedures, elections theoretically will yield a measure of democratization substantively. The matter becomes of increased importance since a country's progress on a scale of 'democratization', as demonstrated in internationally observed elections, may make all the difference to the country's eligibility for continued financial support and other kinds of aid. Assisting in facilitating elections has thus often appeared a logical donor engagement and interest.

However, there is a thin and potentially tricky line between active facilitation of internal processes and intervention into these processes on externally derived terms. Democratization readily translates itself into 'free and fair' elections, and donor preparedness to support elections will generally be contingent upon their expectation that the elections concerned will deserve the label 'free and fair' as they understand it. Donor intentions to give or to withhold electoral support, depending on the modalities of the election system adopted, already place the donors concerned in a crucial umpire role. Donor involvement in monitoring the election process similarly adds weight to the role of the external observer-arbiter. In electoral processes, the role of umpire thus deserves as much attention as the fair play of contenders.

Umpire roles presuppose positive neutrality, which can be a welcome factor especially in tense post-conflict situations.

Through their active involvement, external umpires conceivably might even contribute to reconciliation between parties formerly engaged in violent conflict with one another but now confronting each other in elections. However, it is also of the essence of the role of umpires that they will apply the rules of the game as they know them. When it comes to election procedures, external parties are bound to come with an impressive arsenal of 'best democratic' technologies – Nordic, British, German, Dutch and others. Treating such technologies as possessing a universal validity, umpires will often have little reservation in basing their judgements on them, either when evaluating the electoral system as a whole or in assessing the process and results of a specific election. As experience in election monitoring accumulates and international observers travel from country to country, the umpire role itself gets reinforced, becoming 'professionalized', and based on a growing body of 'known rules' applicable in all situations.

However, it needs bearing in mind that Western electoral procedures have developed in response to numerous needs for modification over time, and that the latest package thus derived is not necessarily the most suitable, or possibly even the most 'neutral', for transplantation (cf. Doornbos 1965). In particular, it should be remembered that electoral procedures in many contexts have been adapted to accommodate the increasingly pivotal role of political parties in electoral processes. But it does not necessarily follow that for democratic processes political parties in all situations are a *sine qua non*, or should now be developed or encouraged in a kind of historical catching-up effort of the utmost priority.

In fact, the 'neutral' umpire role implies dilemmas, as well as qualifications as to its assumptions about the nature of the representative processes it is supposed to serve and promote. In some situations, where two or more groups have emerged from a civil war and are prepared to give elections a chance and participate in them as political parties, an external broker-umpire with some political clout may well make the crucial difference in ensuring the process succeeds. In other situations, though, the almost natural inclination of external umpires to expect to see rival parties climb into the ring, may preclude the possibility of alternative modes of democratic expression being developed which might potentially be more logical and suitable in the context concerned.

This problem, which is essentially one of the justification and limits of external intervention in electoral processes, can be illustrated by the case of Uganda, which in recent years has sought to develop an alternative system of democratic representation that does not start off from the axiom of multi-partyism.

Uganda has a rich experience in the handling of elections. This experience, though, is based less on the frequency with which elections have been held in the country (as there have been only few), and more on the organizational inventiveness with which electoral procedures have been devised as well as circumvented at different times. This chapter will seek to highlight both these tendencies. The assumption underlying the chapter is that the two tendencies are related, as the experience with numerous forms of election cheating in the past appears to have motivated a search for an electoral system which, with 'appropriate technology', would be reasonably fraud proof. We will therefore first look at part of the historical record, and then move on to discussing the electoral system which is currently being used in Uganda. Naturally, this discussion of Ugandan electoral procedures will be conducted against the background of the evolving political scene of the country.

BACKGROUND TO ELECTIONS

Though Uganda has been independent for more than 35 years, nation-wide elections have been held at roughly three intervals only: in 1961–2, in 1980, and in 1994–6. The first round was that of the 1961–2 elections (just before independence in 1962), when a national political arena came to be defined in terms of a triangle constituted by three major political parties: the Democratic Party (DP), the Uganda People's Congress (UPC), and Kabaka Yekka (KY). The DP was formed in the mid-1950s by leading Roman Catholics from Buganda and other districts and had (and potentially still has) a solid Catholic vote as its support base. The UPC was formed in 1960, building partly on the social foundations of its precursor, the Uganda National Congress, which had been formed in 1952 (Leys 1967: 6). The

UPC had its constituency largely in the North and the East of the country, though also with substantial strongholds in the West, drawing its support especially from Protestant voters. KY operated only within Buganda. It had emerged in 1962 as a monarchist-populist movement which stood for the interests of the kingdom of Buganda, which then had a federal relationship with the central government of Uganda.

The first elections in Uganda (excluding Buganda) were won by the DP, and its leader Benedicto Kiwanuka (an ex-service man of the Second World War who was later educated in law in South Africa) became the first elected Prime Minister of Uganda under what the British called 'Internal Self-government'. There had been an initial election round in Buganda, which was won by the DP but declared invalid by the British government (with the encouragement of the UPC). In a second round Buganda opted for the indirect method of having its MPs being nominated by the Lukiko, the Buganda Council. In this second round all Baganda were assumed to be represented by KY. With 21 seats in the National Assembly, the KY then concluded what came to be known as an 'unholy alliance' with the UPC led by Milton Obote, which had 37 seats. The two parties formed the first independence government, with Obote as prime minister and Mutesa, the Kabaka of Buganda, as President of Uganda. Thus, the DP (with 24 seats gained outside Buganda) basically had a strong appeal among Roman Catholics in Buganda as well as in other regions, which would probably have been sufficient for an overall majority. However, KY was successfully established to outmanoeuvre the Catholics from taking power at Mengo, the seat of the Buganda government, and consequently helped to block the DP from retaining power at the national level (Mudoola 1993: 22–5).

In this connection it should be remembered that slightly over half of Uganda's population of about 9 million at the time was Roman Catholic, the remainder mostly Protestant and comprising a small Muslim minority. The identification of Roman Catholics with the DP and Protestants with UPC was very strong and ran across most of the districts and the various ethnic groups in the country. There were some notable exceptions, however, such as in the then Ankole Kingdom where the predominantly Protestant Bahima (a pastoral minority from which historically the political elite had been recruited) voted *en bloc* for the DP, while the majority of Banyankore split their votes in accordance with the standard Protestant = UPC and Catholic = DP pattern. Also the Buganda monarchical elite, though putting their weight behind KY, was largely Protestant.

Several factors had helped to give prominence to a translation of religious denominational distinctions into political party identifications in Uganda.[1] One basic political element was a certain degree of denominationally based social differentiation between Protestants and Catholics. Protestant missionaries, mostly Anglican, enjoyed the support of the British colonial government and had first concentrated their efforts among the circles of the chiefs and elites in the various kingdoms and districts comprised within Uganda. Roman Catholic missionaries, initially mainly French, later also of Italian, Dutch and other origins, came slightly later and began mostly in the periphery of the various districts. Protestant schooling was geared towards the preparation of skills required in the colonial administration, of chiefs, clerks and others, and it has often been observed that there was at least a tacit understanding and collaboration in this regard between the (basically Anglican) colonial government and the Church of Uganda. Protestants thus came to occupy relatively larger numbers of positions within the government structure than was true for the Roman Catholics, and also outside government Protestants tended to have a head-start when it came to setting up commercial ventures or engaging in commercial agriculture. It should not be surprising, therefore, that these differences at some point would find expression in political terms (Mudoola 1993: 41). What is remarkable, none the less, is that this religiously based cleavage between political parties, albeit with notable exceptions as indicated, basically cut across most of the ethnic divisions within the country. At a time such as the present one, when great stress is being laid upon the adage of national unity in Uganda (while the political parties tend to be viewed among the main culprits having sowed disunity), there is not much recognition of the fact that political parties did somehow contribute to a sense of cross-cutting national identities, as opposed to ethnic identities. It is true, however, that the distrust and hostility between supporters of the two parties ran very deep. Yet another key characteristic of Ugandan politics for many years, however, was its pronounced district basis, meaning that it was the district arenas which largely provided the focus for political confrontations, including those between UPC and DP.

It is beyond the scope of this chapter to recount Uganda's turbulent political history during the first two and a half decades after independence (cf. Doornbos 1978). Suffice it to say that the UPC–KY coalition engineered by Obote in 1962 with British support soon got strained over a whole range of issues, and that following a head-on collision between Obote's government and Buganda in 1966, and thus between the Prime Minister and the President, a new, one-party based constitutional framework was introduced in 1967 that abolished the kingdoms and made Obote President. In the late 1960s the Ugandan government increasingly adopted a radical but also authoritarian posture, and in 1969 it adopted the Common Man's Charter, vaguely reminiscent of Tanzania's Arusha Declaration, as its baseline document for policies meant to transform Uganda's social and economic structures. Ensuing internal tensions left little scope for transformations of any kind, however, and in 1971 Idi Amin put an end to these spirals of conflict through his army *coup*, which – initially welcomed and supported as it was in Britain, Israel and Buganda – would soon lead the country into new and graver episodes of misery.

The second time general elections were held in Uganda was in December 1980, a year after the disastrous period of arbitrary rule by Idi Amin had come to an end with the victory of a combined Tanzanian–Ugandan invasion force in the country. This alliance, sponsored by Tanzania's President Julius Nyerere, brought Obote back on to the Ugandan political scene. In addition to UPC and DP, a third party, the Uganda Patriotic Movement (UPM), founded by Yoweri Museveni, took part in these elections. Party symbols, a hoe (DP), a hand (UPC) and a lamp (UPM), were pinned on ballot boxes to enable voters to identify the candidates of their choice. Following these elections, the UPC headed by Obote again came to power, albeit after heavily contested results. Obote and Paul Muwanga, his second in command, did not themselves contest any constituency, but were later appointed (or appointed themselves) President and Vice-president respectively. The UPM had one candidate elected in Kasese in Western Uganda. The DP seemed destined to win, but as results came in and were being announced, Muwanga, who was Chairman of the Military

Commission, ruled that no election results were to be publicized without his permission. In the wake of this, many presumably defeated UPC candidates were announced as having been elected, and in the end the UPC could claim a majority of 'officially announced' elected members (Mutibwa 1992: 142–3). Preparations for a radical overthrow of this kind of politics began within a month after these elections, when Yoweri Museveni, with a now 'historic' party of 27 followers, took to the bush, forming the nucleus which would grow into the National Resistance Army (NRA), later broadened with a political wing, the National Resistance Movement (NRM).

The NRA/NRM made its entry into Kampala in 1986, following its final defeat of what had remained of Uganda's official army. This came after years of bitter guerrilla warfare, with untold civilian casualties, *vis-à-vis* the forces of the Obote II government. Obote II, like the years of Idi Amin preceding it, is remembered as a period of harsh and arbitrary rule, causing havoc with Uganda's economy, infrastructure and above all its social fabric. The NRA/NRM's entry on to the political scene signified a basic shift of the point of gravity in Uganda's politics, namely from the North (which had been the power base of Idi Amin as well as Obote, and finally also of Okello-Lutwa for a brief spell) to the West (from where the NRA draws its main support). However, devising forms of accommodation and power-sharing with centrally located and economically dominant Buganda would soon come high on the new President's – Museveni's – political agenda. Basing itself on forms of direct grassroots representation with which it had already experimented in the areas it had liberated (mainly in the central and western parts of the country), commonly known as the RC (Resistance Councils) system, the NRM sought to establish a new administrative structure and in fact a new kind of political process in Uganda. This 'consultative democracy' model, as Apter (1995) has dubbed it, was further elaborated and modified at various stages, and applied at five levels (that is, from hamlet or village – RC1 – up to district level – RC5). The system was topped by the National Resistance Council, the national parliament. Elections on the basis of this system were held for the Constituent Assembly in 1994, and for Presidential and National Assembly elections both in 1996.

ELECTORAL BEHAVIOUR – THE EARLIER YEARS

Looking back at the way elections were conducted during these different periods, one might begin by observing that what happened in the 1961–2 period represented an example of how elections should *not* be held, or rather, what should not be condoned. On the basis of vivid memories of participants in that electoral process, I had in 1965 begun a small side research project on the manifold ways of cheating elections in Uganda. Although the project never got written up, I had counted about 78 different techniques by the time it was – or rather, remained – shelved. With surprising acumen and inventiveness, voters and party supporters (according to my sources at the time, of *all* parties) experimented with a whole range of methods and techniques to influence or sabotage the election results. These attempts at manipulation occurred in each successive phase of the electoral process, starting with registration in the weeks before polling day (some voters being encouraged to register double, others being discouraged from registering at all), verification at the polling station (at which Christian names with three initials, and especially with the initials F.X., thus recognizable as Roman Catholics, often 'got lost' in voters' registers handled by ballot officers sympathizing with the UPC), as well as in the actual polling (for more on this see below), and finally in the closing and transportation of the – unemptied – ballot boxes (during which a remarkable number of incidents, accidents and even wild chases after 'lost' ballot boxes took place). Lastly, the actual counting and aggregation of the votes from different polling stations similarly lent themselves to active manipulation.[2]

Naturally, polling itself was a key target for 'technical innovations': in Uganda at the time – as in many other African countries – the authorities had in view of the literacy factor opted for a system with two ballot boxes behind a large screen, each one carrying a clearly recognizable party symbol (outside Buganda the competition was only between the DP and UPC). At the end of the day it should have been clear which party had received the largest number of ballot papers in its box. However, long before closing hour many interim transactions would be carried out. An original method, for instance, consisted of the 'tweezers trick': a pair of very long tweezers would be brought into the voting booth, hidden under the coat of a registered voter and, behind the protective screen, could serve to lift a substantial number of ballot papers from one box to the other. The tweezers could then be handed over to a fellow voter or quickly be taken to another polling station. Another trick, demanding close coordination, was the 'screwdriver operation': four same-party voters would come and cast their vote in succession, each in the possession of a screwdriver with which they would loosen one screw of the opposite party's ballot box. The last of these could then lift the lid from the box, take out the ballots and put them into the other box. Other techniques, in contrast, were less sophisticated, and presumably appealing to the hard core of party supporters only: the destruction of ballots of the opposite party by pouring acid or other damaging materials into its ballot box, or by simply setting fire to it.

Predictably, an inverse strategy was to try and ensure that one's own ballot box would become well stuffed: this could be done either in the early hours of the morning – before the first voters would arrive – or by means of a regular infusion of extra ballot papers in the course of the day. A precondition for this route was that one should have sufficient numbers of the official ballot paper available, or at least of a version that would closely resemble it. In the 1961–2 period, however, the scope for this alternative still appeared to be rather limited.

Although the elections in 1961–2 evoked intense partisan interest – as evidenced by the manifold manipulation efforts just sketched – they nevertheless seem to be remembered as relatively 'fair competition'. It was generally assumed that *both* dominant parties, DP as well as UPC, had been indulging in 'extra-electoral' manipulations, and that without these efforts the results might have been more or less the same. Given the demographic realities at the time, however, a slight edge of DP over UPC should not have been improbable.

With the 1980 elections the situation had become entirely different. The context itself was different, as it now concerned the bitter aftermath of the traumatic Amin years, rather than a first dip into the liberties and openings of independence as in 1962. Among the main players, Milton Obote was determined to regain his lawful position, from which he felt he had been unjustly ousted by Idi Amin. Non-UPC voters, however, especially in Buganda, were determined not to see Obote return to power. The international community was determined to see a quick normalization take place in Uganda, as evidenced, perhaps, by the ready endorsement of the elections as 'free and fair' by the Commonwealth Observer Group (COG). In their view, 'surmounting all obstacles, the people of Uganda, like some great tidal wave, carried the electoral process to a worthy and valid conclusion' (COG 1980, quoted in Mutibwa 1992: 139). Many eyes were thus focused on the outcome of these elections. However, at this occasion, what might still have appeared as 'sporting' and amateurish election cheating behaviour in the past, now became rough, nasty and 'professional' manipulation. In many instances, for instance, 'opposition' candidates were physically prevented from registering themselves, leaving the UPC with no less than 17 unopposed representatives in the National Assembly (Mutibwa 1992: 142). The main victim of these and other malversations, which occurred on an unprecedentedly large scale, was inevitably the DP, though the election results of the new party headed by Museveni, the UPM, were almost zero and obviously similarly disappointing to them. The main culprit was generally believed to be Obote's resurrected and overly determined UPC. Hence perhaps the early consolidation of another determination, that by Yoweri Museveni and his followers, to start a guerrilla movement with the aim of replacing what they saw as the illegitimate Obote II government. Consistent with this step, a good deal of fresh thinking about alternative election procedures evidently took place during the years of the guerrilla.

A DEMOCRATIC ALTERNATIVE?

The electoral and representative system that was introduced by the NRM after 1986 is quite novel for Africa (or anywhere else for that matter), and has meanwhile been tested and further modified in several rounds of elections. The core element of the system is that elections for representative roles at all levels, from RC1 upwards to the National Resistance Council, are between *competing individual candidates*, but not party candidates. Thus, candidates can be members of the NRM (in practice the most numerous), but may also be of UPC or DP background (which is by no means exceptional), or just be 'party-less'. But each candidate stands to represent him- or herself as a person, and is not the candidate of a political party. The existence of the formerly dominant parties, the UPC and DP, is none the less condoned, that is, they have offices and memberships, are allowed to make statements on policy issues, and get room to express their views in the media. The key thing they are not permitted to do (but obviously would very much like to do) is draw up and present party lists of electoral candidates, and thus have themselves inserted in the process.

Electoral contests are consequently largely individual contests. In actual practice, this means that in any electoral district the battle can either be between two or more different NRM candidates, between an NRM candidate and a UPC or DP member or supporter, or between different supporters of either party. It should be noted that every candidate who is as such accepted by the electoral commission at the relevant level has, at least formally speaking, an equal chance. For instance, in every electoral district, a series of public pre-election meetings (*barazas*) will be organized, at which each candidate for the available post – the number may be two, but is often more, up to eight – receives an equal amount of time (20 minutes) for his or her presentation. Following this, he or she will have to defend and elaborate that presentation during an intensive 'cross-examination' by the public. Generally, these meetings attract a great deal of attention, and it is by no means exceptional that several hundred people participate and will take their time in an active, comparative scrutinization of the candidates.

The competitive element is also brought out by 'advertising', for example by means of leaflets thrown from aeroplanes, by shirts and hats bearing the name of the candidate, and festive election gatherings with ample food and drink. Some candidates, and some of their supporters, make substantial investments in these campaigns, particularly for seats in the National Resistance Council (Parliament), which entail a fair amount of leverage. Small gifts of soap, salt and sugar, or even cash, are by no means uncommon. This practice is not a monopoly of 'no-party' systems, though, as voters in Southern Italy may recall; what it means is that the 'no-party' system has neither developed an effective antidote against it. Obviously, then, candidates with money to spend have an advantage, as is common in many parts of the world, but those without any means are not *a priori* the losers. There have been several instances of relatively unknown candidates defeating established political figures against all odds.

In contrast to the procedures followed in 1961–2 and 1981, several important 'technical' modifications have been adopted in the system as it is currently practised in Uganda: with the entire process taking place in the open air, one single ballot box is used, which – after first opening it in public to show that it is empty – is centrally placed in a demarcated area and visible for every one during the entire day of the election. Any polling station may serve some 400 to 600 voters. Often after queuing up for a few hours to wait their turn, voters move from one desk to the next, the latter with substantial distance between them: registration, verification, filling in the ballot paper, going to the ballot box, and finally leaving a fingerprint to mark that one has cast the vote. All this takes place in the presence of representatives of the various candidates, who closely observe what the polling officials are doing. There are some relatively marginal opportunities to rig the voting – for instance, some supporters go out of their way to 'assist' elderly people to cast their vote (though in such cases the votes are quite possibly given to candidates which the voters concerned would have favoured in the first place) – but in general the system appears to be quite well protected against possibilities of large-scale fraud. At the end of the day, the ballot box in every polling station is opened, on the spot, upon which counting begins, with hundreds of onlookers at some distance, and in the immediate presence of representatives of the various candidates who closely monitor the whole process. In 1994, I myself had the opportunity to witness this and other aspects of the election as an international observer to the Constituent Assembly election. Based on that experience, my conclusion could only be that the counting procedures, which will not be further detailed here, were quite scrupulously observed.

Election observation in recent years has rapidly become a specialized area of engagement, with more and more fine points for debate, and an emerging academically-oriented literature on different aspects and approaches to the monitoring process. One difference between two 'schools' that has apparently emerged in connection with the most recent Ugandan elections, concerns the question whether observers should limit their assessments strictly to what they can actually witness during polling day, or whether they should try to come to an assessment of the wider electoral process (Cooper and Stroux 1996: 201). The question is not without importance, because it is theoretically possible that the procedures on polling day may be found impeccable while questions will linger on about what takes place, and how, before and after, that is, at registration and in the aggregation of the vote counts. These questions are indeed relevant for the Ugandan context, as one would like to know, for example, whether or to what extent NRM affiliation gives a candidate any particular advantage at registration – both his/her own registration and voters' registration. By their very nature, these particular aspects of the election cycle are much more difficult, if not impossible to verify, which presents observers with something of a dilemma. In turn, this leaves sceptics the option to reserve their opinion or even to conclude that, as one cannot testify that the process as a whole has been in accordance with accepted rules and criteria, one can neither pass a judgement that the elections concerned have been 'free and fair' – the magic formula. When adopting this position, as apparently was the case with the 1996 Parliamentary election observation (Cooper and Stroux 1996: 206–8), observers must realize however that they are in fact passing an *a priori* critical verdict which appears rather at odds with the role of impartiality they usually claim is theirs.

Meanwhile, the national aggregate of election results in 1994 as well as in 1996 appears to indicate that a 'no-party' system can yield a reasonably accurate representation of nation-wide political preferences. NRM candidates in both years were mainly victorious in the west of the country as well as in parts of Buganda, as was to be expected. Furthermore, in Buganda the preference for the DP also remained strong, while several other candidates there attracted votes expressing local Buganda allegiances, some with a traditionalist/monarchist flavour. Large parts of the north and north east, however, showed continued allegiances to candidates associated with the former UPC camp. Again, the fact that in the Presidential elections of May 1996, Museveni was elected with 74.2 per cent of the national vote in his favour (Cooper and Stroux 1996) rather than with any 'classical' 99.8 per cent, seems likewise to point to basically open and realistic processes taking place. Critics – among observers as well as opponents – none the less stress undue advantages that incumbent candidates have over others, but this factor does not really seem to be different from anywhere else in the world, whereas in addition it appears virtually impossible to neutralize the electoral effects of someone already holding office. Besides, it might well work against him/her.

Political parties have not been proscribed in Uganda, but they have had their operations suspended until 1999, when a referendum will have to decide whether they should be allowed re-entry or whether the 'movement' system will be continued. This suspension is based on an agreement between the NRM and the DP of 1986, which conversely opened the door for participation of non-NRM groups in the government. The long-time leader of the DP, Paul Ssemogerere, indeed served for several years as Minister of Foreign Affairs until he stepped down in order to become a candidate in the 1996 Presidential elections (unofficially for a new *ad hoc* coalition between DP and UPC, an arrangement which probably cost him some votes). Meanwhile, the NRM itself will have to decide before 1999 whether it will transform itself into a political party (among other parties), or whether it will try to serve as a strictly neutral umbrella underneath which candidates for political office of all persuasions can contest elections. The present arrangement tends towards a hybrid pattern which in the longer run will be unsustainable (cf. Apter 1995; Geist n.d. (1995); and Kasfir n.d. (1995)).

'NO-PARTY' VS 'MULTI-PARTY': CONTRASTING ASSESSMENTS

The pros and cons of a 'movement' or 'no-party' system versus a multi-party system have often been articulated by Ugandans within and outside the NRM. It seems, though, that there is a certain pattern to the different positions put forward. Those who favour the 'no-party' system tend to point to the specific and negative experiences which Uganda has had with multi-partyism, which in their view call for an approach towards political representation that should be better adapted to the country's conditions. Those who call for the reintroduction of a multi-party system, on the other hand, usually refer to general, universal principles of democratic practice, on the assumption that their intrinsic validity will prove itself in Uganda as much as anywhere else.

Arguments in favour of the suspension of political parties include, *inter alia*, a) that they caused political sectarianism leading to hatred and violence; b) that they were not ideological in the political sense but promoted religious and ethnic conflict; c) that they were not strictly indigenous but had international connections and received foreign support, especially the DP; d) that when Obote terrorized the country, the political parties did nothing to deter him; and e) that the people at large saw (and still see) the political parties as carrying primary responsibility for profound antagonism and national disunity (Mushanga, personal communication, 1997).

Arguments favouring a reinstatement of multi-party democracy stress universal attributes like the following: the requirement of internal democracy within political parties; freedom of association and assembly; good governance; tolerance; regular free and fair elections; openness of government; acceptance of the party in government and those in opposition that their roles are complementary; witnessing peaceful transfer of political power from one political party to another after elections; transparency on electoral laws; freedom to campaign to the electorate without any intimidation; respect of the rule of law, and the like.[3] At times the argument has also been advanced, among others by the DP, that political pluralism and multi-partyism are inherent attributes of democracy, and by themselves represent a basic human right; thus, again, no pluralism, no democracy.

Significantly, an argument that has not been heard on either side is that of possible connections between the existence of political pluralism and the potential for developing alternative policy proposals. In a way this is not too surprising, because experience to date in Uganda and in many other African countries has not really been that opposition parties would derive their main *raison d'être* from the formulation and propagation of alternative policy agendas. The realities of political processes, particularly the limited room for manoeuvre and the economic constraints on developing real policy choices in most parts of

Africa, have largely militated against the articulation of this most 'natural' role of an opposition. Instead, parties or governments coming to power have mostly found themselves condemned to pursue much the same kind of macro-economic policies as their predecessors or neighbours (cf. Doornbos 1977). In turn, this basic given tends to place special emphasis on the representational attributes in the assessment of political and electoral systems, rather than on their capacity to generate or facilitate policy debate. In this light there would also seem to be a case for closer consideration of systems of proportional representation, which generally have only become little known in post-colonial Africa (cf. Hyden 1995).

The position taken in this paper is that advocacy of 'general' validity for either multi-party systems or no-party systems in Africa can be equally unsustainable. Giving due recognition to the dynamics of politics and the balance and balancing of forces is necessary to come to a better appreciation as to what system might offer the best chances of allowing democratic openings in a particular context. In Mozambique, for example, it can be argued that it was precisely due to the careful handling of multi-party elections (with proportional representation) in a social and political context with two major contenders for power (Frelimo and Renamo), that a meaningful and workable basis for national reconstruction and reconciliation could be found (Mazula 1996). In many other situations (for instance, Zambia, Zaire, or Kenya), multi-partyism (though without proportional representation, which is little known in post-colonial Africa) has rather been a recipe for disaster.

In Uganda, in contrast to the constellation of forces such as that in Mozambique, the no-party logic must be seen not only against the background of the country's unfortunate experience with multi-party elections, but also in the light of a new political hegemony established by the NRA/NRM. The latter factor represents a political umbrella as well as the ultimate base of political power, neither of which are to be ignored. *A priori*, however, it is to the credit of this very power base that it has been developing a novel kind of democratic alternative, and it should be recalled in this connection that during the liberation struggle itself the NRA had already begun its experiments with the RC mode of representation. Liberation fronts in other African countries have not always adopted the same route.

During the many years of its struggle, for instance, the Sudan People's Liberation Army (SPLA) has not been particularly noted for its attention to the need to create democratic openings, though recently there have been signs that the SPLA has begun to recognize their importance. In Eritrea, in contrast, the Eritrean People's Liberation Front (EPLF) for a substantial part of the 30 years' liberation war captured the imagination of many outside observers through its non-conventional solutions to many practical issues and its reputedly participatory style of leadership, though since independence in 1993 there have been few steps only to build on and institutionalize these innovations. It is in this comparative perspective, too, that the Uganda model deserves attention.

Various Western critics, however, foremost among them key members of the donor community, approach the question not from any appreciation of the contextual angle but from a 'universal' perspective, and see the Ugandan electoral system as 'non-democratic', if not undemocratic. This verdict again is based on the assumption that elections can only be really democratic if they involve a contest between political parties. Hence there has been persistent donor pressure on Uganda to institute a regular multi-party system. This was clearly evidenced, for example, in the correspondence from the British Ambassador to the Ugandan government, in the course of 1993 and early 1994, on behalf of an international donor consortium which would financially support the 1994 Constitutional Assembly elections and the accompanying election monitoring exercise. As this pressure was steadfastly resisted by the Ugandan leadership, the actual organization and conduct of the Constituent Assembly elections remained uncertain till a very late moment indeed. It was probably due to the standing Uganda had gained as a relatively stable country and its comparative record of economic recovery, that the consortium in the end gave in and allowed the government to proceed with the elections on its own terms, based on the 'no-party' system.

For a variety of reasons, the nature and extent of this international criticism and pressure does not appear justified, and rather seems ill-founded. In the first place, much of the criticism is based on an essentially narrow and ahistorical view of democracy, which is much less principled than it might first appear. Even if it is the case that in a majority of democratic countries today political parties of various kinds play an active role in electoral processes and political representation, it amounts to an unwarranted reductionism to assume that repre sentative systems can only be labelled 'democratic' if such rep-resentation involves intermediate roles for political parties. Party-based representation is historically a relatively recent phenomenon, and critics for whom the equation between multi-partyism and democracy has attained the stature of a *sine qua non*, would find themselves hard pressed to adequately qualify various instances of non-party representative government. Just to mention some historical examples, the New England Town Council, in American textbooks often celebrated as the first example of direct democracy, had no political parties. Its proce-dures were not essentially different from those of RC1 level elections in Uganda today. The first political parties in the Netherlands emerged in the nineteenth century as coalitions of like-minded people already occupying an (elected) seat in par-liament, and were not formed outside parliament or prior to elections. In Britain, the word 'party' had a negative connota-tion at least until the Reform Acts of the early 1830s, as it stood for factions within the parliament which allowed 'selfish' inter-ests to prevail over the 'common good' which members were ex-pected to serve (Calhoun 1982). In democratic theory, finally, political parties are viewed less as the embodiment of basic po-litical rights than as an inevitable adaptation to enable – albeit indirectly – representative processes within complex societies to take place (Schumpeter 1947).

Other important reasons to question the multi-party = democracy equation, however, are of a more pragmatic nature. If political parties dominate the political game, they do this on the basis of the discretion they have acquired to draw up and control lists of electoral candidates.[4] In some countries, and in some parties, the composition of such lists may be based on transparent procedures and internal democracy, but in many others it simply will not. There is no self-evident tendency towards internal democracy within political parties, as Roberto Michels (1915) pointed out early in this century (Michels 1962). The chances of arbitrary manoeuvres taking place when politi-cal parties compose their electoral lists, or of parties deliber-ately blocking someone from putting himself up as a candidate, seems *a priori* much greater than in the present Ugandan system, where theoretically anyone can stand as a candidate, provided he/she meets the non-restrictive conditions. (True, one would want to verify whether the practice in the Ugandan case stands up to the principle, but this does not diminish the value of the principle of self-candidature as such.)

When viewed from the other – the voter's – side, in a system with parties as representative bodies, the voter indeed can be said to have the final say. But voters are generally presented with the top candidates, who are well-known and well-publicized, rather than with the less prominent candidates placed lower down the list. Of course, one would like to expect parties to be picking the right kind of people; that is, we would expect them to properly screen and scrutinize their an-tecedents before putting them on the electoral roll. However, in many countries in Africa and elsewhere such critical procedures are quite difficult to sustain: the centralization of candidates' presentations through political parties facilitates backroom deals allowing the inclusion of less desirable candidates who do not have to prove themselves to the public, but who might get elected as part of a 'package deal'. The Ugandan model, in which individual candidates are responsible for their own candi-dature as a public office-holder and have to respond to and can be held individually accountable by their voters, prevents the possibility of such intra-party deals and priorities occurring, and also for this reason may be preferable in situations where social stability cannot be taken for granted.

Last but not least, within the context of a discussion on two vital aspects of electoral procedures and management, namely the scope for rigging or fraud, and alternative modes of putting up candidates, it is also pertinent to point to the poss-ible connections between these two aspects: elections in which political parties are playing a key role will allow the latter to employ organizational structures and devices which per definition offer much more scope for fraud and malversations than any individual candidate is likely to ever mobilize. Electoral fraud calls for a considerable degree of coordination in a number of respects, of which Uganda's past experience offers numerous examples. The determination to put an end to this has been one of the key motivations for developing Uganda's alternative.

CONCLUSION

There is currently a good deal of thinking, among external as well as local actors, about alternative development strategies in Africa and elsewhere. At the same time there is a growing awareness that the experiences to date with 'multi-party democracy' in Africa have not been particularly encouraging. In the light of present rethinking in these two respects, it appears inconsistent and disappointing that many Western observers remain sceptical or even outright critical about a novel alternative electoral system such as the Ugandan one, which respects the principle of direct representation and has incorporated key checks against various forms of electoral fraud. As a democratic alternative, the system *a priori* seems better suited to Ugandan and various other African contexts than the 'universal' multi-party systems. It would appear that the Ugandan model deserves better, namely to be seriously considered for application in other countries with roughly comparable conditions in Africa, and possibly elsewhere.

NOTES

I should like to thank Dr Tibamanya mwene Mushanga and Asiimwe Godfrey for their constructive comments on a previous draft, and Dr J. Abbink for translating an earlier version from the Dutch.

1. A comparison with the Dutch pattern of political party formation at the end of the nineteenth and beginning of the twentieth centuries is not as far-fetched as it might at first appear. In the Netherlands at that time, political parties served as vehicles for the political emancipation of denominational groups which occupied a modest place on the social ladder, like the Calvinists led by Kuyper and the Roman Catholics led by Schaepman. The step by step introduction of universal suffrage in their cases prompted the recognition of common interests and the logic of developing a common strategy *vis-à-vis* the parties already established in parliament.
2. In addition, at least one attempt at pre-empting results that even preceded this whole chain of electoral procedures should be noted: in one district, that of Ankole, though possibly also elsewhere, an effort was made at one time by the local government officer responsible for demarcating electoral constituency boundaries, to carve them up on the basis of spatial divisions rather than population density. This resulted

in the proposition (which was ultimately to be rejected in court) that a large area sparsely populated by Bahima pastoralists comprising less than 10 per cent of Ankole's population, would be allocated about equal weight of representation as the densely populated agricultural areas containing 90 per cent (Doornbos 1978: 217).

3.   From a communication of the National Democrats Forum (NDF) Party, an aspirant political group, spring, 1997.

4.   At the time of writing (late 1997), several veteran members of the Dutch Parliament, most notably some representing the Christian Democratic Party (CDA), were unpleasantly surprised to learn through the media that the executive bodies of their parties had dropped them from the lists of candidates being prepared for the 1998 elections for parliament. The example illustrates the extent to which MPs in this case are expected to serve as party representatives rather than in their individual capacity.

REFERENCES

Apter, D.E. 1995. 'Democracy for Uganda: a Case for Comparison', *Daedalus* 124(3): 155–90.

Calhoun, C. 1982. *The Question of Class Struggle: Popular Protest in Industrializing Britain, 1790–1832* (Oxford: Blackwell).

Cooper, L. and D. Stroux, 1996. 'International Election Observation in Uganda: Compromise at the Expense of Substance', *Afrika Spectrum* 31(2): 201–9.

Doornbos, M. 1965. 'Afrikaanse Éénpartijstaten en Democratie', in S.W. Couwenberg (ed.), *Problemen der Democratie* (The Hague: Stichting ter Voorlichting over de Oost-West Verhouding), pp. 124–8.

——. 1977. 'Recurring Penetration Strategies in East Africa', in L. Cliffe, J. Coleman and M. Doornbos (eds), *Government and Rural Development in East Africa: Essays on Political Penetration* (The Hague: Martinus Nijhoff), pp. 317–30.

——. 1978. 'Faces and Phases of Uganda Politics: Changing Perceptions of Social Structure and Social Conflict', *African Perspectives* (Leiden), 1978/2: 117–33.

——. 1978. *Not all the King's Men: Inequality as a Political Instrument in Ankole, Uganda* (The Hague: Mouton Publishers).

Ellis, S. (ed.) 1996. *Africa Now: People, Policies, Institutions* (London: James Currey).

Geist, J., n.d. (1995). 'Political Significance of the Constituent Assembly Elections', in H.B. Hansen and M. Twaddle (eds), *From Chaos to Order: the Politics of Constitution-Making in Uganda* (Kampala: Fountain Publishers), pp. 90–113.

Hyden, G. n.d. (1995). 'Political Representation and the Future of Uganda', in H.B. Hansen and M. Twaddle (eds), *From Chaos to Order: the Politics of Constitution-Making in Uganda* (Kampala: Fountain Publishers), pp. 180–91.

Kasfir, N., n.d. (1995).'Ugandan Politics and the Constituent Assembly Elections', in H.B. Hansen and M. Twaddle (eds), *From Chaos to Order: the*

Politics of Constitution-Making in Uganda (Kampala: Fountain Publishers), pp. 148–79.

Leys, C. 1967. *Politicians and Policies: an Essay on Politics in Acholi, Uganda 1962–65* (Nairobi: East African Publishing House).

Mazula, B. (ed.) 1996. *Mozambique: Elections, Democracy and Development* (Maputo: n.p.).

Michels, R. 1962. *Political Parties* (New York: Collier Books, first published 1915).

Mudoola, D.M. 1993. *Religion, Ethnicity and Politics in Uganda* (Kampala: Fountain Publishers).

Mutibwa, Ph. 1992. *Uganda since Independence: a Story of Unfulfilled Hopes* (Trenton, NJ: Africa World Press).

Schumpeter, J. 1947. *Capitalism, Socialism and Democracy*, 2nd edn (New York: Harper and Bros).

World Bank, 1997. 'The State in a Changing World', in *World Development Report 1997* (New York: World Bank/Oxford University Press).

6 Of Ethnicity, Manipulation and Observation: the 1992 and 1997 Elections in Kenya

D. Foeken and T. Dietz

INTRODUCTION

On 29 December 1992, the first multi-party elections – both presidential and parliamentary – since 1966 were held in Kenya. Exactly five years later this happened again. Not only in Kenya, but also in the international community, these elections were followed with special interest, for several interrelated reasons: (1) such elections are considered a major aspect of the 'democratization' process which has been imposed by the western donors on many African states; (2) Kenya has always been a very Western-oriented, open, capitalist and politically fairly stable country amidst a group of countries being quite different in these respects; (3) although less than in the past, it still has strategic importance for the Western countries (for example, Mombasa was an important harbour during the Gulf War); and (4) Kenya is a major 'outlet' for substantial Western donor funds.

The aim of this paper is twofold. First, the results of the elections are analysed in terms of ethnicity and various kinds of manipulation. Second, the importance of election observation is assessed. The two aims are interrelated: given the usual way of election observation (that is, only during a very short period centred around the actual polling day), does observation lead to less manipulation, that is, to more 'free and fair' elections than otherwise? One could go even further: given the ethnic determination of the election results in Kenya, does observation make sense? In the final section of this paper, a cautious answer to these questions is given.

The paper was largely written before the elections of 1997; hence, the main part of it is about the 1992 elections. The 1997 elections are dealt with in the final section, discussing briefly the changes that occurred during the months preceding the polls – including important changes as far as election observation is concerned – as well as the results.

BRIEF HISTORICAL BACKGROUND

In 1989, the Kenyan population counted about 25 million people, subdivided into some 40 ethnic groups. None of the ethnic groups dominates in terms of size. The largest group are the Kikuyu (21 per cent), mainly living in the central part of the country. Then come the Luhya (14 per cent) in western Kenya, the Luo (13 per cent) near Lake Victoria, the Kalenjin (11 per cent) in the central Rift Valley, the Kamba (11 per cent) living east and south-east of Nairobi, the Kisii (6 per cent) in the south-west and the Meru (5 per cent) living east of Mount Kenya. All these groups consist of several subgroups. For instance, the Luhya are known for their internal rivalries, while there is also not much of a group feeling among the different Kikuyu subgroups. However, among the Kalenjin such a group feeling has become apparent since the end of the 1970s (or has been created since Daniel arap Moi, a Kalenjin himself, became president in 1978). During the colonial period, nobody ever mentioned this group as an entity but talked of smaller ethnic groups like the Nandi, the Kipsigis, the Pokot and the Tugen.

After a bloody guerrilla war, known as the Mau Mau, of especially the Kikuyu in the 1950s against the British colonial administration and its African collaborators, Kenya obtained its independence in 1963. Jomo Kenyatta, a Kikuyu, became the first president. During the period prior to independence two political movements were formed, the Kenya African National Union (KANU) and the Kenya African Democratic Union (KADU). KANU combined Kikuyu and Luo interests, while KADU found its political base among some smaller ethnic groups, mainly in the Rift Valley. KANU stood for relatively radical policies, with slogans like 'African socialism' and a preference for a strong central state. KADU represented more moderate political ideas and adhered to a decentralized state apparatus and more room for private initiative. The first president, Kenyatta, originated from KANU, while the incumbent president, Moi, was one of the leaders of KADU. Almost immediately after independence, the two parties melted together into one KANU and most leaders soon moved towards political middle positions. This resulted, in 1966, in the secession of a group led by the first vice-president, Jaramogi Oginga Odinga, a Luo. These dissidents founded the radical Kenya Peoples Union (KPU). In 1969 this party was forbidden by the government and its leaders were put in prison. Hence, a *de facto* one-party state came into existence. However, within the one party, KANU, there were strong differences of opinion as well as a growing resistance to the concentration of power and wealth in the hands of a small Kikuyu group around president Kenyatta.

Kenyatta died in 1978 and was succeeded by Daniel arap Moi, who had been vice-president for ten years. Since Moi was a Tugen, a Kalenjin subgroup, this marked a new era in which political and economic power shifted to the Kalenjin. Of course, especially during the first years of Moi's presidency, this was a precarious process, but by skilfully manoeuvring he succeeded in gradually strengthening his position. He survived a coup attempt in 1982 and from then on he transformed the only permitted political party, KANU, into a state apparatus in his hands and the coterie surrounding him. Kenya had become a *de jure* one-party state.

ETHNICITY AND TERRITORIALITY[1]

Despite more than forty years of 'nation building', subnational/ethnic identities are still very strong, and under President Moi's leadership they have intensified. The 'ethnic question' became a major item at the elections of 1992, and the 'ethnic cleansing' that started in some areas in 1991 (and again occurred in 1997) still has the potential to provoke all-out ethnic warfare and to break the country apart in ethnic zones. If 'ethnicity' has such a potentially devastating power, how 'ethnic' is Kenya? It is interesting to look at the ethno-demographic trends in Kenya before the 1992 elections. After defining 'ethnic clusters'[2] and 'ethnic home areas'[3] we have looked at the changes in the level of concentration of the various ethnic clusters in these home areas, comparing the census years 1969, 1979 and 1989. With one small exception all ethnic clusters in Kenya became less concentrated in their home areas, or, to say it the other way around, became more dispersed. Demographically speaking a considerable ethnic deconcentration took place. The pace of deconcentration was much faster between 1969 and 1979 than during the following decade, though (with two exceptions). Nevertheless, despite the general tendency of dispersal, most ethnic clusters are still rather concentrated in their 'home areas': the Coastal Bantu and the Meru cluster leading with more than 90 per cent, followed by Kisii, Maasai, Somali, Boran, Kamba and Luo with more than 75 per cent. The Luhya, Kalenjin, Kikuyu and Turkana are the groups with the highest dispersal outside their 'home areas'.

We can also look at the changes in ethnic homogeneity at the level of the districts; for instance, the proportion of the district population taken up by the major ethnic group. It appears that most Kenyan districts were less homogeneous in 1989 than in 1969. However, there is a different overall trend 1969–79 and 1979–89. Compared to 1969, 75 per cent of all districts were more heterogeneous in 1979. Out of those 30 districts 18 showed the same trend between 1979 and 1989, but 12 showed a reversed trend of ethnic homogenization during the 1980s.[4] In addition, seven districts had a trend of ethnic homogenization during both periods.[5] This means that during the 1980s – the first decade of President Moi's era – almost half of the Kenyan districts experienced an ethnic homogenization trend, with examples from almost all ethnic groups. Looking at it in a longer time perspective, the ethnic cleansing during the beginning of the 1990s can thus be seen as the violent continuation of a process that started at least a decade earlier.

'DEMOCRATIZATION'

From 1990 onwards, there was so much pressure for democratization from both internal and external forces that Moi had to give in. However, he continuously stressed that multi-partyism would lead to ethnic struggles. And indeed, it is well known that a group of political leaders around him did everything to make this a self-fulfilling prophecy. From the start of the political campaigns, ethnic violence took place, first between Kalenjin and Luhya, thereafter extended to bloody 'tribal clashes' between Kalenjin and Luo, between Kalenjin and Kikuyu, and between Maasai and Kikuyu, while the endemic violence in the northern pastoralist areas developed into a chaos of robberies and looting.

In the beginning of the political campaign for the elections of December 1992 it looked as if the political opposition was heading for an easy victory, since the political dominance of Moi's KANU was limited to the Rift Valley. However, in the course of 1992, the opposition, led by veteran politicians who were each others rivals, fell apart into two main groupings: the Democratic Party (DP) of the former vice-president Mwai Kibaki (a Kikuyu) and the Forum for the Restoration of Democracy (FORD) headed by Oginga Odinga (Luo) and by Kenneth Matiba (Kikuyu), a former minister. A few months before the elections, FORD fell apart into a group led by Matiba (FORD-Asili) and a group led by Oginga Odinga (FORD-Kenya).

A united opposition would easily have won the presidential elections of 29 December 1992. Instead, with only 36 per cent of the votes, Moi was re-elected. And because of the constituency voting system after British design, KANU won an absolute majority in parliament: 100 of the 188 seats, against 31 for FORD-Asili, 31 for FORD-Kenya, 23 for the DP and 3 for smaller parties.

ETHNIC VOTING

Kenya's political system is characterized by ethnic voting. One can speak of 'political ethnicity' when several ethnic groups develop political activities based on their claims to ethnic consciousness (ethnicity in this context refers to a 'we-feeling', an identity based on references to certain perceived (or alleged) common characteristics, which usually include a common language and a common territory but not necessarily so). Closely related to political ethnicity is political clientelism. The political leader has to assure himself of as many political 'clients' as possible in order to safeguard his position. He finds these clients primarily among his own ethnic group. In case of competition between political leaders of one and the same ethnic group, ethnic groups may vote divided, mostly along clan lines. The result is that political parties in Kenya (and in many other African countries as well) are not based on a political programme but on ethnicity, in which ethnic self-interest prevails.

How ethnic were the Kenyan elections of 1992? When looking at the results of the presidential elections at the provincial level, Map 6.1 shows that Moi obtained a majority not only in his 'own' Rift Valley Province, but also in Coast and Northeastern Provinces. The DP candidate, Mwai Kibaki, was strong in one province only (Eastern). The third candidate, Kenneth Matiba (FORD-Asili), had his 'clients' first of all in Central Province and in Nairobi, while Oginga Odinga dominated in Nyanza Province. Only in Western Province was voting strongly divided, mainly between Moi and Matiba, reflecting the two main factions within the Luhya group.

At the district level, ethnic voting was even more conspicuous, which could be expected, since most districts were ethnically defined. For instance, in those districts in Rift Valley Province with a Kikuyu or Luhya majority, Moi lost. In the districts of Eastern Province with groups most related to the Kikuyu, Moi also did not achieve a majority of the votes. Equally revealing is the fact that Oginga Odinga found no support in Kisii, a district in Nyanza Province which is not inhabited by Luo but by Gusii. Finally, the sharing of the votes among the four presidential candidates in the two main urban centres, Nairobi and Mombasa, reflects the ethnic heterogeneity in these areas.

The results of the general election showed a similar pattern. Besides the Kalenjin votes, President Moi's KANU obtained its support among the pastoralist groups (Turkana, Maasai, Somali, Samburu, Boran), among the coastal Mijikenda, as well as among part of the Luhya group in Western Province. These were also the regions where KADU won in the early sixties. The Democratic Party won in the northern Kikuyu districts, in the nearby Meru and Embu areas, and in some Kamba constituencies. FORD-Asili obtained a majority in the southern Kikuyu districts and in Kakamega where Matiba, the FORD-Asili leader, had formed an alliance with a popular Luhya politician.

Map 6.1   Kenyan presidential elections 1992: results by province (% of votes for the four main candidates)

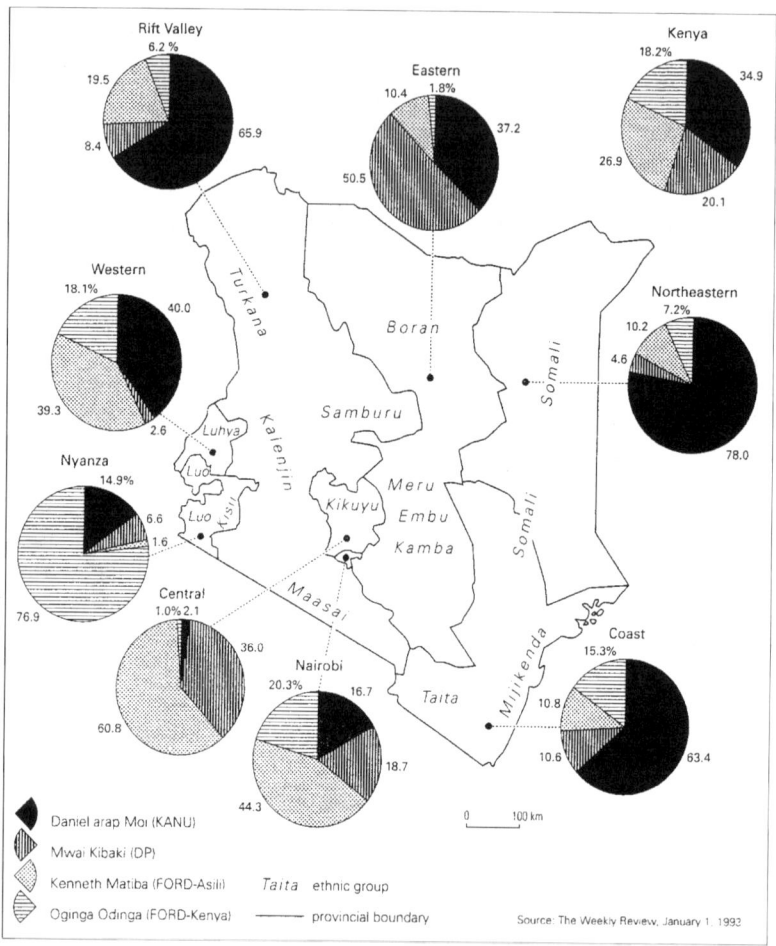

Most of the Nairobi seats went to FORD-Asili, too. Finally, FORD-Kenya, the party of Luo leader Oginga Odinga, won in the whole Luo region. Elsewhere in Kenya, FORD-Kenya won only a few seats, such as in Mombasa where the party had accepted a number of candidates from the Islamic Party of Kenya which had been excluded from the election.

Looking at the ethnic background of the elected opposition members of parliament, we see that 67 per cent of the FORD-

Asili members were Kikuyu, 61 per cent of FORD-Kenya Luo and 52 per cent of the Democratic Party again Kikuyu. In KANU, however, not a single Luo or Kikuyu won a seat. Among the KANU members of parliament, we find all Kalenjin representatives, 12 out of 17 elected Kamba from the south-east, 9 out of 10 elected Somali from the north-east, all 6 elected Maasai, 6 out of 9 elected Gusii, as well as representatives from all the smaller ethnic groups. The numerically second group in Kenya, the Luhya, was strongly divided: 9 representatives for FORD-Asili, 7 for KANU and 5 for FORD-Kenya. Despite this, the influential Kenyan weekly *The Weekly Review* wrote: 'The seventh parliament will be a living example of the reality of ethnic politics in Kenya.' Even in the multicultural capital Nairobi ethnic voting seemed to have been dominant. The percentages of votes for FORD-Asili and FORD-Kenya reflected the percentages of the population being Kikuyu and Luo, respectively.

LEGAL MANIPULATION

In retrospect, President Moi and his party had an easy victory in the 1992 elections. A few months before the day the elections were held (29 December), their prospects were not so bright, however. The opposition was still fairly united: that is, the Democratic Party and FORD. Especially the latter party, combining about half the Kikuyu and the whole Luo communities, as well as a then still unknown part of the Luhya community (in short: based on the support from the three largest ethnic groups), formed a formidable threat for both the president and KANU. Indeed, a candidate of any combination of the three main opposition parties would have won more votes than Moi. However, even in case of a united opposition, becoming the new president was another thing.

In August 1992, the Constitution of Kenya (Amendment) Bill passed the Kenyan parliament. Among other things, this bill made it mandatory for a successful presidential candidate to muster at least 25 per cent of the votes in at least five (out of eight) provinces (besides the requirements of having the greatest number of votes and being elected a member of parliament for a constituency). In case none of the candidates would achieve this, a run-off should have to be held between the two leading candidates. What the bill did not specify were various other possibilities. What had to be done if the leading candidate did not meet this requirement but the second one did? And what had to happen if after the run-off elections, the two candidates still did not muster the 25 per cent clause? At the time of the passing of the bill, these possibilities were not merely theoretical. Nevertheless, the bill sailed smoothly through parliament without any amendments and with only one vote against. This was less surprising than it may seem. Parliament was made up of members of only one party, KANU, and it was widely believed that if there was a party and a presidential candidate capable of meeting this requirement, it was KANU and Moi. Perhaps more surprising was the silence from the opposition. An explanation might be the one given by the attorney-general, Amos Wako, asking: 'Are [the opposition] admitting that the current president can fulfil that 25 per cent requirement and that any other presidential candidate cannot?' (*The Weekly Review*, 14 Aug. 1992: 15).

If this requirement can be regarded as a strong, legal move towards the re-election of president Moi, another article in the same bill had to safeguard KANU's governing power. The bill also mandated the candidate who was elected president to form a government from among the members of his own political party, even if that party would not have the parliamentary majority. In other words, as long as Moi would be re-elected, KANU would always retain (complete) power. The clause also prevented the other parties from forming a coalition government in case one of the opposition candidates might win the presidential elections. It is remarkable that this clause passed even more unnoticed than the 25 per cent requirement. Perhaps it is an indication that in the end all candidates and parties aim for the same: absolute majority, meaning unshared power.

What was more controversial, however, was the Electoral Commission, which had responsibility for the organization and conduct of the elections. According to the Kenyan constitution, the Commission is appointed by the president. In order to be acceptable to all parties, it was evident that at least its chairman, Justice Zacchaeus Chesoni, would have to be considered by everybody as being impartial. The opposition leaders were never consulted, however, and Chesoni was widely regarded as a puppet of president Moi. This was serious, since the Electoral Commission's powers were far-reaching. Its functions included not only the preparation and supervision of the elections, the maintenance and revision of voters' registers, and the promotion of voters' education, but also the determination of the number and boundaries of constituencies based on the most recent census: the one of 1989 (Kenya 1992a). It is the latter responsibility which may have decisively influenced the outcome of the parliamentary election in KANU's favour.

There are two ways in which manipulation is possible by means of defining constituencies. The first one is known as 'gerrymandering': the boundary of a constituency is drawn in such a way that the group one does not want to win forms a minority.[6] Even though there were allegations of 'Moimandering' (*Finance*, 15 Nov. 1994), it is doubtful whether this actually happened because of the ethnic homogeneity of nearly all districts, and hence constituencies, at least outside the main urban centres.

That cannot be said of the second manipulation method, namely the determination of the number of constituencies, or more specifically the degree of representation per district. According to the Constitution of Kenya, chapter III, section 42(3), 'all constituencies shall contain as nearly equal numbers of inhabitants as appears to the Commission to be reasonably practicable.' In 1966, 158 constituencies were created and in 1987 another 30 were added. Although at the time of the expansion of the number of seats, KANU was still the only political party, it is conspicuous that it created a surplus of small constituencies (in terms of population) in areas with strong support for the ruling party.

On average, there should have been about 42,000 voters per constituency (7.9 million registered voters divided by 188 parliamentary seats). Reality was very different, however. North-eastern Province (141,000 voters), a KANU stronghold, allocated 10 constituencies (on average 14,100 voters per seat), while Nairobi (674,000 voters), an opposition stronghold, counted only 8 seats (more than 84,000 voters per constituency). A district like Taita Taveta (66,900 voters), another KANU stronghold, had four constituencies, while Kisumu Town (100,000 voters), a FORD-Kenya stronghold, was just a single constituency. There are many more examples, all pointing in the same direction: areas where KANU was known to be strong (Rift Valley, Coast Province and the sparsely populated areas in the north) are quite over-represented in the Kenyan parliament. This explains why KANU, with only 34 per cent of the votes in the parliamentary election, was able to win 53 per cent of the seats. Seats won by KANU required on average about 33,000 registered voters as against 52,000 for the opposition. If constituencies had been defined on a more equal basis, the balance in parliament between KANU on the one hand, and the joint opposition on the other, would have been reversed, meaning the opposition would have had a majority of seats.

There is another method of legal manipulation, which may not have such a direct impact as the previous one, but which can influence the outcome in an indirect way. This concerns control by the different political parties of the mass media and particularly television. There are two national television companies in Kenya. The oldest one is the Kenya Broadcasting Corporation (KBC), which is state owned. The other one is the Kenyan Television Network (KTN), which is owned by KANU. In other words, television is avowedly pro-government. That cannot be said of the press, however. The biggest newspaper, *The Daily Nation*, is independent, the second largest, *The Standard*, takes a 'central' position, while the third one, *The Kenya Times*, is owned by KANU. Moreover, among the weeklies and monthlies there are some highly critical journals, which are widely read.

Finally, legal manipulation can also take place by announcing popular policy measures shortly before election day. This was the case at the annual Jamhuri Day, two weeks before the election of 29 December 1992. Minimum wages for all workers went up by 12 per cent, married women in the civil service were awarded house allowance (a very sensitive point in Kenya), travelling allowances for Muslims going to Mecca were more than doubled, and over 4,500 prisoners serving sentences of up to six months were released. That same Jamhuri Day, which is supposed to be a national celebration, turned into an outright KANU rally (covered by television, of course), prompting several foreign diplomats (among whom the ambassadors of the United States, Germany and Sweden) to demonstratively leave the Nairobi stadium where it was held.

ILLEGAL MANIPULATION

As said, the above-mentioned ways of legal manipulation did not receive very much attention from the press, the opposition and others. More criticisms could be heard regarding various types of illegal manipulation. This concerns not only all kinds of irregularities on election day itself (see below), but also events during the preparation stages in the months prior to the actual elections to which we will turn now.

Complaints started as soon as the registration of voters started on 8 June 1992. According to the opposition, malpractice was widespread and the Electoral Commission disorganized; hence, they called for a boycott. When nothing happened, the opposition decided to make the best of a bad job, and registration went on for 43 days (in 1988 it took three months!). The final deadline came amidst widespread complaints, especially in Nairobi, from people who said they had not been able to obtain identity cards, which are a prerequisite to registration. The relatively short period of voter registration may have been the cause for the low number of voters that were registered in the end: 7.9 million. Compared with an adult population of about 11 million, one can only conclude that at least a few million potential voters were not registered.

The essential questions, then, are: where did most of these unregistered voters live? Or: to which ethnic groups did they belong? Or: did KANU benefit from the non-registration of so many potential voters? According to *Africa Confidential* (of 18 Dec. 1992), the latter question should be answered with a 'yes'. At district level, this cannot be confirmed, however. Compared with the total populations in all districts, voters' registration ranged from a low 25 per cent in Kwale District to a 'high' 56 per cent in Mombasa District. But one cannot find evidence that registration in 'KANU districts' was higher than in 'opposition districts'.

As for the nomination of candidates for the parliamentary election, the story was different, however. There were reported incidents of violence, abductions and obstructions directed mainly at opposition candidates during the parliamentary and civic nominations in December. A number of opposition candidates were physically prevented from presenting their nomination papers in their constituencies, particularly in Rift Valley Province, which many KANU activists had declared a 'KANU zone'. The opposition leaders demanded from the Electoral Commission a repeat of the nominations in all areas where the opposition had cried foul. Strong protests also came from the Commonwealth observation team, as well as from several diplomatic missions. The only thing Chesoni was prepared to do was set up a five-man commission, composed of members of the Electoral Commission, with the task of investigating the reported irregularities. The final result was, first, that the cases where candidates had been physically obstructed from presenting their nomination papers fell outside the authority of the Commission and had to be referred to the High Court and, second, that in the 16 constituencies where opposition candidates had not presented their papers, the Commission had decided that the KANU candidates would stand unopposed, thus giving KANU a comfortable head start.

Several other irregularities and malpractices were reported, mostly shortly before and on election day. Some of these were directly attributable to the Electoral Commission. For instance, a number of polling stations opened with a considerable delay – in some cases as late as the afternoon – due to the late arrival of election materials, mainly ballot boxes, ballot papers and stamps. There were also cases where the names of some party candidates were omitted from the ballot papers, but nevertheless voting went ahead in the constituencies concerned. In some places ballot papers destined for one constituency ended up in a different constituency. In over 40 constituencies, the number of presidential and parliamentary ballots failed to match by more than 800 papers (equivalent to a ballot box full of papers), which is regarded as a characteristic sign of ballot box stuffing. Finally, vote counting and release of results were also seriously delayed. In all, a representative of one of the major observer teams, the Washington-based International Republican Institute, was openly wondering whether the whole process was 'systematic or indicative of a focused effort to disadvantage specific regions, constituencies or candidates' (*The Weekly Review*, 1 Jan. 1993: 48).

There were also irregularities which fell outside the responsibilities of the Electoral Commission. Among these were harassment and intimidation of voters – particularly by the Youth of

KANU '92 (YK '92) – and vote buying. The latter took place on a large scale, predominantly by YK '92 and the other KANU support groups Operation Moi Wins and Toroitich Till 2000 (Toroitich is Moi's middle name). Unlike the opposition parties, KANU disposed of large sums of money (state money, according to many), and was, for instance, able to set up national and provincial secretariats for its support groups with full-time staff. An estimated US$60 million was spent on vote buying, mostly by KANU supporters. Expenses ranged from hiring transport for voters and bodyguards for candidates, to employing thugs and distributing party T-shirts or even cash money to passers-by.

OBSERVATION

Not only in Kenya itself, but also from the perspective of the donor-countries, the 1992 elections were seen as a major event in the process of democratization. After all, Moi had to agree with multi-partyism and elections after maximum external pressure, notably by suspending foreign aid. Hence, in order to restore the financial relations between Kenya and its donors, the elections had to be labelled 'free and fair'. This explains the great interest in the elections from outside Kenya.

There were several international observation teams. Besides the above-mentioned International Republican Institute (IRI) team, there were officials of two other institutions from the United States, namely the Federal Electoral Commission and the International Foundation for Electoral Systems (a third American-based group, the National Democratic Institute, had been rejected by President Moi because of its supposed bias in favour of the opposition). Another important group was the Commonwealth team, led by Sir Telford Georges, a former chief justice in Zimbabwe and Tanzania. The Commonwealth team was the largest ever sent out by the body on such an assignment, which was in Kenya considered an indication of the seriousness with which the conduct of the elections was being regarded in the Western world. There were also national teams from Canada/Sweden (the so-called Scancan team), Denmark, Egypt, Finland, Germany, Japan, the Netherlands and Switzerland. In all, more than 150 external observers watched the elections.

The most important local observation team was the National Election Monitoring Unit (NEMU), consisting of several professional and church-related organizations in Kenya. Funded by external donors and chaired by Rev. Samwel Kobia (Secretary-general of the National Council of Churches of Kenya), NEMU was set up to coordinate local bodies planning to monitor the forthcoming elections and to educate the public on matters relating to the holding of free and fair polls. Among the 20 members of its 'council of elders' were a former governor of the Central Bank of Kenya, two former permanent secretaries and a leading banker, which were intended to give NEMU much-needed credibility. Other local monitoring groups were the Bureau for Education, Research and Monitoring, the National Council of Women of Kenya and the National Committee for the Status of Women in Kenya.

At this point it is important to distinguish between observation and monitoring. Usually the distinction is made by the length of the period during which the election process is being watched. Observation, then, is restricted to the actual election day(s) and (part of) the counting of the votes during the day(s) afterwards. Monitoring covers a much longer period and includes the months prior to the actual election day(s). All international teams were observation teams (although the IRI organized two missions to Kenya in order to get at least an impression of the nomination process and the campaigns), while the local teams were more of the monitoring type. Interestingly, the Electoral Commission of Kenya used the official status of the person involved as the distinctive criterion, an observer simply being 'a spectator' but a monitor 'almost [being] an official participant within the polling station at which he/she must exclusively operate' (Kenya 1992b: 1). According to the Commission, observers should in particular scrutinize the following aspects of the actual elections (Kenya 1992b: 2–3):

- maintenance of peaceful and orderly voting process;
- documentation and recording of accountable equipment and papers;
- display of empty boxes before voting;
- sealing before and after polling;
- transportation of ballot boxes from the polling stations to the counting centres;

- checking of the seals to the aperture and elsewhere before opening of ballot boxes;
- noting the sealed packets of accountable stationery from the polling stations and the presiding officers' statement of ballot papers issued;
- the manner in which votes are counted;
- collating and correlating of results; and
- visible indication that the presiding officer is in control of the entire polling situation.

On the day the Commonwealth team arrived in Kenya – on 16 December, two weeks before the election day – the IRI just released a press statement of findings on the campaign and nomination process. The report was based on a two-week observation mission and was fairly negative, stating for instance that the electoral process had been 'severely damaged by the centralized and systematic manipulation of the administrative and security structure of the state to the ruling party's advantage' (*The Weekly Review*, 18 Dec. 1992: 14). The statement also spoke of 'political harassment' of opposition candidates and 'illegal' use of KANU money to influence voters. There was a furious reaction from the YK '92 chairman, Cyrus Jirongo, heatedly accusing the IRI of siding with the opposition, asking the Electoral Commission to cancel the accreditation of the US team and deport them, and if not, threatening to bar the IRI observers from visiting polling stations on polling day (a threat which could not be seen as entirely imaginative).

At the same media briefing, the spokesperson of the IRI team, Margaret Thompson, also stressed that the observer teams were in Kenya to observe and report, not to monitor the polls. As she explained, monitoring would mean virtually overseeing the whole election process (at least a period of six months), while observing involved mainly placing personnel at selected stations in order to get an impression of whether or not the polls were free and fair. But even within this limited scope, this was precisely one of the major weaknesses of the observation process, because there were far too few international observers. The result was that only a minority of all polling stations could be visited by the observation teams, and the time spent at each station was usually very short, certainly not the whole day. This can be exemplified by the following account (Geisler 1993: 620):

> In Kenya, covering an area more than twice the size of Britain, 160 international observers were confronted with over 7,000 polling stations (roughly 45 for each of them), not to mention the 10,500 or so 'streams' with their separate voting procedures. The 56 members of the International Republican Institute managed to visit 2.3 per cent of the polling stations in a quarter of all constituencies, while the 33-strong Commonwealth Observer Group claimed to have seen roughly three per cent of all polling stations in 75 per cent of the 188 constituencies. The coverage of other observation missions was altogether more patchy. A Swedish team of four, for example, visited 22 stations in two constituencies, and others did not fare much better.

The observation team from the Netherlands consisted of seven representatives from the Ministry of Foreign Affairs in The Hague. The large majority of them had had experience with or in Kenya before, which was felt as 'very useful'.[7] According to the terms of reference, the mission's observations only concerned the election day itself and, to a limited extent, also the counting of the votes. More specifically, the aspects which were to be watched in particular were the opening of the polling station (including the sealing of the ballot boxes), the closing of the ballot boxes, the transportation of the ballot boxes to the central counting station, as well as the start of the counting of the votes.

Together with a representative from the Netherlands Embassy in Nairobi, each team member 'covered' a specific area in Kenya. These were parts of the following districts: Nairobi, Embu/Meru, Laikipia, Kajiado, Uasin Gishu/Elgeyo Marakwet, West Pokot, and Turkana (the former three being opposition strongholds and the latter four being KANU strongholds). In all, the seven teams visited 68 polling stations and 9 counting offices. Most stations opened too late, some even in the afternoon, the main reason being late arrival of ballot boxes and papers due to transport problems. In several stations, there was a shortage of ink and stamps, in a few also of ballot papers. The lack of privacy was conspicuous in the eyes of the Western observers: the voting booths were hardly screened, while the illiterates (of which there are many, especially in the rural areas) had to be aided by the officials. Nevertheless, the observers' impression was that the voters seemed not to have any problem with this lack of privacy while casting one's vote. In all polling stations, NEMU observers were present, although many of them were very young and remained quite 'invisible' during the election day. Also present in most stations were 'agents' of the four major political parties. In a few cases, it was witnessed that these agents played a rather intimidating role towards the illiterate voters. Finally, in one of the districts, people from a nearby refugee camp (victims of the 'ethnic clashes' during the campaigns) were not given the opportunity to vote, despite their strong wish to do so.

The counting of the votes took place with an enormous delay, for several reasons. First, many polling stations closed later because their opening was delayed. Second, some presiding officers did not give permission to start counting before all ballot boxes had arrived, which because of the transport problems took many hours. Third, the whole counting process was very inefficient, partly because of the exaggerating attempts to let it look 'transparent'. In addition, it was observed that no specific identification had been attached to the ballot boxes brought in, although this was legally prescribed. It was also noted that party agents did not check the numbers on the ballot boxes, even though they had written these down in the morning. This check would have been the only proof that the boxes had not been opened between times.

Despite all these imperfections, the judgement of all seven sub-teams was moderately positive. The general 'impression' was that, despite the fact that many voters had to queue for hours in the hot sun, the people had been able to cast their votes in the way they intended to. There were hardly any irregularities noticed. It was also felt that voters and officials, as well as party agents, were very positive regarding the presence of the international observers.

Of major concern for the Kenyan government were the final statements by the international observation teams. In private, none of the international monitoring teams and virtually no Nairobi-based diplomats could state that the elections had been fair. In its official statement released on the eve of its departure (when, according to Geisler 1993, the counting of the votes had not yet been concluded in many constituencies!), the Commonwealth team even admitted this:

> This was an election that proved difficult to evaluate in terms of freeness and fairness. It was evident to us from the start that some aspects of the election were not fair. These included:
>
> * the registration process in many parts of the country;
> * the nomination process, particularly in the Rift Valley, resulting in the unopposed return of 16 KANU parliamentary candidates;
> * the lack of transparency on the part of the Electoral Commission;
> * the intimidation, administrative obstacles and violence that marked the political campaign;
> * the partisanship of the state-owned radio and television;
> * the reluctance of the government to delink itself from the KANU party.
>
> These negative aspects were compounded by the numerous administrative problems that can be directly attributed to the inability of the Electoral Commission to plan ahead and pay adequate attention to the many basic and essential elements of the electoral process. This resulted in late delivery of materials, polls with too many voters, lack of adequate training officials and a non-effective public education programme. (*The Weekly Review*, 1 Jan. 1993: 9)

The statement went on in a more positive tone by stressing the inexperience of the Electoral Commission, the dedication and enthusiasm with which the millions of people had exercised their right to vote, the commitment of the thousands of polling officials, and so on. Its main conclusion was that the elections constituted 'a giant step on the road to multi-party democracy'. The latter was underscored in the official statements of all other international observation teams, including the one from the Netherlands. However, some additional remarks in the report of one of the seven Dutch sub-teams may be revealing. From reliable sources in the district concerned it became clear that strong manipulation practices had occurred during the period before the elections, with the sole aim to limit the anti-Moi and anti-KANU votes in the district. Examples were high payments to potential opposition candidates who were willing to withdraw, harassment of (potential) candidates, and opposition offices pelted with stones.

The national monitoring teams had between 7,500 and 10,000 observers deployed in the field, and their judgement of the actual elections was much more critical than that of the international teams. Almost immediately after the election day, the largest, the National Election Monitoring Unit (NEMU), declared that the 'electoral process has been seriously compromised' and in its final report the unit concluded 'that the December 1992 elections were not free and fair' (Geisler 1993: 627).

THE 1997 ELECTIONS[8]

Exactly five years after the 1992 elections, the next elections were held. Before presenting the results, it is important to (briefly) discuss the developments prior to polling day. These can best be dealt with in terms of changes on the one hand and continuities on the other. The continuities refer to renewed ethnic clashes and to a divided opposition. The changes concern the political reforms of September 1997 and the monitoring activities by the donor community.

In August and September 1997, very serious ethnic conflicts emerged at the Coast and later in the south-west as well. The resemblance with the clashes that occurred in Rift Valley Province in 1992 was conspicuous. First, the attacks were carried out by large, well-organized groups. Second, the violence involved was very brutal, and hundreds of people were killed. Third, the violence at the Coast was solely directed at people from up-country: people known to vote for the opposition in an area dominated by KANU. Finally, the cases were never solved: it never became clear who the real leaders were, let alone that any of the perpetrators were tried in a court of law.

The opposition was even more divided than during the 1992 elections. There were 14 opposition candidates for the presidency, while 24 parties took part in the general elections. The two FORD parties fell further apart. FORD-Kenya – in 1992 a coalition of the Luo and part of the Luhya communities – split into two because the Luo political leader, Raila Odinga (son of the late Oginga Odinga) stepped out to form his own Luo party, the National Development Party (NDP). Hence, FORD-Kenya became a Luhya party led by Kijana Wamalwa. The same happened with FORD-Asili, which combined part of the Kikuyu and part of the Luhya communities. Partly because its leader, Kenneth Matiba, refused to stand for the presidential elections, the party split into a Luhya faction (FORD-Asili) and a Kikuyu faction (FORD-People). Several other parties took part in the elections, two of which were of some importance, notably the Kamba-based Social Democratic Party (SDP, with the first female presidential candidate Charity Ngilu) and Safina, the only party which pretends to have a non-ethnic base (hence its name, which means 'the Ark'). The largest ethnic group in Kenya, the Kikuyu, was also the most divided one, since there were five Kikuyu candidates for the presidency, although only one of them, Mwai Kibaki (Democratic Party), was a serious one.

An important change compared with the previous elections concerned the constitutional and legal reforms of September 1997. For years KANU had refused to comply with the widely-voiced desire – under the leadership of the NCEC, the National Convention Executive Council, representing a broad range of church-related and other societal organizations – for political reforms in the country. However, in order to avert complete chaos, a group of about 75 members of parliament from both KANU and the opposition parties decided to take the initiative by forming the so-called Inter-Parties Parliamentary Group (IPPG), which had to formulate a wide range of constitutional and legal reforms. Among the more important reforms were the extension of the Electoral Commission by 10 members suggested by opposition parties (but still forming a minority against the 11 members from KANU), the provision for a coalition government (in practice meaning that the president can appoint ministers in his cabinet from opposition parties, which is precisely the way Moi became a minister in 1964), the recommendation to register all parties (which led to the registration of Safina but not of the Coast-based Islamic Party of Kenya), and the equal allocation of broadcasting time for all parties on television and radio. However, two issues of decisive importance for the election results and for the power distribution in the country were left untouched. This was the 25 per cent rule for the presidential elections and the determination of the constituency boundaries (by the Electoral Commission); hence the general conclusion of the NCEC that the reforms 'are massively deficient in ensuring a representative parliament for Kenyans' and that it is 'not possible to achieve free and fair elections under these conditions' (*The Sunday Nation*, 14 Sept. 1997).

Another important change was in the field of monitoring and observation of the electoral process. Initiated and coordinated by the Dutch embassy in Nairobi and chaired by the Canadian embassy, a group of 22 donor-countries (also including the United States, Britain, France, Germany, Japan and the Scandinavian countries) formed the Donors' Democratic Development Group (DDDG) in order to monitor the whole election process, including such critical phases as voter registration, party primaries, nomination of candidates, political campaigning, the polling itself and counting (see Rutten below). The reason to do so was the conviction that manipulation did take place in 1992, perhaps not so much during the actual elections but during the preceding stages. The actual monitoring was carried out by a group of researchers from various donor countries (the Election Observation Centre or EOC), as well as by teams from the diplomatic missions. Voter registration, party primaries and nominations of candidates were followed in 25 districts. Presidential and parliamentary campaign meetings were attended in all provinces except one (North-eastern). On election day, 90 teams visited over 500 polling stations in 118 (of the 210) constituencies and counting was monitored in 50 counting halls (DDDG 1998).

At the national level, the 1997 elections were observed by a group, funded by several European countries, whose motto was 'Together for Peaceful Elections' and consisting of the National Council of Churches of Kenya (NCCK), the Institute for Education in Democracy (IED) and the Catholic Justice and Peace Commission (CJPC). Just like the donor community, not only the poll itself was observed – by over 28,000 watchers, working in teams of two in all the 210 electoral constituencies and of three present at the counting centres – but also the voter registration, the nomination process, the campaigns and the role of the media, by 840 monitors (*The Weekly Review*, 9 Jan. 1998).

Because of the splintered opposition, largely along 'tribal' lines, the results of the 1997 election were very much like those of the previous polls. In the presidential election, Moi won most votes (40 per cent) and was again the only candidate with more than 25 per cent of the votes in five of the eight provinces. The only serious rival was Kibaki, who got 30 per cent of the votes, with more than 25 per cent in three provinces. The three other candidates who prior to the polls were also seen as rivals – Odinga, Wamalwa and Ngilu – were far behind and only managed to get a substantial number of votes in their 'home' provinces. In the general elections, KANU again won the majority of the seats, notably 107 out of 210 (against 100 out of 188 in 1992), of which 11 unopposed. Kibaki's Democratic Party won 39 seats (23 in 1992), Odinga's National Development Party 21 and Wamalwa's FORD-Kenya 17 (against 31 in 1992 for the two combined), while newcomers Social Democratic Party and Safina won 15 and 5 seats, respectively.[9] The ethnic factor in both the presidential and the parliamentary elections is clear again: Kibaki and his DP profited from the withdrawal of Matiba, thus obtaining many votes from that part of the Kikuyu–Embu–Meru cluster that voted for Matiba and his FORD-Asili in 1992. Both the NDP and FORD-Kenya are much smaller now than the original FORD-Kenya in 1992, because of the split of the latter in a Luo and a Luhya party, respectively.

The election itself was described as 'chaotic'. According to *The Daily Nation* of 30 December 1997, 'just about anything that could go wrong did go wrong'.[10] The newspaper talked about a 'Chaplinesque performance', a 'national disgrace' and 'an insult to voters', but admitted that not only the Electoral Commission was to blame for this, but certainly also the extremely bad weather. In a first analysis of the 'Together for Peaceful Elections' group, it was stated that 56 per cent of the polling stations failed to open on time, because voting materials were not available or election officials were not present. The poll watchers reported concerns about the lack of secrecy in about 6 per cent of the stations. Also during the nomination process and the political campaigns, many irregularities had been observed, mostly bribery and vote buying, particularly by 'the ruling party'. On the other hand, the voting itself was reported to have taken place in 'a serious and largely satisfactory manner'. The same applied to the counting process. The group's general conclusion was that despite the many irregularities and the chaotic character of the elections, 'the results reflected the wishes of the voters'. At the same time, however, it was recommended that the institutional bias for KANU, such as the domination of the state media and the unfair delineation of electoral constituencies, ought to be seriously addressed (*The Weekly Review*, 9 Jan. 1998). Much more critical were the NCEC, the Kenya Human Rights Commission (KHRC) and the Citizens Coalition for Constitutional Change (or '4Cs'). They rejected the results as null and void, demanding new elections (*The Economic Review*, 5 Jan. 1998).

In its final report, the DDDG (1998) also mentioned irregularities during the various stages of the election process. About four million potential voters were not registered as such: two million aged 18–23 who had not been issued identity cards and another two million who just failed to do so. However, as in 1992, there was no proof that non-registration occurred more in opposition than in KANU areas. The party primaries were 'peaceful and transparent' in most areas, although problems were evident in several others. On the whole, the primaries were 'flawed but acceptable'. The nominations of parliamentary candidates on 8 and 9 December went 'satisfactorily', although in a number of areas there was violence and tension. As in 1992, media coverage of the campaigns was very disproportionately in favour of KANU and president Moi, notwithstanding the reforms regarding this point by the IPPG. Moreover, opposition coverage by the two national television channels (KBC and KTN) was negative throughout and positive as far as KANU was concerned. Despite the reporting by the written media of the very chaotic character of the voting day, it was established that almost 90 per cent of the 7,500 polling stations on which information was available were well organized. Nevertheless, the DDDG report mentions some serious problems. First, there were cases of misprints and omissions of candidates' names on the ballot papers. Even the Electoral Commission itself had to admit (in a press release of 31 December 1997) that under such circumstances 'it cannot be said such elections were fair'. Second, in 13 per cent of the stations the secrecy of the vote was not guaranteed. Third, bribery and vote buying were common, even on election day. Counting of the votes was generally conducted 'in a fair and transparent manner', albeit that there were substantial delays largely due to ill-prepared returning officers. In eight constituencies, however, serious irregularities were noticed. In three of these – Westlands (Nairobi), Kitui West (Eastern) and Changamwe (Mombasa) – the KANU candidate narrowly won under very suspicious circumstances. This is the more serious because otherwise the combined opposition would have had the majority of the seats in parliament instead of the ruling party. The counting of the votes for the presidential elections was 'satisfactory' in most constituencies.

Despite all this, on 7 January 1998 the European Union released a statement through its president, the British High Commission in Nairobi, saying that it accepted the results of not only the presidential but also the parliamentary elections, describing it as 'a further step in Kenya's development towards greater democracy'. At the same time it was noted that the elections fell short of 'normal democratic standards', that there were incidents of violence, bribery and intimidation of voters. Moreover, 'voter registration was incomplete, the media, the TV, and radio controlled by the State did not provide balanced coverage' (*The Daily Nation*, 8 Jan. 1998).

CONCLUSION

As in most other African countries, ethnic rivalries play an overwhelming role in Kenyan politics. In such a system, political parties play a role as vehicles in order to get access to the political centre and, hence, to state resources. The easy switching by candidates for the parliamentary nominations from one party to another is telling in this respect. With them, the voters switch as well. FORD-Kenya is a clear illustration: in 1992 it was a Luo party with some Luhya support, but with the defection of the main Luo political leader, it became a pure Luhya party and lost in 1997 all its support in the province in which it won overwhelmingly in 1992.

The practice of ethnic voting makes it possible to determine to a certain extent each party's strong and weak electoral areas. In a constituency voting system after the British example, combined with control by the ruling party of the Electoral Commission, this can easily lead to (legal) manipulation and constituency boundaries which strongly favour KANU. Besides several other legal and illegal manipulation practices, this was a major factor in KANU's large victory in the parliamentary elections of 1992.

Does election observation make sense in a system in which the outcome of the elections is to a certain extent known in advance? That was a key question after the 1992 elections. It was felt that because the major manipulation practices took place during the stages prior to the actual polling day, monitoring of the whole election process was necessary, and in as many areas as possible. Five years later, this was indeed done by both a national monitoring group ('Together for Peaceful Elections') and a group of 22 donor-countries (the Donors' Democratic Development Group). For the latter group, this was a unique 'experiment' leading to a critical report in which many irregularities were noticed. A careful reader of the report can only come to the conclusion that the 1997 elections were not really 'free and fair' and that the results of the parliamentary election (not the presidential election) are at least questionable.

It is still too early to say what lessons can be drawn from this 'experiment', not only for the group of donor-countries but also for election observation in general. It is beyond question that such monitoring is far more useful (but also far more expensive) in assessing the 'free and fair'-ness of such elections than short-term observation alone. But the main question that remains is whether the whole election process was positively influenced because of monitoring activities by the two monitoring groups. What is clear is that despite the monitoring activities, the election process was *not* entirely 'free and fair'. Nevertheless, two tentative conclusions can be drawn from the DDDG 'experiment'. First, in its role as an objective 'third party', it is likely that at least it prevented the election process from being even more 'unfree and unfair'. And second, it served to legitimize the role of the local monitoring organizations.

NOTES

1. This section is based on data derived from the Population Censuses of 1969, 1979 and 1989. We are grateful to Deborah IJsendijk and Luuk Dietz for their assistance with data collection and analysis.
2. An ethnic cluster consists of one or more 'ethnic groups' as distinguished by the Kenyan Central Bureau of Statistics during the

Population Census of 1989. For instance, the Kikuyu, Luhya, Luo, Kalenjin, Kamba, Somali and Turkana are all different ethnic clusters, while the Kisii, Maasai, Coastal Bantu, Meru and Boran are clusters consisting of more than one ethnic group.

3.   It is quite easy to define 'home areas' since the Kenyan Districts are demarcated along ethnic boundaries. For instance, the Kikuyu home area constitutes Kiambu, Murang'a, Nyeri, Kirinyaga and Nyandarua Districts, the Luo home area consists of Kisumu, Siaya and South Nyanza Districts, while the Somali home area is made up of Garissa, Mandera and Wajir Districts. Only Nairobi and Mombasa are exceptions to the rule. It should be noted that the 'original' 40 districts are used in this analysis: before the many subdivisions that started at the end of the 1980s.

4.   Kwale: Coastal Bantu (85 per cent, 84 per cent and 85 per cent in 1969, 1979 and 1989, respectively); Kilifi: Coastal Bantu (94–93–93); Tana River: Coastal Bantu (64–39–42); Machakos: Kamba (98–97–97); Embu: Meru cluster (89–86–86); Garissa: Somali (96–83–91); Mandera: Somali (96–89–98); Wajir: Somali (98–92–98); Murang'a: Kikuyu (96–96–96); Nandi: Kalenjin (78–71–74); Bungoma: Luhya (84–81–83); and Busia: Luhya (65–60–61). NB: figures are rounded.

5.   Mombasa: Coastal Bantu (35–37–40); Kirinyaga: Kikuyu (96–97–97); Nyandarua: Kikuyu (95–95–96); Laikipia: Kikuyu (57–64–68); Samburu: Maasai cluster (74–75–75); Kericho: Kalenjin (82–83–83); and Trans Nzoia: Luhya (47–49–52).

6.   The term 'gerrymandering' is derived from an American governor, Eldridge Gerry of Massachussets, who concocted a constituency that looked like a salamander. Well-known examples could also be found in Northern Ireland, where boundaries cut Catholic neighbourhoods in two, so that in both constituencies the Protestants formed a majority.

7.   The information concerning the Dutch observation team is derived from Memorandum – 02/93, The Hague: Ministry of Foreign Affairs, 5 Jan. 1993.

8.   Since this section was written shortly after the elections, only first impressions can be presented here.

9.   The remaining six seats went to FORD-People (3), FORD-Asili (1), Kenya Social Congress (1) and the Shirikisho Party of Kenya (1). In addition, twelve members of parliament were nominated: six for KANU, two for the DP and one for NDPK, SDP and Safina. The fact that half of the nominated members were proposed by the opposition was one of the results of the political reforms of September 1997, because in 1992 all twelve were KANU representatives. In all, KANU now occupies 113 seats in parliament and the combined opposition 109.

10.   Ballot boxes arrived too late, were insufficient and/or improperly secured. Ballot papers were not present at all, or too few or the wrong ones or with the wrong symbols or with no names, and so on. Polling stations could not open as no security guards were at hand or no officials turned up or staff wanted more money. Hence, in a number of polling stations people could vote the next day as well.

REFERENCES

DDDG, 1998. *Final Report: Kenya General Elections 1997* (Nairobi: The Donors' Democratic Development Group).

Dietz, T., D. Foeken and A. van Haastrecht, 1996. *Kenya: Mensen, Politiek, Economie, Cultuur* (Amsterdam/The Hague/Brussels: KIT/Novib/NCOS).

Doornbos, M. 1991. 'Linking the Future to the Past: Ethnicity and Pluralism', *Review of African Political Economy* 52: 53–65.

Foeken, D. and T. Dietz, 1993. 'Leidt Afrikaanse Democratisering tot Etnische Polarisatie?', *Geografie* 3(1): 30–4.

Fox, R. 1996. 'Bleak Future for Multi-Party Elections in Kenya'. *The Journal of Modern African Studies* 34(4): 597–607.

Geisler, G. 1993. 'Fair? What has Fairness got to do with it? Vagaries of Election Observations and Democratic Standards', *The Journal of Modern African Studies* 31(4): 613–37.

Haugerud, A. 1995. *The Culture of Politics in Modern Kenya* (Cambridge: Cambridge University Press).

Holmquist, F. and M. Ford, 1992. 'Kenya: Sloughing toward Democracy', *Africa Today* 39(3): 97–111.

Hornsby, C. and D. Throup, 1992. 'Elections and Political Change in Kenya', *Journal of Commonwealth and Comparative Politics* 30(2): 172–99.

IED, 1997. *National Elections Data Book Kenya 1963–1997* (Nairobi: Institute for Education in Democracy).

Kenya, Government of, 1992a. *Election '92: Towards Free and Fair Elections* (Nairobi: Ministry of Foreign Affairs and International Cooperation).

Kenya, Government of, 1992b. *The Role of Election Observers and the Code of Ethics* (Nairobi: Government Printer).

Kenya, Government of, 1994. *Population Census 1989* (Nairobi: Ministry of Planning and National Development/Office of the Vice-president, Central Bureau of Statistics).

Lemarchand, R. 1992. 'African Transitions to Democracy: an Interim (and Mostly Pessimistic) Assessment', *Africa Insight* 22(3): 178–85.

Osaghae, E.E. 1993. 'A Re-examination of the Concept of Ethnicity in Africa as an Ideology of Inter-elite Competition', *African Study Monographs* 12(1): 43–60.

Periodicals and Papers

Africa Confidential, various issues.
The Daily Nation, Nairobi, various issues.
The Economic Review, Nairobi, 5 Jan. 1998.
Finance, Nairobi, 15 Nov. 1994.
The Sunday Nation, Nairobi, 14 Sept. 1997.
The Weekly Review, Nairobi, various issues.

7 The Organization and Observation of Elections in Federal Ethiopia: Retrospect and Prospect

J. Abbink

INTRODUCTION[1]

In several strands of political theory, multi-party elections are considered as a prerequisite for real and effective democracy: in order to let the people exercise choice between programmes and candidates without the outcome being a foregone conclusion. In Africa, multi-party elections are seen by the Western donor community and the UN as one of the most important ingredients of the political democratization process in Africa, and international election observers have been a familiar part of the political landscape in countries perceived as carrying a promise of democratization. Ethiopia has been one of these countries. Both for economic and political reasons, it has been, and still is, a popular country with the Western donor community (the EU, the USA, and also the World Bank) on a continent which has seen the so-called 'third wave' of democratization run into the sands of neo-autocracy and economic stagnation (cf. Lemarchand 1993; Ihonvbere 1996).

In this chapter I examine the nature of Ethiopia's recent process of post-1991 political change and its institutional underpinnings, in the light of questions of representativeness, legitimacy, and sustainability of democratization. The focus will be on the electoral processes that have taken place, while the role of (especially international) election observers in possibly enhancing liberalization and democracy in the country will also be discussed. The *economic* aspects of political liberalization will only be marginally dealt with here, although they are very important in the case of Ethiopia.

150

Since the fall of the communist Mengistu regime in May 1991, Ethiopia, one of the poorest[2] and most populous[3] countries in Africa, has been experimenting with a political model based on ethnicity as an organizing principle. The country has now entered a phase of 'consolidation' of new political structures (see Lyons 1996) after a 'transitional period' of some three and a half years initiated by a 'National Conference of Peace and Reconciliation' in June 1991. The processes of both transition and consolidation were led by the victor in the long civil war in the north, the Tigray Peoples' Liberation Front, allied with three other groups, largely its own creation,[4] with which it forms the 'Ethiopian Peoples' Revolutionary Democratic Front' (EPRDF).

In any study of the contemporary Ethiopian political scene it is necessary to remember the adjective 'revolutionary' in the above party name: firstly because the democratic tradition as now espoused by this dominant party was shaped by its past allegiance to Marxism and to hegemonic vanguard-thinking as they emerged as elements of all revolutionary parties and liberation movements in Ethiopia in the 1970s, and secondly because the second adjective is qualified by the first in many important respects. The EPRDF differs, however, from the classic Marxist-inspired revolutionary movements in that it has emphasized ethnic relations (the 'nationalities question') as the main historical problem of Ethiopia, over and above questions of class and economic oppression.[5]

In 1994, after a transition period led by the EPRDF-dominated TGE (Transitional Government of Ethiopia), Ethiopia became a 'democratic federation', composed of nine 'regional states', and a 'city state' (Addis Ababa, which has its own separate charter since mid-1997).[6] An anomaly is Dire Dawa, detached from the Somali Regional State in 1995 and directly ruled by the federal government after ethnic clashes and internal disorder. The regional states all bear the name of their majority ethnic group,[7] except Gambela and the Southern Region (where more than 40 ethnic groups live).

Since 1991 there have been several rounds of elections in Ethiopia: the 1992 regional elections for local authorities, the 1994 Constituent Assembly elections, in 1995 the federal elections for the House of Peoples' Representatives, and in 1996 again elections on the local level for the *woredas* (districts) and *k'ebeles* (local authorities). In all elections, the ruling EPRDF was victorious by a very wide margin and was never threatened in its power position at any level. These elections, though perceived to mark the advent of a new, more open political process, were in several respects peculiar. Before looking at the nature and function of the elections in federal Ethiopia, a brief survey of the country's political structure, institutions and party organization is needed.

DEMOCRACY AND ETHNICITY: THE ETHIOPIAN APPROACH

Ethiopia's political system, and by implication that of the elections, is based on an interesting but controversial assumption. Democratization is primarily seen as equalling the recognition and realization of 'nationality' rights, meaning of ethnic group rights. These include not only use of the 'indigenous' language, cultural expression, and regional self-administration, but also the 'unconditional right to self-determination, including the right to secession', as the new 1995 Constitution says in art. 39.1.[8] While all kinds of individual rights are also generously recognized in the Constitution and the country is claimed to have the rule of law, the status and impact of the collective ethnic (nationality) rights tends to override all others. In the ideological view of the present Ethiopian regime, all previously suppressed ethnic groups[9] in Ethiopia should realize their ethnic, linguistic and cultural identity, preferably in their own region, and not be dominated by any other group, as was claimed to be the case in the empire state under Haile Sellassie and Mengistu. Ethnicity thus has made its entry in the *official* political discourse of Ethiopia and perhaps indeed of Africa.[10]

Part of the new democratized order is also the recognition of a private, independent press,[11] a definite improvement compared to the *Derg* period. Nevertheless, it is frequently harassed and lives in insecurity, with some ten to fifteen journalists in jail and independent papers and magazines feeling the threat of closure over their heads. These papers are neither freely available nor tolerated everywhere outside Addis Ababa.

Democratic thinking and institution-building was never well-developed in Ethiopia, which was, until 1974, an autocratic monarchy allowing no organized opposition, and (after a three-year transitional period) from 1977 to 1991 a totalitarian communist republic. Even the revolutionary underground opposition movements of the latter period, like the EPRP,[12] had no clear idea of how democracy should institutionally be installed in a country without a sufficiently literate rural population, with substantial linguistic and regional diversity, and which lacked a more or less integrated, nation-wide middle class. The 'national question' (a Marxist-Leninist preoccupation popular in the Ethiopian student movement and the later liberation movements) was – next to the land question – declared to be the main socio-political problem of Ethiopia. The TPLF (started as an ethno-regional movement of young people, sidetracked by the new revolutionary regime in 1975 when it turned to oppressive violence to quell the struggle for democratic rights) came to power in the name of this nationalities issue (later phrased in terms of regional autonomy for Tigray, against centralist 'Shewan-Amhara'[13] oppression), although the revolt was not started because of 'ethnic oppression' (compare Gebru 1991: 221). When the TPLF came to power, in combination with the EPLF in Eritrea, it imposed this model of ethnic rights and ethno-federation on the rest of the country.[14] This is not the place to further discuss the history and the constitutional shaping[15] of this issue (which, however, has great relevance for many other African countries). Suffice it to say that ethnic group identity has been declared the basis for the entire political process: for party formation, for the delineation of regions and electoral districts (gerrymandering), for registration of voters (ethnic group membership should be stated here), for eligibility of a candidate to one of the two chambers of parliament, and for the administration of local and regional governments (including appointments of administrators and civil servants). This is quite far-reaching but it is not easily imagined by Western observers what the implications are of this organizational model both in the political process and in everyday social relations between people. A region-based ethnic identity is both a resource and a label which all Ethiopians now have to work with, often overriding criteria like professional achievements or experience.[16]

Among the many African multi-ethnic polities, Ethiopia is the only one which recognizes ethnicity in such an explicit manner as an organizing principle and goes to such an extent of de-emphasizing the idea of a unitary state and national identity.[17] This is perhaps understandable in view of the recent history of ethno-regional violence in the country, but all the more ironic in one of the most ancient and strong central states that the continent has known.

THE POST-1991 POLITICAL STRUCTURE

The emergence of the post-*Derg*[18] political structure has been conditioned largely by the blueprints of the TPLF, prepared before its entrance in Addis Ababa in May 1991. At this juncture there was little organized political life in Ethiopia: no active political parties, no strong civil society organizations, and no free press, everything having been either co-opted or eliminated by the Mengistu regime. The National Defence Forces had melted away in the final months of the civil war, and the EPRDF armed forces took over the role of national army. The EPRDF took the initiative in calling the National Conference mentioned above, the members of whom were invited – not elected – from a selection of ethnic and liberation organizations, and thus initiated the transitional period.

The stated aims of the EPRDF regime are a democratization of centralist structures of the old unitary state, decentralization of decision-making to the regions through devolution and federalization along ethnic lines (to prevent dominance of one group over others), a liberalized, more market-oriented economic development led by the agricultural sector, and a quest for economic self-sufficiency, for example in food production.

The new Constitution of federal Ethiopia, adopted in December 1994 by the House of Peoples' Representatives on 8 December 1994, and coming into effect on 21 August 1995, outlines the political structure of federal Ethiopia, to the effect that power of the federal government under the prime minister appointed from the dominant party is still the core element of the state, despite decentralization efforts. The upper house of parliament is the Federal Council, the 108 members of which are elected on the basis of ethnic representation by the regional parliaments. It is a body with little power, holding only two sessions annually. The second chamber, the 548-member House of

Peoples' Representatives, is formally the main legislative body, and is elected by the people through an intricate system of district elections with ethnic parties as the main contenders (see below). The House does not have the right of initiative and is in practice not a sufficient countervailing power *vis-à-vis* the executive.

The prime minister (the head of the EPRDF) is the most important political figure and is supported by a circle of advisers in the Prime Minister's Office and in the Ministries (under the Ministers themselves). Ministers and advisers are primarily accountable to the prime minister and not to the parliament. This in effect means that the EPRDF as a party is very powerful in shaping and executing national policy without meaningful debate or opposition. The President of the republic is a largely ceremonial figure.

It is also notable – but nothing surprising in the context of African politics – that not only key political positions but also numerous economic positions in Ethiopia have been occupied by newly appointed loyalists with a certain (Tigrawi) background. The privatization policy of the government (sale of state building companies, hotels, insurance companies, and book publishers) tends to reinforce this tendency. Opposition groups claim that members from other ethnic groups were massively replaced by loyalists regardless of their professional qualifications and experience. Neo-patrimonial traits on a seemingly ethnic basis are thus being retained in the Ethiopian political system – though this statement must be seen as a hypothesis which needs further substantiation.

POLITICAL PARTIES

In the wake of the democratization process started in 1991, numerous parties have been emerging in Ethiopia, with most of them having also been officially registered with the National Electoral Commission. Whether this is an index of a sustainable democratic process, however, remains to be seen. This point holds generally in Africa: compare the example of Kenya after president Moi's bow to 'multi-partyism', where the intergroup ethnic violence and unabashed 'divide-and-rule' politics of the reigning elite have led to more instability in the political system and to a downturn in the national economy. In Ethiopia there are three problems with the parties: 1) Most of them have – by the clear admission of the EPRDF itself – been created from above as satellite parties of the ruling party for an ethnic constituency (and as there are about 80 recognized ethnic groups or nationalities, the number of parties can reach that number). We saw that the EPRDF itself was composed of groups claiming to represent the Tigrawi, the Oromo, the Amhara and the numerous southern peoples of Ethiopia. 2) Most parties are too recent and too poor in resources to have a significant constituency. They have no firm roots in the past, partly because of the systematic suppression of parties under previous regimes and the absence of a civic democratic tradition in a country where politics is regarded with deep suspicion by the population, especially after the 1976–8 'Red Terror' period.[19] The number of parties is also confusing to the wider public. Some of them emerged in response to harassment and persecution of certain populations (for example, the All-Amhara People's Organization in 1992). 3) The government, and especially the EPRDF, are ambivalent in their attitude towards parties not associated with the regime, and also to the idea of political opposition as such. Scathing remarks and veiled threats are often heard, even by the Prime Minister.[20] There is no effort to cultivate the idea of issue politics and compromise. The EPRDF model of ethnic political organization may indeed also pre-empt the need for trans-ethnic issue parties, because, in its view the first condition for real democracy, next to the recognition of basis human rights, is the right to express and realize ethnic identity, through regional organization, 'indigenous' language use in education, and development of their respective cultural traditions.[21]

Be that as it may, there are many parties, and some of them have a vocal opposition to the government and the dominant party. None are so well organized as the EPRDF, the core of which (TPLF) was forged in seventeen years of guerrilla warfare. Under the present regime, the fact that these political parties have been emerging and recognized is less important than the fact that they virtually all have been formed on an ethnic basis, especially the EPRDF-supported ones (recognizable under their name of 'democratic organization' or 'democratic movement'). Among almost all officially recognized ethnic groups in Ethiopia there was a political party, sometimes two. (This proliferation of groups is presently being reduced by lumping together small groups adjacent to each other.)[22]

The opposition parties also partly have an ethno-regional constituency: for example, the Oromo Liberation Front (OLF, now outlawed because of its armed resistance to the government), the AAPO, the Southern Ethiopian Peoples' Democratic Union (SEPDU), the Afar Revolutionary Democratic Unity Front (ARDUF), or the Ogaden National Liberation Front (ONLF).[23] But one of the most important groups, the CAFPDE,[24] is not based on ethnicity, despite a predominance of Southern groups.

Although some parties (AAPO and CAFPDE) have been able to stage huge mass rallies, they have not had the opportunity to become a significant counter-force. They have no influence in the political process, also due to their past boycott of the electoral process. Government threats and harassment (arbitrary arrests, frequent confiscation of their papers and accounts, prevention of campaigning and, according to human rights groups, extra-judicial killings and kidnapping of party members) are reported to have contributed to this low profile. Especially in the rural areas, opposition party activity is not possible.

Hence, most opposition parties have felt marginalized from the start (since 1991). A case in point is the Oromo Liberation Front, which (despite its uncertain constituency and controversial political programme) has support among Oromo-speaking people: it was removed from the Transitional Government at the time of the first elections in June 1992. The same fate befell members of the Southern Coalition. As a result of this marginalization, most opposition parties boycotted the electoral process thereafter, not only because they were being harassed and downplayed, but also because they disagreed fundamentally on the ethnicized political structures put in place by the EPRDF as the very context and precondition for the electoral process.

ELECTIONS IN ETHIOPIA: THE HAILE SELLASSIE AND MENGISTU YEARS

Present-day Uganda under Museveni has a non-party political system whereby individuals stand as political candidates for a district and are judged by the voters on their programme and performance. The system has innovative aspects and does fulfil certain criteria for 'direct democracy', despite the fact that the position of the President and his party remains predominant. Few people know that a somewhat similar system was in force in the later years of Emperor Haile Sellassie's reign, with the exception that the Ethiopian system was more elitist and that the emperor's position was unassailable. The 1957 elections for the Chamber of Deputies (the lower house) were the first elections which created the beginning of some kind of independent power bloc next to the emperor (Clapham 1969: 142). The members of the Chamber were elected under universal adult suffrage. Two candidates for each constituency were chosen. The number of deputies grew with the population and with the number of constituencies delineated. According to Clapham (1969: 143), each candidate stood 'on the strength of his personal connections in the district'. This meant in practice that candidates with social standing, wealth and a good network were most likely to stand and to win. It was not yet democracy. But there was genuine competition at least on the constituency level, and thus some measure of choice for the voters.

In the *Derg* period, there were also some sort of elections, but only between alternate candidates on the list of the Workers' Party of Ethiopia, the single party. There was no real choice and no way to influence political decisions, and elections had the character of a mass mobilization to give the incumbent regime some stamp of approval (Dawit 1990: 68–9). The organizational work necessary for this was called in Amharic *dirigitawi sera*, 'organizational operation', a euphemism for election engineering by political cadres on all levels to get the desired result. While in 1987 (year of the new Constitution and of the proclamation of the People's Democratic Republic) an effort was made to have representatives of all ethnic groups in the *Shengo* (the parliament), the real exercise of choice was never in the cards.

The *Derg* electoral system was thus a step backwards in the slow evolution of democratic elections that was begun under Emperor Haile Sellassie,[25] and it was of course utterly subverted by the systematic abuse of both the idea and practice of the rule of law in that period. Finally, neither under Haile Sellassie nor under the *Derg* were any international election observers ever present.

However, in assessing these previous episodes of elections in Ethiopia, one has to keep in mind an enduring characteristic of Ethiopian 'political culture': the lack of the idea of political neutrality and of equal competition of political groups. The 'taking of sides' was – and is – seen as inevitable in a political tradition where power emanates from above, either of a divine (up to Emperor Haile Sellassie) or of a secular-ideological (*Derg* and present regime) nature. Political power is also held to be indivisible and is grounded in ideas of a zero-sum game. This *a fortiori* also holds for the 'observation' of the political process, for example elections, either by domestic or foreign observers.

ELECTIONS UNDER EPRDF RULE: THE ORGANIZATION OF VICTORY (1992–6)

Background

Elections are only one of the aspects of the process of political reform in post-*Derg* Ethiopia, and perhaps not the most important one. They have, however, opened up a promise of democratic choice which might eventually lead to substantial representative democracy in the future, especially when combined with a reorientation of the political process away from confrontation politics, and a respecting of the free press and of the rule of law. In present conditions the EPRDF has a hegemonic position in determining the conditions and climate of politics and is creating interests which tie persons and elite groups to its power structure. It is out of the question that they would lose power, or would permit this to happen. EPRDF members, some in the parliament, to which I put the question of what would happen after possible electoral loss in the 1995 elections, did not understand what I was talking about: it was unthinkable that they would lose. The claim of course was that they had come to power with immense sacrifice for the whole of Ethiopia and had 'the mandate of the rural masses', but the subtext was that they just would not allow electoral loss. Indeed, the institutional and other resources of the EPRDF, as the governing party controlling the state apparatus and with its army as the ultimate pillar of support, were obvious (see Lyons 1996: 126–7).

Nevertheless, a good organization of the electoral victory was deemed necessary. The old term 'organizational operation' (see above) to describe the process is still applicable here, and the role of well-placed political activists or cadres was indispensable. This aspect indicates some of the continuity in Ethiopian political culture.

In assessing the elections, it is therefore essential to recognize the wider context and background of the power relations, the nature of regime politics and the political culture which shape the electoral process itself. In almost any African country, state power is deeply contested, and scarcity of resources and access to them evoke patron–client politics and elite rule. Combined with the gap between traditions of local democracy and law on the one hand and state politics on the other, this leads to persistent problems of legitimacy and accountability, which elections and multi-party activity cannot mitigate. This also means that *between* elections, a government resorts to other means to further its aims and assert its hegemony.

For instance, in Ethiopia the reform of public administration in the context of the 'democratization process' has brought some other, non-electoral, ways to replace administrators and political dignitaries. The most important one is the *gimgema*. This is a critical group evaluation session, in the presence of a candidate who has to defend his/her record and/or admit mistakes. If one fails to justify one's performance one is dismissed forthwith. This was a method already used by the EPRDF in a milder form in the guerrilla struggle, and its origins are not difficult to see. In the context of these 'evaluation sessions' there is room for manipulation, and also, the procedure is recognized neither in the Constitution nor in law. The *gimgema* is now the most widespread method to remove people from their job, and explains the extraordinarily rapid turnover of administrators and officials in the country in the last few years. Whether it can be considered as an asset to democracy and furthers good governance stands to be seen.[26]

Elections: the First Round

The first elections under the EPRDF were those of 21 June 1992, for local governments (zones, districts (*woredas*), and local councils or *k'ebeles*). For the EPRDF they were a first experience with nation-wide election,[27] but purposely not for national institutions. In the large majority of constituencies EPRDF candidates were chosen, often by default, because in many areas no political groups, parties or individuals had been forthcoming (all WPE personnel were removed and forbidden to stand). In most rural areas, local candidates had associated themselves quickly with the EPRDF and were thus elected or nominated. The EPRDF won with 96.6 per cent of the vote (1,108 of the 1,147 regional seats).

The preparations for these elections had been less than perfect in terms of voter education and campaigning. The aim of the EPRDF was to quickly gain a kind of mandate to consolidate its rule in the name of peace and stability (the local councils were called 'peace and stability' – committees) and go on with its transitional policy.

Due to alleged pressure and intimidation, groups like the OLF (which had a request for delay of the elections turned down) boycotted the elections and left the Transitional Government. A subsequent military conflict between forces of the OLF and the government was won by the latter. Mediation efforts between the EPRDF government and the opposition groups, with or without the support of Western intermediaries, failed, largely due to EPRDF refusal to budge (Lyons 1996: 129). Renewed secret negotiations between the two in 1997 have not yet led to a *rapprochement*.

The Second Round

In the course of 1993–4, a new Constitution was drafted, and elections for a *Constituent Assembly* (CA) were prepared by the Transitional Government, whose basis had been further narrowed by a forced exodus of 11 groups (including OLF in 1992 and the Southern Coalition in 1993) that disagreed with EPRDF policy.

The elections took place on 5 June 1994 and were the first on the national level after 1991. The political structure of new regions and ethnic districts had in the meantime been extended, and a complex procedure of voting on the basis of these districts was prepared. It implied that in regions predominantly inhabited by a certain ethnic group, a representative of other, 'non-ethnic' parties could not stand. This meant in effect that, for instance in the Oromiya region, no 'Tigrawi' or 'Amhara' party could put up candidates. In the Tigray region, no party except the TPLF was allowed to run: on the 'obvious assumptions' that another ethnic party would have no support, and that a non-ethnic party could not represent the interests of the Tigrawi population. (The few trans-ethnic national parties which existed had few chances to make themselves known, and were often actively barred from campaigning in the regions. The first of these, the National Democratic Union, was denied free operation already in 1992 (though not officially banned), when it became successful in mobilizing mass support in Addis Ababa.)[28]

In the nine regions and in Addis Ababa 548 candidates had to be chosen for the CA. Both the delineation of electoral districts, the selection and screening of candidates, and the technical aspects of the electoral procedure were well-planned, although again there was no serious multi-party campaigning or information dissemination for opposition candidates. The dominant position of the EPRDF, as the party organizing the process and as the authorities, needs no comment. The Norwegian team was the only serious observer group at these elections, and while they agreed that the procedures on election day itself were 'without violence and major flaws', they noted all kinds of small problems suggesting the underlying problem of EPRDF dominance prohibiting the free expression of choice (Pausewang 1994: 27–8). A domestic observer noted that the EPRDF had resorted 'to political gimmick and patronage' (Kassahun 1995: 133).

The opposition parties had been dissatisfied with the non-negotiated extension of the two-and-a-half-year transitional period by the EPRDF after the deadline of January 1994 (five months before the finalizing of the draft Constitution) . They did not agree to the unilateral course of action taken by the EPRDF in imposing its new political order, its regionalization and its Constitution without national dialogue. Neither did they acquiesce in the creating of the ethnicized, compartmentalized framework for the elections. Hence they proclaimed a boycott, saying it was better not to participate at all than to win a few seats here and there in an unfair competition. In the actual election campaign, there were also repeated cases of intimidation and pressure by EPRDF soldiers and sympathizers.

Of the total of 1,471 candidates for the 548 seats, 534 were party candidates, while 936 were 'independents'. In fact there were only elections for 526 seats, because 22 candidates from officially recognized 'nationalities' with less than a 100,000 people (that is, the size of a constituency) automatically received a seat in the Assembly. This was seen as democratic, because they would otherwise be represented by members of the 'ethnic majority' in their district or region. It is democratic in the minimal sense of having direct group representation, but remarkably here again is the assumption that people can or should only be represented by their 'own' ethnic candidates. It goes without saying that these 22 delegates are loyal supporters of the EPRDF, on which they are totally dependent.

According to official statistics, only some 57 per cent of all eligible voters in Ethiopia participated in the 1994 elections. This is not as bad as in the US national elections, but still, with the massive mobilization effort of the EPRDF in the countryside, it was a disappointing result;[29] also in view of the manifest psychological and other pressure on especially the poorer and rural electorate to come and vote correctly.

Results of the 1994 elections did not come as a surprise: a huge majority for the EPRDF candidates. The EPRDF and its affiliates won 484 of the total of 548 seats. In Addis Ababa, the EPRDF won 13 of the 23 seats, which was its lowest score country-wide. The independent candidates won 8 seats. Less than half of the eligible voters turned up in the capital.

Some details of the election were puzzling: many of the independent candidates (who had to submit 500 signatures beforehand to endorse their candidature) often did not get even 500 votes. The question arose who put them up, and had it been to artificially enhance the idea of 'choice'?[30] Puzzling also was that almost all seats in the two big regions of Amhara and Oromiya (where one would expect at least some real opposition to the EPRDF) were won by the EPRDF: 289 of the total of 294.

Before the elections, the opposition parties had manoeuvred themselves into a difficult position: to participate would mean to accord legitimacy to the, for them, dubious political structure and the orchestrated electoral process. To opt out would mean self-marginalization and the loss of any chance to make their voice heard in a national forum. The EPRDF counted on such a position, and knew that Western donor-countries would disapprove of the attitude of the opposition. Consequently, the party could reap the benefits both ways: getting the large majority of seats – which they would have had in any case, also if the opposition would have gone along – and the approval of the donor community which reproached the opposition for not taking a chance.

The Third Round

After the approval of the new Constitution – with only token amendments – by the CA on 8 December 1994 after some nine weeks of discussion, preparations were made for the May 1995 parliamentary elections, which would finally 'install a government with a real popular mandate'. The vote would be for the 548-seat House of People's Representatives (HPR) and the Regional governments (1,368 posts). The organization and preparation of these elections built upon the experience of the CA elections. Candidates of the opposition parties were again not present due to the continued boycott; the more than 60 political parties were almost exclusively ethnic parties affiliated to EPRDF. There were also hundreds of independent candidates, who came both from some opposition groups and from the EPRDF. Voter registration was officially reported to be about 25 per cent higher.[31]

The elections on 5 May 1995 thus led to an even higher score of success for the EPRDF, reminiscent of communist voting percentages. The EPRDF won 502 of the 535 eligible seats in the HPR (the remaining 13 for the Afar and Somali regions remained empty for some time because of a delay of the elections there.)[32] Again, 22 seats of the total of 548 were assigned to ethnic minorities. Only 7 independents won a seat.

In the preparations for these elections no risks were taken by the EPRDF, and it tried to mobilize more voters especially during the registration phase. As if the organizational and political context of the process itself would not have been enough, there were various subtle tricks – left largely to the liberty of the EPRDF-led local electoral committees – to enhance the vote for the party. For example, not only was the electoral emblem of the EPRDF the most known one, it was usually placed no.1 on the ballot paper. The fate of ballot boxes after closure of the polling station was not known, especially in the rural districts.

Some polling booths had a – for international observers, invisible – ballot paper in the booth itself, attached as an 'example' for the less literate voters, with the emblem of EPRDF already filled in.

This time in Addis Ababa all seats were won by the EPRDF, an in many ways surprising result. Even some loyal allies of the EPRDF like the Ethiopian National Democratic Party (ENDP, the small party of Kifle Wodajo, ex-chairman of the Constitutional Commission, and of former TGE Vice-president Fecadu Gadamu), who surely counted on winning some seats, initially did not get even one.[33]

Subsequent Rounds

A later round of elections, which passed virtually unnoticed by international observers, was the one in 1996 for the *k'ebeles*, the local authorities. They were swept by the EPRDF in a manner fairly reminiscent of the *Derg* system of elections, as very few alternative or opposition candidates were fielded or had a chance. Organization of the elections, voting itself (location, procedure) and vote-counting was controlled by the local administration, which was largely in the hands of the EPRDF. No foreign election-observer reports exist on these elections. It should be recalled that in the sphere of local administration the *gimgema* system of evaluation (see above) is much more important than that of elections.

In addition, various regional states held district council elections in the course of 1997; for instance in December in the Southern Regional State, partly because of a relatively high 'rate of attrition' of council members voted in two years before. Again no local or foreign observers were present here. Reports from local voters and from one of the main opposition parties that tried to participate, the Southern Ethiopian Peoples' Democratic Coalition (SEPDC) (in a press statement of 13 January 1998, issued from Addis Ababa) about these elections suggest that these elections could not be considered free and fair. There were reliable reports of intimidation of the opposition groupings and of acts of preventing them from campaigning and even registering their candidates. House-to-house visits were even made by EPRDF party cadres to the people who had submitted their name as a supporter of an opposition candidate in order to pressurize them to retract their support (the electoral law requires a minimum number of such supporters when candidates register).

ELECTION OBSERVATION

The first three rounds of the elections in post-*Derg* Ethiopia saw the presence of international observers. But interest declined with every round. For the CA and parliamentary elections of 1995, the Ethiopian government also refused to give accreditation to several proposed observers (as, for example, in the case of the Netherlands).

Important, however, was the fact that more *local* observers and monitors became active. Their gradual emergence has been one positive aspect of the presence of international election observers: under their aegis the idea of local observers gained some acceptance. Nevertheless they were limited in number and in experience. The local observers (often members of recently founded NGOs supported by Western donor money, both those regime-friendly and some of the more critical) may in principle (but not always) be more reliable and critical than the foreign observers. Nevertheless, a problem with the domestic observer groups is that they tend to be more partisan, or are identified as partisan, by the government. They are often not recognized as observers. It might be best if they worked in close conjunction with external observers.

In the 1995 elections, foreign observers had to submit to stricter operational guidelines and conditions set by the Ethiopian government. But their judgement on the 1994 and 1995 elections in general was moderately optimistic.

The international observers in Ethiopia were all short-term observers. Embassies of the Western countries were supposed to be monitoring, also in order to develop a more long-term perspective on the political process. However, staff of the various embassies also tended to concentrate on short-term observation – spot checks – in the capital and in some major towns. They did not delve deeply in the preparation and organization of the elections in the months preceding polling day. Some embassy personnel neither knew the correct number of parties, what their names stood for, nor their presumed constituency or affiliation. Their briefing of short-term observers was also superficial and casual. The effect was that both resident personnel and observer missions chiefly looked at the technical aspects of the voting process on polling day itself.

In general it can be said that international observers had little understanding of local political culture, and little contact with the average Ethiopian citizen in normal social interaction (partly due to the language problem). On polling day itself and afterwards, the presence of foreign observers could have had a mitigating effect on all-too-obvious vote-rigging, and in that sense was positive. But their numbers were insignificant in view of the thousands of polling stations, and the ultimate normative impact of observers was very limited. They cannot prevent election engineering. It is remarkable how many incidents or 'mistakes' were noticed by the international and domestic observers, which gives one cause to think about the polling stations where no observer ever set foot. This is not to say that in the Ethiopian elections of 1994 and 1995 vote-rigging of the obvious kind was predominant: the procedures spelled out were generally observed (cf. Pausewang 1994: 28), and the National Electoral Board of Ethiopia has to be commended for having done a remarkable job in the logistical and technical aspects of the enterprise. Critical issues, however, were the general atmosphere of the electoral process, marked by heavy psychological and material domination if not intimidation of the government and party in power. Indeed, one wonders how it could have been otherwise in a country emerging from civil war where the new elites 'cannot afford to lose elections'. In close relation to this point, the preparation phase was critical, because here one saw the problems of an ethnic district system, of lack of transparency, screening of candidates, a lack of campaigning and information dissemination, and subtle or sometimes outright intimidation, especially in the rural areas. A general feature of Ethiopian political culture – which has great difficulty in accepting the idea of the legitimacy of political opposition – is that people when called to vote are expected to vote for the incumbent party or government. There is hidden fear and insecurity among the electorate (half of whom are not literate and have no access to information) that the government can find out whether one has voted for the adversary, and therefore it is deemed safer just to vote for the ruling party.

These factors are difficult for short-term observers to measure, but are relevant nevertheless. The above aspects are quite common in other African countries as well, and remind us not to expect to much from election observation by foreigners, even though their presence may be appreciated by locals.

1992

According to most international observers who were present at the 1992 elections (cooperating in the Joint International Observer Group), there was no way that these could be called 'free and fair', not even in their procedural aspects (see NDI 1992, NIHR 1992, Gamst 1995), and this did not only depend on poor logistics. True, there was a lack of campaigning, a lack of information among voters on the stakes and on candidates, and a shortage of ballot papers. But according to Lyons (1996: 127), before and during election day 'intimidation, violence and fraud' were widespread (for a vivid case study, see Gamst 1995). This was substantiated in many field reports. The observers were also critical of the attitude of the TGE toward their own activities. A positive point was that due to serious criticism of the international observers, the Ethiopian public was informed of the problems with the elections and the TGE was forced to respond to some of the charges made.

However, the rules of the game were not changed nor could they prevent EPRDF dominance on virtually all fronts. On the basis of these faulty elections Lyons concludes: 'Instead of working to sustain the initial broad coalition and implicit pact behind the July 1991 National Conference, the EPRDF backed its ethnic affiliates and created a single-party dominant political system' (1996: 128).

1994

Compared to the 1992 round, there were fewer international observers present at the CA elections: 148 (Kassahun 1995: 133). There were also local Ethiopian observers, those appointed by the government and other from local NGOs like A-Bu-Gi-Da, a civil organization formed by intellectuals and teachers (funded by some Western NGOs committed to civic education). This organization took the challenge of democratization and civic political education seriously, and set up courses on political reform, democracy and civic rights in Addis Ababa and various provincial capitals. Observers from this group – and local observers in general – were more perceptive than the foreign observers (Kassahun 1995: 133–4; A-Bu-Gi-Da 1994: 3–4) of flaws like poor voter education and guidance, disrespect of secret voting, veiled threats to voters, occasional obstruction of local observers, and obscurities in the counting phase.[34]

The foreign observers were mostly recruited from resident Western embassy staff of seven donor-countries, which formed a Donor Election Unit (DEU) in March 1995. They were assisted by four external advisers (experts on elections) and the members of the DEU made many observational field missions. But it is important to recognize that such diplomatic observers are – bound by diplmatic convention itself – usually not willing to compromise in any serious way their relations to the host-country government.They cannot and will not report in a critical or sometimes even in a balanced manner.[35] In the 1994 Ethiopian elections, they gave substantially more positive reports than in 1992. Though they regretted the lack of meaningful choice, ascribed largely to the 'opposition boycott', they mentioned the improved technical aspects and the peaceful proceedings (cf. Lyons 1996: 130; Pausewang 1994: 27). Structural constraints on the political process, the election system, the campaigning, and on obtrusive and unobtrusive methods of intimidation, though in many respects the same as in 1992, were suddenly no longer seriously commented upon. This reflects the lack of independent foreign observer teams present (except for the Norwegians): embassy diplomats are interested in maintaining good relations with the host country.

The major background reason for a lenient attitude is probably that the Ethiopian regime showed itself serious about economic reforms, was open to World Bank and IMF suggestions, and had largely maintained law and order in the country, certainly as compared to the notorious cases on the rest of the African continent, including neighbouring Somalia. These two features – willingness to open up and marketize the economy, and keeping law and order from a relatively strong centre – have proved to be decisive in donor-country perception ever since, and led these donors to continue to give Ethiopia the benefit of the doubt, whatever problems there may be with the furthering of a culture of democracy, the implementation of representative democratic institutions, the observation of human rights, and building of a rule of law.

After the CA had done its job – approving the Draft Constitution – the 'Donors Group' of 18 Western countries felt the need to congratulate the CA for the result, saying that it was an important milestone on the path towards the establishment of democracy in Ethiopia (see Lyons 1996: 131). This superfluous statement glossed easily over the lack of substantial debate and virtually complete EPRDF domination in the CA meetings.

1995

According to June Rock (1996: 98) there were 220 accredited international observers (including embassy staff), and 60 local observers during the parliamentary elections. There were no organized foreign NGO teams, and the observers were mainly from the countries wishing to remain friendly with the regime, like the US and some EU countries.

Observers noted a lack of privacy in polling booths, insistence by election officials that the public vote for certain candidates, and lack of clear differentiation of electoral symbols of contending parties or individuals on the ballot paper (cf. Rock 1996), problems remedied by the officials after they were criticized on these points. What happened in polling stations not observed can only be guessed. Some observers (the Norwegian group) registered a similar atmosphere of forced participation, apathy and intimidation to that which had characterized earlier rounds. While some of these general charges may be debatable, there were certainly cases of pre-election disappearances and even killings of (lesser-known, often local) political opposition figures, arrests of campaigners, and the prohibition of holding party rallies or opening branch offices of opposition parties (see Lyons 1996: 135–6, 139), which may show that these elections simply were not conducted in the proper atmosphere. There were also disturbances in the eastern cities of Dire Dawa and Harar, where grenades were thrown in public places a few days before election day. The tricks mentioned above were usually noted by local not international observers. Their extent is not known.

Neither hindered by the critical sounds from observers nor bothered by the highly skewed and problematic context of the electoral process in Ethiopia, the US Embassy released a press statement praising the elections in terms like 'free and fair; ... important milestone along Ethiopia's road to greater democracy ...' (cited in Lyons 1996: 141). Such facile statements (remarkably similar to those issued in 1994), bypassing long-term and contextual factors in evaluating democratization, undermine the critical function of election observation.

CONCLUSIONS

There is no doubt that from a Western point of view, Ethiopia is going through an interesting experimental phase of national redefinition and reconstruction. In 1991 a regime assumed power that offered a significant opening for a more democratic political order as well as for an economic fresh start, released from the burden of civil war. While Ethiopia effected a historic break with a violent and authoritarian regime in 1991 and still has a possibility to realize important democratic gains, the incumbent government seems much less committed to democratization than in 1991. Reasons may be: a) its institutional difficulties and insecurity as an elite regime based on an ethno-regional minority; b) a deadlock over the road it has to follow after having taken an, in several respects, uncontrollable ethnic regionalization policy as its political strategy; and c) the tendency to subsume erstwhile democratic commitments to its economic policies and its wish to retain power.

In comparing the reports of international and local observers on the election rounds held so far in Ethiopia, one notes an interesting paradox: with every round of elections, the reports of field observers seem to lose their relevance for the political opinion of donor-countries of the democratic credentials of the incumbent regime: a paradox, because it becomes obvious that Western governments' and donors' assessments of the Ethiopian experiment are not made on the basis of intrinsic values related to democracy and to public opinion in the country itself, but on strategic geo-political motives, on pragmatism and on comparisons with the worst cases of social breakdown and violent disorder, as in Liberia, Sierra Leone,

Rwanda or Sudan. Ethiopia is thus always seen as 'better off than in the Mengistu era' (this criterion is easily met) and as far more promising than its neighbours Somalia or Sudan. This is their good right, and of course a predictable, realistic position in international politics. However, what counts in the final instance is not only the attitude of Western donor-countries, but that of the larger population of the country in question. It is difficult to hold massive opinion-survey research on the political attitudes and aspirations of the Ethiopian population. It can certainly be said that they appreciate the end of the civil war, the period of relative peace and the opening up of political and economic life. But what seems clear also (especially among large sections of the rising middle classes) is a serious lack of political confidence in the government, not assuaged by the four rounds of elections. Neither does the ethnic interpretation of democracy (even apart from the huge additional costs of having to finance an extra layer of fully-fledged regional state administrations) have the *a priori* sympathy of Ethiopians. Historically, ethnicity as such has rarely if ever been a legal, let alone constitutional, value among Ethiopian populations.

There also seems to emerge a lack of *trust* not only between large parts of the population and the government but also increasingly between sections of the population itself. The heightened awareness of 'ethnicity' as a result of government regionalization and education policy may be playing a role here. A far-reaching ethnicization may sharpen competition, inequality, negatively affect mobility and social interaction, and evoke violent protests. Ethiopia has always been characterized by a balance between regional (not ethnic) and central affirmations of political authority (Clapham 1995: 39), and the politicization of ethnic identities may lead to divisions where there were none before. It has reshaped voting constituencies in ethnic terms, away from material issues which may be shared on a regional basis.

In retrospect, it is difficult to say what the elections in Ethiopia have accomplished, except to solidify a rather autocratic dominant-party system. For the EPRDF regime, going through the motions of elections has been a means to formally ground its legitimacy. Whether these have indeed been representative – that is, have been measuring the real political preferences and choices of the wider population – is doubtful (Cayla

1997: 123; Lyons 1996: 142). They might have been a beginning of possible democratization, but appeared as a ritual or a game of self-affirmation of a regime comfortably holding the reigns of power acquired by other means.

The Western donor-countries do not see (or have ceased to see) their own universalist assumptions on democracy and the rule of law as applicable to non-Western countries with different cultural and historical traditions (compare Huntington's influential concept of the 'clash of civilizations').[36] This perhaps explains the non-committed, easy-going response of many observer missions on African elections, in Ethiopia and elsewhere, as well as the equally frequent response of Western governments to simply shelve critical reports from the field.

New elections in Ethiopia will be held in the year 2000. In prospect it can easily be said that the preconditions for meaningful democratization and establishing of a sound justice system should at least be: growth and better organization of the legal opposition parties and of the independent civil society organizations; government toleration of these opposition forces – for example, as parties which can campaign, offer plans for the future, engage in debate, make propositions and the like, and the government's acceptance of the idea of opposition as a normal part of an open political system; making the electoral process accessible from the start to all contesting forces; enhancing the quality of the legal system as an independent – and as much as possible depoliticized – domain. The law can give body to the realization of democratic political and social rights. There is probably room for the improvement of the legal training of Ethiopian judges, for more respect toward their independent decisions, and for a formal reorganization of the system so as to give the common people engaged in legal cases transparent decisions within a reasonable period of time. This latter point is not the case at present, but is crucial. Public trust in a government is corroded most seriously by perceptions of systematic injustice and unfairness and lack of timely procedure.[37]

While any judgement on political reform in Ethiopia cannot be given here, one could say that there is little doubt that the ethnicized character of Ethiopian politics will continue to pose new practical and personal problems for many Ethiopians. Political shaping of ethnicity will also remain a sort of theoretical challenge to 'democratic politics'. For instance, how will individual rights to personal identity, to political choice (for example on non-ethnic parties and candidates) and to social and economic mobility reconcile with collective, ethnic identity, especially when the latter tends to be stimulated by state discourse and policy? Can ethnic groups always be expected to be united in their interests and their stands on policy if they are made up of a plurality of regional and clan groups? Must voting go according to the ethnic district system and is proportional representation on the basis of country-wide issue politics not feasible? Democracy entails institutionalized respect for minorities in a system where majorities make decisions, but there are unresolved difficulties in the effort to realize democracy within the bounds of ethnic or ethno-regional groups. These factors still await resolution. They might be tackled within a framework which, more than is the case now, demands compromise politics and a firmer approach to the consolidation of a rule-of-law regime, which should build on the rich legal traditions of Ethiopia.

In the specific case of Ethiopia, the challenges to their group and national identity (or the idea of nationhood) are also relevant. While ethnic diversity has been a fact of life for two millennia, boundaries between 'ethnic groups' were never fixed nor even very clear. Intermingling, intermarriage and cooperation between 'ethnic group' members was a continuous process, and did not diminish in the era of modernization after 1941. A common Ethiopian identity, though situational, has been emerging in the shadow of the national polity, and contrasted Ethiopia with most African countries. Historically, indigenous traditions of customary law of the various ethno-regional groups tended to blend and assimilate in the border regions and yielded common core values. It is in this sphere, of reconciling customary law traditions with modern ideas of rule of law, as initiated by the six law codes promulgated under Emperor Haile Sellassie (in 1957–65), that lies one of the enduring challenges for the grounding of a new political order of Ethiopia. Here much remains to be done, and it seems that the contribution of Western experts and democracy observers has been less than helpful.

A theoretical point is that if elections are held under a regime which is negligent in the observation of the rule of law and in respecting an independent judiciary, they do not signify a democratic breakthrough. The construction of a regime of rule of law, while a Western concept in its theoretical formulation, has its antecedents in African societies and must stand central in the assessment of whether a country is on the road to sustainable democracy. An independent judiciary which can efficiently, within a reasonable time limit and without harassment from the executive, let the law run its course is the most powerful constitutional check on undemocratic rule. In principle, the new Ethiopian constitution has created the framework for it (arts. 14 to 32, except that art. 39.1 is anomalous, see note 8). The judiciary may thus gradually enhance legitimacy and accountability in a political system on purely judicial, not political, grounds. An improved historical and cultural understanding of the local society in this light will help to redefine the mission of observers and monitors and to stimulate critical dialogue with governments and public opinion in the country observed.[38]

NOTES

1. I am grateful to Professor Christopher Clapham (Lancaster University) for critical comments on an earlier version of this chapter.
2. Per capita cash income is *c*. US$120 per year.
3. *c*. 58 million people, excluding the 2.8 million in Eritrea.
4. The Oromo Peoples' Democratic Organization (OPDO), set up in 1990, the Southern Ethiopian Peoples' Democratic Union (SEPDU), and the Amhara National Democratic Movement (ANDM), before 1994 called the Ethiopian Peoples' Democratic Movement, which emerged from a splinter group of the Ethiopian Peoples' Revolutionary Party which was defeated in a rural battle by the TPLF in Tigray region in 1981.

    A study of the Ethiopian political scene demands an interest in and mastery of abbreviations: there are dozens of parties, mostly on an ethnic basis (foreigners are not good in remembering or recognizing them). Most of them were created or stimulated by the TPLF/EPRDF, the party which has set the political agenda of post-Mengistu Ethiopia (see below).
5. An excellent overview of rural rebellion in post-1941 Ethiopia is given in Gebru 1991, a study of the ideas of the student movement is Balsvik 1985, and an analysis of the 1974 revolution and its aftermath is found in Andargatchew 1993.
6. Harar Regional State is in effect also a city state, comprising only the city of Harar, with some 134,000 inhabitants.
7. Oromiya, Amhara, Tigray, Afar, Harar, Beni Shangul-Gumuz, and Somali. In actual fact all these states are multi-ethnic, as the recent National Census reports have shown.

8. An in constitutional law very exceptional article, which no constitution has ever included in this form. The Soviet Constitution of 1936 (art. 17) had the 'right of secession' for the various republics (although not according clear potential sovereignty to ethnic units), but this was ambiguous because it was said to be 'limited' in art. 15. In addition, other Soviet laws prohibited 'agitation for secession'. In Western theory, of course, the notion of secession is incompatible with federalism.

9. I will continue to speak of ethnic groups – the more neutral term used by social scientists – instead of nationalities – a basically Stalinist term which *a priori* accords a potentially political character to all such groups.

10. In most other African countries ethnicity is the *unofficial* discourse of political relations, as for instance in Kenya: rhetorical denial of the political relevance of ethnic organization and ethnic (or what is called there 'tribal') power blocks but a neo-patrimonial political practice of divide-and-rule. See Dietz and Foeken in this volume.

11. Radio and television remain a government monopoly, although the ruling party has its own radio station, Radio FANA.

12. The leftist-Marxist Ethiopian Peoples' Revolutionary Party.

13. Shewa: the region around Addis Ababa, and the area of origin of many members of the dominant elite in the Haile Sellassie era.

14. It should be remembered that the Tigrigna-speaking population (or Tigrawi) only form *c*. 8 per cent of the total population, not counting those in Eritrea.

15. See my 'Ethnicity and Constitutionalism in Contemporary Ethiopia', in *Journal of African Law* 1997.

16. See Prime Minister Meles Zenawi's statements in an interview with the Amharic news magazine *Reporter* (25 *Ginbot* 1989 E.C., which is 2 June 1997): 'There are two types of placements, namely political and civil service placements. Political placements apply to appointments, while recruitment based on civil service criteria is aimed purely at ensuring proficiency and professionalism. In the case of political appointments, we take ethnic representation as a major criterion. Competent advisers are assigned to political appointees who may not be professionally competent' (which might, he suggested, go so far as not being literate). It should be added that the civil service placements are graduates from the newly founded Civil Service College, where candidates from one ethnic group are trained in different programme-tracks, to be sent back to their ethnic region of origin. Hence, also here the ethnic criterion is becoming stronger.

17. Dawit Yohannis, the current Speaker of the House of Peoples' Representatives and a close adviser to the prime minister, is reported to have said in 1995: 'We say there is no country called Ethiopia, no state that defends the interests of this multi-ethnic community grouped under the name Ethiopia.' Cited in Lyons 1996: 124.

18. *Derg* is the Amharic term for the Armed Forces Committee that ruled Ethiopia after 1974, led by Lt.-Col. Mengistu Haile Mariam as dictator. The entire 1974–91 period has thus come to be known as the *Derg* period, although since 1987 Ethiopia was nominally governed by the Workers' Party of Ethiopia and was a People's Democratic Republic.

19. See also Abbink 1995.
20. For example, in the interview mentioned in note 16, where he stated that 'there is no opposition political party in Ethiopia in the true sense of the word'. Also in a press statement after a bomb attack by Somali Islamist groups in Ethiopia in May 1997, the prime minister tried to associate the terrorists with legal opposition groups, which 'would be smashed if they give safe haven to terrorist individuals or organisations' (Reuters news message, 27 May 1997).
21. In addition, political figures and members of the former regime's political party as well as members of the former army are barred from participating in political life. Until the 1995 elections, they could not vote either.
22. For instance, in August 1997 four ethnic organizations (the Ethiopian Berta Democratic Organization, the Gumuz People Democratic Organization, the Mao-Komo Democratic Organization and the Boro-Shinasha Democratic Movement) in the small Beni Shangul-Gumuz state were united in one party (Ethiopian News Agency, 1 Sept. 1997).
23. Since 1996 split in at least two factions, one of them now cooperating with the EPRDF.
24. Coalition of Alternative Forces for Peace and Democracy in Ethiopia.
25. The aborted 1974 constitution commissioned by Haile Sellassie and offered to the *Derg* in August that year, would have made Ethiopia more like a constitutional monarchy, with parties, proportional representation and a sharply reduced political role for the monarch. It was swept aside by the *Derg*, which soon thereafter assumed dictatorial power.
26. Dr John Young, a Canadian political scientist until recently at Addis Ababa University and with profound knowledge of the TPLF and its history, has been doing research on the *gimgema* system.
27. Although they were preceded by 'snap elections' in the form of public meetings, not secret voting, in January–April, to clear the ground and to install local '*k'ebele* election commissions' to prepare the June event. The members elected were almost all EPRDF candidates.
28. According to Vestal 1996.
29. At least 10 per cent of the potential electorate (some 2 million ex-members of the Armed Forces, security services and of the Workers' Party of Ethiopia) could not vote.
30. Lyons (1996: 133) mentions the case of a TPLF (EPRDF) member in Tigray who had been put up as an 'independent' candidate. See also Kassahun 1995: 132.
31. The measure of excluding armed forces members and WPE members (see note 21 above) was allegedly lifted for the parliamentary elections of 1995; see Rock 1996: 97.
32. Due to logistic and security problems.
33. There was genuine shock in the head office of the party after the results were made public, and some top men said the EPRDF had shown 'its real autocratic face': 'We were just used. They want to have it all. They did not even grant us *one* seat, after all our close co-operation!' Interview, 14 May 1995. In the end, the ENDP won one candidate in Dessie town for the House of People's Representatives .

34.   A-Bu-Gi-Da has since had internal troubles, but still functions as a relatively successful independent civic educational organization, with
branch offices in various larger towns (e.g., Dessie, Jimma and Awasa).
Its funds and reach are limited but their activities are popular.

35.   External foreign observers are often more critical but they are as a rule
handicapped by their brief stay and lack of familiarity with local conditions and non-elite perceptions in the country observed.

36.   See Huntington 1997.

37.   It is doubtful whether the 1996 government programme of upgrading
the judicial system has been a success from the legal-judicial point of
view. The majority of practising judges was then dismissed on unclear
and sometimes faulty grounds to make way for a new batch of judges
who had been trained in a crash course of only six months. These new
candidates were young and inexperienced persons, often with only secondary school education. It is unclear why they were nominated as
judges without making the usual gradual climb through the court
system to gain knowledge and experience in a legal and human sense.
Apart from having led to a long closure of the courts in 1996 and 1997,
the programme also affected the quality and independence of the
judicial system.

38.   Western observers and political scientists are perhaps ill-equipped to
research the nature of the 'political process' in African settings (unless
they have long experience, good social and historical knowledge, and
know something of the relevant language). It is not difficult to recognize the external trappings of a democratic process in such settings, but
whether this means that a country is 'democratizing' is unclear. There
is a need to better understand what 'democracy' and related political
values of dialogue, openness, and respect for lawful procedure mean in
their historical and cultural setting, and how they relate to economic
and cultural values.

REFERENCES

Abbink, J. 1995. 'Transformations of Violence in Twentieth-century Ethiopia:
Cultural Roots, Political Conjunctures', *Focaal. Tijdschrift voor Antropologie*
25: 57–77.

A-Bu-Gi-Da, 1994. *June 5, 1994 Constitutional Elections Monitoring Mission
Summary Report* (Addis Ababa: A-Bu-Gi-Da).

Andargatchew Tiruneh, 1993. *The Ethiopian Revolution, 1974–1987: a
Transformation from an Aristocratic to a Totalitarian Autocracy* (New York:
Cambridge University Press).

Balsvik, R.R. 1985. *Haile Selassie's Students: the Intellectual and Social Background
to a Revolution, 1952–1977* (East Lansing: African Studies Center, Michigan
State University).

Cayla, F. 1997. 'Ethiopie: le Nouveau Modèle, un Réalisme Ethnique?', in
L'Afrique Politique (Paris: Karthala), pp. 111–28.

Clapham, C., 1969. *Haile Selassie's Government* (London: Longman/New York:
Praeger).

——. 1995. 'Ethnicity and the National Question in Ethiopia', in P. Woodward and M. Forsyth (eds), *Conflict and Peace in the Horn of Africa: Federalism and its Alternatives* (Aldershot: Dartmouth), pp. 27–40.

Dawit Wolde-Giorgis, 1990. 'The Power of Decision-Making in Post-Revolutionary Ethiopia', in M. Ottaway (ed.), *The Political Economy of Ethiopia* (New York–Westport–London: Praeger), pp. 53–72.

Gamst, F.C. 1995. 'Experiential Reflections on the 1992 Elections in Southwest Ethiopia', *Human Peace* 10(3): 3–8.

Gebru Tareke, 1991. *Ethiopia: Power and Protest. Peasant Revolts in the Twentieth Century* (Cambridge: Cambridge University Press).

Huntington, S.P. 1997. *The Clash of Civilizations and the Remaking of World Order* (London: Simon and Schuster).

Ihonvbere, J. 1996. 'Where is the Third Wave? a Critical Evaluation of Africa's Non-transition to Democracy', *Africa Today* 43(3): 343–68.

Kassahun Berhanu, 1995. 'Ethiopia Elects a Constituent Assembly', *Review of African Political Economy* 63: 129–35.

Lemarchand, R. 1993. 'African Transitions to Democracy: an Interim (and mostly Pessimistic) Assessment', *Africa Insight* 22(3): 178–85.

Lyons, T. 1996. 'Closing the Transition: the May 1995 Elections in Ethiopia', *Journal of African Studies* 34(1): 121–42.

National Democratic Institute, 1992. *An Evaluation of the June 21, 1992 Elections in Ethiopia* (Washington, DC–New York: National Democratic Institute for International Affairs and African-American Institute).

Norwegian Institute of Human Rights, 1992. *Local Elections in Ethiopia 21 June 1992: Report of the Norwegian Observer Group* (Oslo: Norwegian Institute of Human Rights).

Pausewang, S. 1994. *The 1994 Election and Democracy in Ethiopia*. Human Rights Report no. 4 (Oslo: Norwegian Institute of Human Rights).

Rock, J. 1996. 'Ethiopia Elects a New Parliament', *Review of African Political Economy* 65: 92–102.

Vestal, Th. 1994. 'Deficits of Democracy in the Transitional Government of Ethiopia since 1991', in H.G. Marcus (ed.), *New Trends in Ethiopian Studies* (Lawrenceville, NJ: Red Sea Press), vol. 2: 188–204.

——. 1996. 'Promises to Keep: Human Rights in Post *Derg* Ethiopia.' Paper read at the Annual Meeting of the Oklahoma Political Science Association, 15 Nov. 1996 (Rogers University – University Center at Tulsa, Tulsa, Oklahoma).

8 Secret Worlds, Democratization and Election Observation in Malawi

R. van Dijk

INTRODUCTION

One day in April 1994 a remarkable event occurred in a small village in the Mchinji district in Malawi, where the United Democratic Front was holding a political rally in preparation for the May 1994 general and presidential elections. The elections were going to be the first 'free and fair' elections in Malawi after 30 years of single-party rule. People were gathering in great numbers to hear what this newly formed opposition party would say. As a member of the Lilongwe-based core group of United Nations international observers,[1] I was present that day observing this rally where a large number of UDF officials, all in yellow blouses, happened to be present. Suddenly, I became aware that the atmosphere became tense among the officials and the general public when a group of masked *Nyau* dancers appeared on the scene and stopped about a hundred metres away from the place of the rally. There they hid themselves behind some trees and shrubs and started to sing and ring their bells. They made it clear they intended to dance where the rally was being held and began to work themselves into an emotional state, as is usually the case on such occasions. People whispered to each another: '*Zilombo! zilombo!*' (literally meaning: 'wild animals!'), and some officials began to move around nervously, confused about what should be done next. Clearly there was some fear that violence would break out – which is common to *Nyau* dance occasions – particularly against the local population, who knew the way these things can develop. The UDF leaders, aware that they were holding a rally in an area where the *Nyau* were strong, decided to bribe them to allow the political meeting to proceed. At intervals, piles of *Kwacha* bank notes would openly be carried from the UDF platform to the waiting *Nyau*, in the hope that it would be enough to prevent the rally from being broken up by the dancing. But by 4 p.m., all the banknotes had gone and time had come to end the rally and make a fast exit.

This event may indicate that, apart from political there are also specific *cultural* dimensions to the process of 'democratization' and to projects of international intervention in Africa such as election observing. Although political science studies of democratization in sub-Saharan Africa have become numerous (see Buijtenhuijs and Rijnierse 1993, Buijtenhuijs and Thiriot 1995), studies of political culture have only received little attention (notable exceptions are Schatzberg 1993, Martin 1993 and Robinson 1994). Most of the literature on the subject of monitoring the democratic process deals with the inherent problems of election observing in Africa's recent democratic transition processes (see Buijtenhuijs and Thiriot 1995: 51–2, Geisler 1993, Meyns 1995, Hyden 1996, Bjornlund, Bratton and Gibson 1992). Regarding countries like Zambia, Uganda, Kenya, Ghana and Malawi, the donor community increasingly imposed political conditions for the continuation of aid and financial assistance. In most cases, democratic changes were demanded, to be monitored by independent international organizations. Election observation thus became a hallmark of political conditionality (Geisler 1993: 630–1).

However, in their practical execution election observation missions often turned out to be nightmares, as the procedures they were supposed to witness were seldom in conformity with Western ideal standards. Most authors therefore highlight the intrinsic problems of election observing, such as the many ways in which elections can be rigged, absence of fraud-resistant voter identification and registration procedures, contradicting views of different observer groups during elections, and difficulties in arriving at sound and univocal verdicts over the free-and-fairness of an election.

Indeed, the *cultural* implications of the imposition of democratic procedures and their monitoring are rarely being considered (Robinson 1994). Not without cynicism one could say that whereas the nation-state has been called the 'black man's

burden' (cf. Davidson 1992), its extension in terms of a democratic system with all that is presupposed by it has become a
'white man's burden' in Africa. Indeed, many of the 'problems'
election observers encounter in the execution of a democratic
procedure boil down to a clash of cultures, and cannot be translated into 'mere' practical technicalities only. One such area is
the recording of personal identities. Referring to Michel
Foucault's term, in his analysis of the development of the
Western nation state, the 'micro-physics of power' that the
state came to command when dealing with the identity of each
of its subjects developed into one of its corner-stones in the
West. Individuals with their name and identity became registered in records that represented a fixed and independent
memory. The state became centralized, lending a central core
or framework to this identity. Political authority became dependent on enlisting a majority of these subject identities as voters
in discrete election procedures.

In comparison, however, much of this 'micro-power' of gov-
ernmentality is absent in the African context. Political authority does not exist in this form (see Bayart 1992 and Schatzberg
1993 for an elaboration of this point), and a centralized state
with undisputed access to each of its subjects' identities does
not exist either. In Ghana and Malawi, for instance, the two
countries in Africa with which I am most familiar, names and
identities of individuals are not fixed and are not recorded in a
state-controlled independent memory. Names and identities
rather exist on the basis of the person's social relationships and
the phase in life s/he is in. In such cases the often recorded
problems election observers meet in establishing voters' identities should be partly explained in terms of cultural differences
in what the meaning and political significance of a centralized
state actually is and implies.

The literature on election observing therefore faces a
problem in that it accepts the formation of nation-states as a
reality taken for granted, as a natural order of things, and along
with it a process of 'self-evident' democratic participation in
state power. The international donor community promotes the
establishment of centralized states in Africa as this belongs to
what it perceives as a global order of things. Hence it seeks the
imposition of democratic systems which in the West have come
to be regarded as the only legitimizing procedure for the estab-

lishment of a centralized state. Election observing primarily appears to serve this purpose, irrespective of the cultural differences that exist in the appreciation of political power and political legitimation.

A fundamental question social scientists therefore face is whether their efforts in suggesting ways of improving election observing are not in fact part of a rhetoric of power that persistently defines cultural differences between African political systems and the West as 'problems' and 'irregularities'. What is required is a more culturally oriented approach which empirically seeks to understand when and how people perceive a system as legitimate or illegitimate, or a specific procedure as fraudulent or trustworthy. In other words, what is required is a cultural exploration of normative schemes and imagination before any sensible improvement in the 'political tourism' (cf. Geisler 1993) of election observing can be suggested.

As a large number of studies of processes of democratization in Africa have now been able to show, democratization is both imposed and imagined. In most cases, international pressure to democratize was met by a desire from local groups in society to change the system, a desire most of the time expressed in a myriad of cultural ways. In further defence of cultural relativism here, it is not at all clear from the literature what in most cases the local desire and imagination entailed with regard to the procedures that would lead to a democratic structure; largely because they have not been studied yet. It is this field of popular imagination with regard to election procedures – where cultural factors come into play which usually remain unnoticed by the outside political observer – which I contend as crucial to the 'success' or 'failure' of any attempt at democratization of a society. In this sense, what is striking in the scholarly debate about the democratization process in Africa is the lack of attention to the significance of the 'secretive' and the 'imaginary' in local political culture. As a rare example, Geschiere in his study of the secretive in the context of Cameroonian political changes notes:

> The recent democratization movements are accompanied ... by a veritable blooming in politics of occult forces. At the very least, their political role is brought into the open.
> (Geschiere 1995: 12, cited in Buijtenhuijs and Thiriot 1995).

He provides various examples of the complex relationship between notions of witchcraft, the occult on the one hand and democratic procedures on the other, which also have been studied by Tall (1995) in Benin and by Meyns (1995) in Mozambique. Here Meyns for instance points at the magical *cum* ritual power of traditional healers with regard to the supposed 'secrecy' of casting a vote in the democratic transition of 1994. He cites the following report of the *Moçambique Peace Process Bulletin*:

> It is widely reported that Renamo has told peasants in its zones that the ballot would not be secret because 'curandeiros' (traditional healers) will know how people vote and that they must vote for Renamo.
>
> (Meyns 1995: 42, citing *MPPB* 1994, vol. 12: 8)

The relevance of this imagination also extends to the Malawian case. The two-staged process of democratic change in this country (in June 1993 the National Referendum, in May 1994 multi-party general and presidential elections) has mainly been studied from the angle of national politics and its different elites – political, religious and ethnic – that became the important players in the field (see Chirwa 1994, Cullen 1994, Kaunda 1995, Kaspin 1995, Newell 1995, Van Donge 1995). Few authors have looked at the local understanding and perception of what the political change might mean to the common people in their own terms (see for instance Englund 1996 for a welcome exception) or by looking at the role non-elite religious groups played in the process (see, for instance, Fiedler 1995 and Van Dijk 1998a, 1998b).

It is, however, clear that in Malawi a local world of secrecy, in which specific secret societies play a dominant part, suddenly came face to face with notions of secrecy which are implied in a democratic procedure. In this chapter I intend to explore some dimensions of what I will phrase as the 'meeting of secret worlds' in the unfolding process of democratic transition. Obviously, an important subsequent question is what the chances of success are for a Western-style democracy if local worlds of secrecy remain untouched by such 'superficial' processes of political transition, leaving the deeper structures of political culture virtually unscathed.

Although much more should be said about the fact that secret worlds and societies may remain intact and in place after a process of democratic transition has taken place, thereby lending support to a thesis of cultural continuity, the focus of this chapter is explicitly on the implications for election observing. It will explore some dimensions of this 'meeting of secret worlds', thus bringing a specific cultural perspective to the understanding of what observing election procedures and political compaigning actually meant in the *local* context.

On the one hand, democracy and the democratic execution of an electoral process, ideologically and practically, imply and presuppose secrecy. Behind the prescribed 'democratic procedures' – with a distinctly Western cultural origin and logic and not immediately translatable into a local African setting – there is, however, a world of the imaginative, of different connotations and meanings. The local understandings of what secrecy in voting is, what it 'guarantees', by whom it is protected and to whom it allows political access, may thus have distinct features as compared to Western political understandings.

On the other hand, in Malawi, as in other Central African countries, communities have their own cultural models, organizations and social groups of secrecy, one of which, the secret society of the *Nyau*, is the most important example. In many localities, secrecy relates to hidden powers – 'powers of the earth' (*zinthu za kunthaka*) – to which one cannot gain unmediated, direct access. Those who gain access to such powers of secrecy are mostly perceived to be in a state of moral ambiguity. In this sense, witches, healers/medicine men, chiefs, and members of the *Nyau* secret society do not differ much as far as common perceptions are concerned. In the process of democratization therefore, domains of secrecy and imagination seem to meet, whereby the role of the election observer, as I hope to show in this contribution, can perform mediating or intermediary functions between the two.

In the first section, a chronology of events is presented leading up to the democratic transition in Malawi in 1994. It will be shown what importance the established mainstream churches had in this process and how they paved the way for international election observing. One of the issues here is that these mission churches from the very onset of their presence in

Malawian society have waged a battle against *Nyau* and its secretive world of ritual practice, initiation and violence. In the
following section more is explained about the linkage between
Nyau and the political machinery. In the final section some conclusions will be drawn concerning the role of international election observing in a situation whereby those involved as
observers are hardly aware of such a meeting of secret worlds
which the advent of democracy in Malawi *de facto* entailed.

CHURCHES VYING FOR DEMOCRACY

Starting in March 1992, a democratic revolution took place in
Malawi which in 1994 led to the removal from power of
'President-for-life' Dr Kamuzu Banda – until then, one of the
longest-surviving dictators in Africa. Banda's regime had for 30
years been marked by a despotism which a badly-informed
foreign press often described as 'benevolent', but which in
reality rested on systematic repression. Although Malawi was
one of the ten poorest nations in the world, its government
managed to operate and maintain very efficiently-organized
police agencies. The only political party allowed in the country,
the Malawi Congress Party (MCP), was in direct control of
paramilitary groups, particularly the widely feared Malawi
Young Pioneers (MYP) and the intelligence services. Moreover,
in the years following independence in 1964, gradually and systematically, all connections with the outside world were brought
under the aegis of the Banda-controlled police apparatus, free
news-gathering by both the domestic and foreign media was
made impossible, the intelligentsia was silenced and international exchange of people and ideas was drastically curtailed
(see Williams 1978, Médard 1991). In view of all this Malawi
came to be known as the 'Albania of Africa'.

The first free elections, held in 1994, led to the victory of one
of the new opposition groups, the United Democratic Front,
and its leader, Bakili Muluzi, forced Dr Banda to step down as
president. Although they condemned the many incidents of
intimidation which preceded the election period, the election
procedure itself was greatly commended by national and international observers, media and intellectuals for its remarkable
freedom and fairness and virtual absence of any form of intimi-

dation. Compared with preceding instances in Zambia and Kenya, the Malawian elections appeared to stand out, and were highly praised as such, for the fair reflection of 'the will of the people' they seemed to offer.

In the period immediately preceding the elections, the established churches of Malawi, particularly the Roman Catholic, Presbyterian and Anglican churches, had begun to play a significant public role in the process of democratic transition.[2] At the same time groups representing the 'traditional' political culture also started to make their voices heard. In what follows, I shall be looking at both these developments, particularly at what they meant for the cultural significance of international election monitoring.

Under the rule of president Banda, churches and other religious organizations had become the only places where people could meet in an atmosphere of relative freedom from close political supervision. Other types of independent social or ideological organizations had gradually been subjected to the MCP's political control, and their freedom to meet was seriously curtailed. This did not mean, of course, that churches were free to criticize the regime openly, as the Jehovah's Witnesses experienced in the late 1960s when they were brutally expelled from Malawi for publicly questioning the legitimacy of Dr Banda's rule. The MCP's paramilitary youth groups, the Malawi Young Pioneers, were sent against the Jehovah's Witnesses and forced many of them to seek safety in neighbouring countries. Unconfirmed reports still speak of hundreds killed in these pogroms.

Although the large established churches in Malawi had, since independence, largely gone along with what the regime expected of them, they nevertheless formed one of the few channels through which reports of the regime's use of terror against the population could reach the outside world. In addition, starting in the late eighties, a growing protest began to be heard within the Roman Catholic church against the worsening economic situation in Malawi and the increasing gap between the poor majority and the small political elite, which had been very successful in filling its own pockets. The first big push in this direction came from the Papal visit in 1989. Not so much because of anything the Pope actually said – his speeches remained rather uncritical of the Malawian government – as from the discussion brought about by the renewed attention for Malawi from the international media as a result of the coverage of the visit.

In March 1992, following secret discussions within the clergy, the Roman Catholic Bishops published a Lenten-letter in which they, for the first time in post-independence history, protested against the repression, poverty and harassment of political opponents that had become the trademark and result of 30 years of Banda's dictatorship (see Cullen 1994, Newell 1995, Nzunda and Ross 1995, Lwanda 1996). As had been the case for other parts of Africa (see Schatzberg 1993, Diamond 1993, Witte 1993), in Malawi the religious elite called for a democratization of the political system. This represented the first truly open criticism of the Banda regime for many years. The blame for the increasing poverty in the country was placed squarely on the shoulders of the failing political system and the policies it enforced. Corruption, censorship and officially-sanctioned political violence were roundly condemned in unambiguous terms.

The appearance of this Lenten-letter rocked the government profoundly and landed the country in a deep political crisis. It was, after all, the first time that an organisation had been able to publish a critical appraisal of the political and economic situation at more than 2,000 places throughout the country without any of the many branches of the secret services getting wind of it. The political elite reacted violently and, as they did at all other instances when dissenting voices could be heard, deployed the MYP to intimidate Catholic clergy and church members and to install a general reign of terror against all who wanted to take the protests further. Locally the *Nyau* society, sometimes in collaboration with the MYP (see Englund 1996: 117) also installed a reign of terror in an attempt to influence and curb the growing popularity of the religious and later the opposition group's protests (Kaspin 1995: 617, Van Dijk 1998b).

Although the bishops and the other parties involved were initially denounced by the regime as criminals, and the police in many parts of the country started to round-up anyone they thought might have a copy of the letter, there was sufficient international pressure to ensure that in the months that followed the government *did* negotiate with the religious leaders. At this point, representatives of the other established churches in

Malawi, with the help of international mediators, were also able to join these negotiations with the government.

The aim of the churches in entering the negotiation was to bring about a democratization of Malawian society in the hope that this would bring a halt to the continuing spread of poverty. A greater participation of the population in political decision-making, freedom of thought, freedom to form political organizations and political parties, free elections and a dismantling of the repressive paramilitary organizations, particularly those of the youth organizations, were placed at the top of the long list of objectives the churches presented to the government.

The churches, with the help of a number of other civil organizations, established the Public Affairs Committee (PAC) which provided an umbrella-function to the opposition groups that slowly began to emerge in various parts of the country (Ross 1995: 31–2). The PAC began to negotiate the terms for an eventual democratic transition with the Presidential Committee on Dialogue (PCD), and by November 1992 at the so-called 'Kwacha-Conference' an understanding was reached. A National Referendum was to be held on the issue of changing from a single to a multi-party system. The country's opposition was allowed to form itself into 'pressure-groups' which were given the liberty to present their views in public and to run campaigns. In reality, however, intimidation by the two political youth-bodies was rife and proved to be extremely effective in closing off entire districts from activities and propaganda material of the opposition (Englund 1996: 116–19, Kaspin 1995: 617).

These two oppositional groups were named the Alliance for Democracy (AFORD), with a stronghold in the Northern Region, and the United Democratic Front (UDF) with a power-base in the South and who, as was mentioned earlier, gained victory in the general elections in the end. At the same time, both the government and the MCP, as the only legal political party, would spare neither effort nor expense to persuade the Malawian population of the advantages of staying with a one-party state.

As the 'pressure-groups' were still rather weak in their organizational structure and resources, the churches, the Roman Catholic and the Presbyterian in particular, ran the better part of the multi-party campaign: they negotiated a 'free and fair process', mobilized massive support particularly from the youth (see for the implications on generational power-relations Van Dijk 1998b, Englund 1996: 120), and distributed civic education material, monitored the registration and voting centres, and reported cases of intimidation and harassment or any other violation of what in the negotiations had been agreed upon (see for different aspects of the churches' involvement on various levels, Cullen 1994, Newell 1995, Nzunda and Ross 1995). It became extremely fashionable to wear and show the insignia of the PAC, which were a mixture of Christian symbolism of the cross, the rosary, and the *nyali*, the lamp, as the sign of the light that multi-partyism would bring against the powers of the dark that came to be associated with single-party rule (the symbol for the MCP was the black rooster, or in local parlance the 'black cock').

As I myself witnessed many times, PAC youth spend hours and hours on civic education, in explaining to the elderly people in the villages that '*mattipatty*' was not just another party but instead an entire different system that would allow greater participation in the political running of the country. AFORD and UDF rallies were usually opened by young PAC representatives who in prayers and religious songs would request the benevolent heavenly powers to lend support to their just cause.

However, in many parts of Malawi a reign of terror from the combined sources of MCP paramilitary groups, the MYP in particular, the local chiefs and party-headmen and local *Nyau* groups continued, which to a large extent went unnoticed by outsider agencies (see Englund about the secretive forms of oppression in local communities, 1996: 116–19). It was in this period (first quarter of 1993) that international pressure began to bring this still fragile democratization process to the conclusion desired by, amongst others, the donor-country community. The United Nations Development Programme (UNDP) stood guarantee for the international and independent monitoring of the National Referendum, while the churches took charge of the local monitoring, working through the new opposition groups. The UNDP supervised the registration of voters and organized the media campaign and programme of civic education that preceded the referendum. It also provided the logistical and financial support for the whole operation. The election monitoring would also monitor the operation of the UNDP and other services associated with it. The UNDP effort was partly supported by the Dutch government and the author became one of the first two international observers sent from the Netherlands to join the UNDP team in Malawi.

The referendum itself was held in May 1993 and two-thirds of the Malawian population voted for a change to a multi-party system. In the months that followed, the pressure groups managed to become recognized as legitimate political parties and new, until then unknown, political parties were permitted to operate. The new political parties worked with the churches to negotiate with the government for the first free general elections, which would include an election for the head of state. Despite the outcome of the referendum, it should be stressed that in the second half of 1993 the machinery of political repression remained menacingly present. There was still no freedom of speech, the new political groups had little access to the media and the logistical and financial resources available to them – in contrast to those available to the government – were insufficient to reach and mobilize supporters in every part of the country.

This, then, was the situation when in December 1993 a dispute between soldiers and members of one of the governing party's paramilitary youth groups, the Malawi Young Pioneers (MYP), got out of control in a northern town. The army, which interestingly had been able to maintain a markedly independent position within the existing political structure, seized its chance and began a hunt for members of the MYP paramilitary organizations that lasted many days (Van Donge 1995: 9, Lwanda 1996: 183–90). Eventually, after a number of fierce, sometimes deadly armed struggles, the power of the paramilitary organizations was broken and some of their members fled abroad. (More than 2,000 of these well-armed paramilitaries presently occupy former territory of the Renamo guerrillas in Mozambique – there had always been strong links between the Malawian paramilitary and RENAMO, dating from when the latter still controlled important parts of the border with Malawi.)

The general and presidential elections were moved back to mid-1994 and the first half of that year was marked by a clear drop in the number of incidents of intimidation and political violence. Freedom of speech was slowly extended by a reluctant government and opposition groups gained more access to the media. 'Civic education' was set up to inform the public about the rather complicated electoral procedure the various parties had eventually agreed to, and about the positions of the various political parties and presidential candidates.

As the election time drew closer, the largest political parties seemed to differ less and less on matters of policy and, instead, increasingly began to reflect the regional and ethnic identities of their supporters (see Forster 1994, Chirwa 1994, Kaspin 1995, Van Donge 1995 for a further analysis of the intertwined ethnic and regional dimensions of the election results). The governing MCP seemed to draw most of its support from the central region of Malawi, the traditional homeland of the Chewa. This is the ethnic group to which Dr Banda and the most important members of his political elite always had claimed to belong (for locally held critical views of the supposed Chewa ethnic background of Banda see Lwanda 1993, Englund 1996). The Tumbuka-speaking northern region seemed to be a bulwark of AFORD, and the party's political leadership – including its leader, the trade unionist Chikufwa Chihana – still consists mostly of Tumbuka speakers. The southern region has become the heartland of the UDF, which gets much of its financial and logistical support from the Indian population living in the main urban and commercial areas located in this part of Malawi.

The elections were won by the UDF and the presidential campaign was won comfortably by the UDF leader Bakili Muluzi, a member of the Islamized Yao-ethnic minority in Malawi which since Independence had been marginalized under Banda's ethnic policies (see Thorold 1997 on the Yao's dissenting position). The elections also made it plain that Dr Kamuzu Banda was a spent force in Malawian politics. The way in which the elections were carried out, the discipline of the millions of voters and the remarkable radio speech in which Dr Banda accepted defeat, received general international praise. Apart from a number of incidents, partly caused by a group of Commonwealth Observers declaring the elections 'free and fair' before counting the cast votes had even begun in some districts (see also Geisler 1993 for profound criticism of the Commonwealth Observers' problematic participation in other instances of democratic transition), the elections were judged by the international observers to have been sufficiently well conducted to allow them to be regarded as reliable. (Irregularities which required voting to be repeated were found in only two districts.) Even the transfer of power to the new UDF-dominated government went fairly smoothly.

The attention of international news-services was drawn to Malawi again in 1995 when a committee of investigation brought out its report of inquiry into an incident in 1993 that had taken the lives of one minister and a number of members of parliament. In that year they had all fallen from grace with Dr Banda and their bodies were later found riddled with bullets at the bottom of a ravine in Mwanza-district. A judicial commission tried to have Dr Banda arraigned on grounds of direct involvement in the killings, but his failing mental and physical condition led the court to decide to dismiss the case. This was not an isolated incident and international critics have pointed out that the judicial commissions in Malawi so far have had little success in bringing to trial those responsible for past political crimes.

In general terms it is safe to say that Muluzi's government still deals with a legacy of open and covert political coercion and violence. In remote areas the power of the former MCP party chairmen continues to be significant, despite their defeat in the general elections and despite the UDF control of all government positions. Usually, these party chairmen, unofficially but effectively, still form the main contact persons for outside agencies, NGOs for example, as they maintain to have the longest experience in dealing with such exchanges. Other elements of the former political culture, in which secret societies played an important role such as chiefly authority at the village level, have likewise remained largely unaffected by the democratic changes at the national level and it is here that the cultural construction of secrecy is a dominant factor. Secrecy belongs, so to speak, to the ground layer of the local political culture, and it was clear from the onset of the democratization effort that the international organizations had very little understanding of its salience. In the following section this aspect of the local political culture in its confrontation with a Western-inspired democratization process is further explored.

POLITICAL CULTURE, SECRECY AND DEMOCRATIZATION

Returning to the moment when the first international observers arrived in Malawi, the micro-political process that unfolded can be described and analysed as a meeting of two 'secret worlds' – that of 'democracy' as it is understood in the West, and what might be called the dominant , partly traditional, political culture. To begin with the latter, from the inception of his rule Banda continuously referred to the cultural values and political traditions of the largest ethnic unit in the country, the Chewa, and took the Chewa models of authority as the ideal for the post-colonial political order he intended to create. Vail and White note:

> As a cultural broker for the Chewa, Banda had a broader vision, however, than formulating an ideological statement for his ethnic group alone. He has instead equated 'Malawian-ness' with Chewa-ness, and he has depicted the Chewa as the very soul of the country.
>
> (Vail and White 1989: 182)

Within this 'reconstructed' political tradition the *Nyau* secret society was and still is perceived as a key institution belonging to the very heart of its culture (Kaspin 1993: 54). Only initiated men are members of the society. When they appear at important public occasions the Nyau group consists of masked dancers, drummers, the *akapoli* (free running guardians of the performance/helpers) and others who in their normal outfit participate, sing songs and clap their hands. The masked characters are known as 'animals' (*zilombo*), whereby some of them indeed represent animal figures, while others represent a mockery of important social, political or religious types (for instance, a man dressed up as a white lady and wearing a white facial mask; see for a fuller picture of *Nyau* symbolism: Aguilar 1996). The masked dances were and still are particularly performed at certain rituals, such as funerals, girls' initiation ceremonies and installations of chiefs.

However, in large parts of Central and Southern Malawi the authority of traditional leaders such as village headmen and chiefs is underwritten by the *Nyau* not in the performative sense, but rather in the sense of a masked and concealed form of control and coercion. Developing from forming the backbone of traditional authority, it became after independence in 1964 a secretive instrument of oppression by Banda's government at the local village level. Close connections were developed between village headmen and local party chairmen, hence between respectively *Nyau* and the Malawi Young Pioneers who became very central in the execution of authority for the local MCP party cadres.

In many villages, the *Nyau* mainly exercised coercive political power at night and as unrecognizable strangers. Writers who have described these acts emphasize the ritual terror and occasional political murders the *Nyau* carry out, and which usually rarely came to light in the daily world of formal authority (see Schoffeleers and Linden 1972, Linden and Linden 1974, Schoffeleers 1976). Englund, writing from his experiences in a village in the Dedza district just prior to the elections, gives a vivid account of what became common practice in the implementation of coercive government regulations:

> Although village headmen and local party officials were responsible for seeing that the orders of the government were obeyed, the harshest measures of coercion were usually left for strangers and, significantly, for the masked characters of *Nyau*. The so-called party membership renewal campaigns were initiated by party chairmen in villages, but because they seldom succeeded in persuading all villagers to renew their memberships, the names of defiant villagers were passed on to officials in other areas. These officials, strangers to the villagers in question, came to visit their houses during the night. They were often accompanied by members of the Malawi Young Pioneers ... or by *zilombo*. If the door was not opened, the visitors would break into the house. If its occupants still refused to pay for the renewal of their party memberships, the visitors confiscated property in order to cover the costs of renewal. The possibility of resistance was extremely limited. The Young Pioneers were notorious for their readiness to use violence: the sight and sound of *zilombo* in the middle of the night have prompted many villagers to make, in horror, the required payments.
>
> (Englund 1996: 117)

Professor M. Schoffeleers mentions in personal communication that in the Central region the group of *akapoli* usually was made up of young 'hooligans' who either with or without the formal consent of the *Nyau* elders to a large extent were responsible for forms of uncontrolled terror. In the Southern part of Malawi where Nyau is also active, the young were much more re-strained and some *Nyau* groups would prefer not to have *akapoli*.

In terms of a historical perspective, it is interesting to note that in pre-colonial and colonial times with the advent of missioniza-tion a dispute developed between the mainline churches, the Roman Catholic in particular, and the *Nyau* societies. As Schoffeleers and Linden (1972) show, the missionaries tried to 'save' the younger generation from hidden and heathen rituals at which *Nyau* was involved, to turn this generation into the bulwark of new nationhood, the generation from which the leaders of tomorrow would emerge (see also Mandala 1990: 154). fighting *Nyau* in this way became a way of contributing to the building of the nation-state.[3]

However, in the coming to power, after independence, of Banda and the MCP regime, a mirroring process occurred. As Ross (1969) has shown for certain types of witch-hunters in Southern Malawi, Independence became the time of revealing the concealed and of turning what once was concealed into an element of public nationhood. In Southern Malawi *mbisalila*, a specific type of witch-finder, began operating, usually invited to villages by local headmen and by the new party cadres. The term *mbisalila* refers to *ku bisa*, the act of hiding, and to bringing out into the open (*ku tuluka*) of what once was hidden. In other words, political power on the village level made it clearly un-derstood that it could command, control and bring out into the open what once was hidden through another powerful force: witchcraft (*ufiti*).

At the national level, at public ceremonies and celebrations where Dr Banda would be present, *Nyau* dancers paraded out into the open, such as that of the huge Kamuzu Stadium in Blantyre, for all too see; the initiated as well as the uninitiated. For Banda, displaying and applying the hidden elements of a central cultural heritage, formed an essential element in pro-moting Malawian nationhood.

With it, however, the antagonistic relations between the regime and the mainstream churches were revealed. As I argue elsewhere (Van Dijk 1998b) the mainline churches increasingly were curtailed in controlling or influencing the position of the

younger generation in the development of Malawian nationhood. From the onset of the Malawian independent state, post-
colonial nationhood locally associated itself with the effective
political force of *Nyau* as something 'of the government' (see
Englund 1996: 118). The regime took a position as a protector
and defender of this secretive political tradition against other
forces, among them particularly the power of the mainline
churches. Indeed adding to the perception of the *Nyau* societies
as the signs and symbols that constitute the 'substructure of
rural Chewa consciousness' as Kaspin defines it (Kaspin 1993:
54), a deliberate political and ideological dimension was introduced to the relationship between coercion and secrecy in
Malawian society. To use a felicitous phrase from Taussig, in
these public displays there was an element of skilled revelation
and of skilled concealment: the state displaying a specific 'selection' of its secretive political apparatus while concealing the
rest of it from the public gaze.

The 'formal' political power exercised by the MCP and its
leaders during its years in power was not perceived by the
local population as being fundamentally different in operation
from the political power of the *Nyau*. Both were just as likely
to be described in terms of witchcraft which, in its way, was
not really very surprising. After all, people simply 'disappeared' without any kind of explanation being offered as to
their fate, open political discussion of any kind was forbidden,
and real power remained the preserve of initiated individuals.
Political power was exercised by bringing out into the open in
the villages the *zilombo* (the wild animals), who would
then coerce people into participating in the compulsory political rituals of the ruling MCP party. Like witchcraft as a power
of the night, political power hence 'devoured' people, killed
and destroyed property, while effective protection was hard to
find.

The great majority of observers[4] who arrived in Malawi in 1993
were not aware of this cultural dimension of the political situation. Their activities were coordinated by the UNDP in
Malawi, which, of course, had other priorities. During the elections themselves, the observers were mainly concerned with the
technical aspects of running polling stations and concentrated
on monitoring those parts of the electoral process most open to

fraud. Prior to the elections they needed to pay a lot of attention to the way in which political activities were carried out in public, in order to assess whether freedom of speech and of political organization really was being taken seriously by the authorities. The cultural dimension of Malawian politics therefore tended to be overlooked.

Nevertheless, observers present just prior to both elections (the referendum of 1993 and the general elections in 1994) were increasingly tipped off by local monitors about the influence the secret society could have on the elections. Under the aegis of the PAC, *de facto* the mainstream churches, these local monitors were sent by the political parties to keep an eye on the procedures and to report irregularities to their party or to the PAC. They tended to come from nearby villages and urban districts and were therefore familiar with the local political situation.

In some places the international observers, for instance, were told that the *Nyau* had threatened to turn up at the polling stations before they opened, in full dress, complete with ritual masks. The implication of this, which may not have been apparent to the non-Malawians, was, firstly, that the *Nyau* would then be 'taking possession' of the location, which would then be inaccessible to non-initiates and, secondly, that ritually sanctioned violence against the local population could result. In other locations, the *Nyau* threatened to turn up and demand to inspect the ballot papers. Since the balloting procedure consisted of removing the ballot paper with the symbol of the selected party and disposing of the rest in a sealed box, it would be immediately apparent which party someone had voted for if the remaining papers were taken out of the polling station. In this way, the *Nyau* sought to control the voting in favour of one party. Elsewhere, it was rumoured that the *Nyau* would be placing 'magic eyes' in polling booths.

In a way, as I argued elsewhere (Van Dijk 1998b), the system of local monitoring, as organized by the PAC, allowed the mainstream churches to move back in again, influencing the younger generation's political position within the Malawi nation. It was clear that these young, zealous local monitors would react strongly against the threats of *Nyau* in the process of democratization. Englund writes of a village in the Dedza district of Malawi:

The tensions over the appearances in MCP rallies [of *Nyau*] became apparent shortly before the referendum. Junior members [of the *Nyau*] were increasingly reluctant to force villagers to attend rallies, and some even refused to dance there. At least some members were afraid that they could be attacked by angry supporters of the multiparty cause. Thus according to this view, a complete inversion was possible; instead of being feared for their fierceness, *zilombo* would themselves be attacked by villagers.

(Englund 1996: 118)

An example like this should make it clear that political tension, next to its more open and manifest forms, is also expressed in ways that are indirect but quite perceptible, and it is the latter aspect that gave all the familiar problems of election observing (language barrier, administrative preoccupation, logistics, political pressure) a specific cultural dimension. Local monitors indeed engaged themselves in a process of skilled revelation (namely to the international observers) and of skilled concealment (that of *Nyau* threats) on the basis of a very different political objective as compared to, and running counter to, that of the ruling party and its regime. The term 'skilled' here received a double meaning as local monitors became skilled in terms of the training they received (organized by the PAC), on how the election procedure was set up, on how monitoring should be conducted, and in terms of the academic skills of reading and writing which were expected of them. On the other hand, 'skilled' here also has the meaning of mastering the techniques by which *Nyau* and MYP acts of intimidation could be reported to higher authorities and the international observers without running the risk of becoming the next targets of political violence. The hope and expectation was that the international observers in their turn could report such matters to the Electoral Commission which would have the authority to intervene. Although the Electoral Commission was informed by the core group of international observers and in addition also had its own sources of information in the country, as far as I am aware, traditional authorities were never confronted by the Commission to curtail the activity of the *Nyau* in particular.

Subsequently, and despite the local monitors' efforts in laying bare the concealed forms of coercion and violence, writers familiar with the influence and social dynamics of the *Nyau* have pointed to the considerable overlap between the areas where the *Nyau* remained active and the districts in which the MCP enjoyed electoral success (see Kaspin 1995).

From the point of view of the local population, the arrival of multi-party elections brought the new, unknown and secret world of 'democracy' into view, next to the 'old' secret world of the *Nyau*. Under the old power monopoly of the MCP, the local population 'voted' by openly and publicly supporting one of the candidates put forward by the regional MCP council. In other words, the MCP did put forward a slate of candidates and the winner was simply the one with the largest number of supporters lined up next to him. In this way, it was quite obvious who had voted for whom, and commonly the government would brag about the openness of its 'democratic' system.

At the referendum and the general elections the voting booth, the ballot paper, the envelope and the sealed ballot box, however, appeared to evoke only rather poorly understood notions of electoral secrecy. For instance, observers would certainly report as an 'irregularity' two persons seen entering a polling booth (usually this happened if one person intended to assist another person in the complicated procedure of casting separate votes for the parliamentary and presidential elections, while not being aware that 'secrecy' prohibits this). Moreover, for many people it was not at all clear what the concept of multi-party democracy actually meant in the first place. 'Mattypatty', as it is called in the local tongue, was seen by many, and particularly the older generation, as 'just another party' and not as a system for making a choice in secret of one of a number of parties and one of a number of candidates.

It was therefore not surprising that during the negotiations between the PAC and the government about the form the elections would take that the MCP insisted that instead of 'secret' voting, the voters would line up behind their preferred candidate in the traditional way. Although, obviously, they were only acting out of self-interest, hoping that people would be intimidated into supporting them, in popular understanding it indeed signalled a relationship with the dark, hidden world of politics which had threatening connotations for many Malawians. In spite of the 'openness' in voting in the MCP system, politics and political activity had long been associated with a violent, coercive and dark world of powers from which protection was almost impossible to find. Dark, hidden and secret dealings belong to a realm connected with witchcraft and amoral behaviour that fears the light of day. In the PAC campaign of promoting 'mattypatty' the symbol of the *nyali*, the lamp, was therefore well chosen, as it contrasted light with dark, thereby turning the secrecy of the democratic system into something morally acceptable.

The international observers were, in my experience, often regarded by the local people and by the local monitors as persons with special, almost esoteric knowledge about the rituals of democracy and their intricacies. Particularly for the local monitors the international observers remained persons who could not become subject to, nor engulfed in, the secretive machinations of the *Nyau* and intimidation by the MYP. The source of power and authority of the international observers remained unaffected by the local political forces and lay beyond the local political system of control. Furthermore, the international observers were clearly initiated into the secrets of how the democratic system could be tricked and what ways there were to influence the result of the election by means largely unknown to the local political system. International observers therefore sometimes became part of local powerplays in which local monitors, young men as they usually were, attacked the power of the 'old' bearers of authority (a case of this nature has been described in Van Dijk 1998b) under the protection of the observers. Local monitors zealously sought to be 'initiated' in the knowledge about the secrets of the democratic system, the ways in which esoteric means could be applied by those opposing *mattypatty* to befraud the election procedure.

In some cases, as I myself experienced, local monitors of the oppostion groups in particular seemed to be suspicious and ambiguous about the international observers' position. After all, such knowledge could also have been placed in the hands of the ruling party, the MYP and even the *Nyau* for that matter, giving these groups an advantage over the local monitors and the oppostion groups they represented. The international observers naturally responded to this by going into lengthy technical explanations of such things as what can go wrong with registration cards, but they remained under suspicion as holders of potentially dangerous, almost esoteric knowledge about the rituals of democracy and the ways in which certain 'techniques' could be applied affecting voting behaviour. International observers hardly ever saw themselves as bearers of such secretive knowledge and seemed not unaware of their culturally mediating position between the two worlds of secrecy in which they operated. Such positions, which in society are occupied for instance by medicine-men and chiefs (as they mediate between the world of men and the world of the ancestors and their spirits), are always regarded with ambiguous feelings of esteem, respect, awe and fear. The long presence of international observers in Malawi (for nearly two years in all), through which they became increasingly aware of at least some of the dynamics of local culture, and in addition the fact that international observers gained access to places where ordinary Malawians never dared to go (such as MYP bases throughout the country), lent force to such feelings of ambiguity.

On the side of the *Nyau* societies, it has remained unknown how they reacted to the presence of international observers to whom their acts of intimidation surreptitiously were reported. There are, however, indications that the power of the secret societies, as the backbone of traditional authority, has remained largely unaffected by the democratic change and implementation of a new political structure after 1994. It is only recently that scholars have begun to record the *Nyau*'s responses to the process of democratization on a systematic basis, as the present political situation in Malawi seems to allow for the exploration of this field of study once heavily embargoed (personal communication with Prof. Schoffeleers).[5]

CONCLUSION

In this chapter I have argued that in understanding the process of democratization in Malawi, and perhaps elsewhere for that matter, the exploration of the secretive, the hidden and the concealed needs to be included. They form part of the cultural understanding upon which local normative schemes and perceptions have been built. In discussing the role and position of the observers with regard to the elections in Malawi, I have pointed out that there was in fact on the local level and in the perception of the local population a meeting of two secret worlds. It was a meeting of which the observers themselves were hardly aware, but which at the same time made them subject to a culturally perceived position as representatives of a political order which presupposes secrecy. In exploring their position in the Malawian local political culture, first of all, the role of secret societies needs to be taken into account. Particularly in the Central and Southern regions, where the ruling MCP had to been forming local alliances with the *Nyau*, the *Nyau* had been making it clear from their actions that both the traditional authority of the chiefs and headmen and political power in general were something exercised in secret. The international observers only became gradually aware of this local political culture. For the greater part the international observers only received note of such forms of intimidation by *Nyau* and MYP groups as second-hand information through the local monitors; and their means to respond to it were indeed very limited. Other than occasional reporting to the Electoral Commission in charge of the entire election effort, the relative and cultural distance between the international observers and the local political practices prevented deeper interaction.

Secondly, democratic rituals themselves, as introduced through the intervention of outside agencies, appeared to have their own secretive dimensions in the eyes of the population, and these were therefore not always immediately accepted (for instance, in some cases people would insist they wanted to go into the polling booth only if accompanied by somebody else). This being the case, democratic rituals were not directly separated from the partly tangible and partly imaginary world of hidden evil forces to which local forms of political intimidation – for instance, *Nyau* magic eyes in polling booths – alluded to.

Some important insights emerge from the Malawi experience. In order to perceive and understand the more subtle and, to Western eyes, often somewhat 'irrational' ways of influencing voter behaviour, it would be advisable if election observers have more time to get acquainted with fears and anxieties of the local population as they exist both in the realm of 'day' as well as in the realm of the imaginary. The observers in the Malawi case had inadequate knowledge of the local culture and lacked sufficient time to prepare themselves adequately for it. Moreover, attention to the 'non-rational' and the imaginary in local culture was lacking as well. This led to an over-emphasis on the more 'rational' technical aspects of the election with the result that the actual observing, as was the case in Malawi, ended up narrowly focused on election procedures, usually concentrated in the periods just before, during and for a few days after the elections. To have a good chance of uncovering the more subtle and cultural forms of intimidation and influencing of voters, the observer would certainly need to be present for a longer time before the election and preferably in one place.

Secondly, in support of Geisler's conclusions (1993: 634) the *local* monitors are crucial in the empirical understanding of local popular culture and its normative schemes. With their continued presence, their broad-based composition and their very broad coverage of the entire election process and the polling stations, they would be the ideal partners of foreign observers. As Carothers also notes:

> Domestic election monitors, if properly organized and prepared, have important advantages over foreign observers. ... They know the political culture, the language, and the territory in question and consequently are capable of seeing many things that short-term foreign observers cannot.
>
> (Carothers 1997: 26)

But as Geisler correctly said, this partnership is obstructed by the fact that they remained in the margins of funding by the international community and in the shadow of their foreign colleagues as far as proclamations on the conduct of the election are concerned (Geisler 1993: 634). Certainly in Malawi the continued lack of financial support for their activities as well as the persistent surreptitious threat with regard to their activities from the side of the *Nyau* and MYP affected their stamina. Hence there is a great deal to be said for an increased and direct partnership between local monitors and international observers in all the aspects of the election observing effort. Further, Nevitte and Canton (1997) make a plea for an increased sense of complementarity between domestic and international observers. Instead of pointing at the 'dangers' of the local background and political bias of domestic observers, they stress the fact that becoming a local monitor may provide 'ordinary' citizens with greater knowledge of the 'nuts and bolts' of the democratic process (ibid.: 58). In my contribution, however, I have hopefully been able to show that there is no one-way process. It is not only domestic observers who have to be led into the secrecies of what a democratic system implies and presupposes, but it is also the international observers who need to have a much greater sensitivity to the secrecies of a local political culture.

Thirdly, with regard to the effect of the internal observing activities in Malawi, the conclusion should be that despite their lack of knowledge of the local political culture, the international election observers contributed to the process precisely because of their intermediary position. In their contacts with local monitors, surreptitious acts of intimidation could be presented and openly discussed, information on the various means of 'rigging' the election procedures could be shared and questions on some of the technical aspects of these procedures could be answered (in fact half of my time as an international observer in Malawi was devoted to such 'educational' activities as explaining what the complex voting process consisted of, what a discard box actually was meant to be, and so on). In this way, both the international observers and the local monitors would feel that their status, efficacy and safety were enhanced by mutual close contact and collaboration. The general conclusion from the Malawi case therefore should be that close partnership will prove to be beneficial to a deeper empirical understanding of local political culture and thereby of the effectiveness of international observing.

The elections, finally, led to a greater regionalization and ethnicization of Malawian politics (see Chirwa 1994, Kaspin 1995). When the election result became known, the consequences of the heavily regionalized voting were regularly and widely discussed amongst the UNDP's election observers. Would the country fall apart into warring regions, with an AFORD-dominated North, a UDF-dominated South and a still vigorous MCP in control of the Central region? Despite these concerns, the UNDP presence, with all the civic education and media support services that went with it, ended soon after the elections, with the result that the organization did not remain to look at how the results would be accepted.

To judge from the developments – or the lack of them – in Malawi in the second half of 1994 and into 1995, it looks as if elections and democratization have remained two quite different things. The old political culture of the former MCP (particularly its gerontocratic nature: see Van Dijk 1998b) have remained largely intact, albeit in a somewhat altered form. This continuity takes many forms, among them the continuing influence at village level of the former MCP party chairmen and the way that many important members of the old political elite have found themselves a place within the UDF. Freedom of news-gathering for the sole radio broadcasting corporation is still not in place, and Malawi remains the only African country without TV: a direct legacy of political thinking under the Banda regime. In addition, the power of the *Nyau* secret society – which helped form the backbone of traditional forms of authority in large parts of Malawi – remains virtually unchanged and contributes to a picture of substantial continuity surviving in spite of elections and democratization. No public debate has ever started on the legacies of that political culture and the atrocities that took place in the period of 30 years of dictatorship that shaped this specific culture. Neither is there a public debate about the tenets of what democratization in Malawi is supposed to mean and what the places of *Nyau* and traditional authority is to be. So far there has been no indication that the new government of Bakili Muluzi is prepared to step into this arena, as it remains preoccupied with defending itself against the many accusations of undemocratic government it receives from the national and international communities. This once more seems to be an indication that the local political culture is of greater 'resilience' than some had hoped for after the advent of democratic change in this country.

NOTES

1.   The United Nations Development Programme brought together a group of observers from a variety of Western and African countries under the umbrella of the JIOG (Joint International Observer Group) that also assisted the Malawian Electoral Committee in the execution of the election procedures.

2.   The role of the established churches in Malawi's democratic transition is by no means unique. See Buijtenhuijs and Rijnierse (1993: 65) and Buijtenhuijs and Thiriot (1995: 59) for a discussion of the actual influence of particularly the Roman Catholic and various Protestant churches elsewhere in sub-Saharan Africa.

3.   It needs to be specified here that these local political conflicts between the *Nyau* and the churches mainly relate to the Central and Southern

parts of Malawi. In the much smaller Northern region of Malawi, where the *Nyau* were absent, local-level contestation between Christianity and traditional authorities developed very differently (see McCracken 1977). Nevertheless, Christianity contributed to the development of a national elite most importantly through the establishment of the first institute for higher education in Malawi in this particular region.

4. The distinction between observers and monitors is that, as will be explained in more detail below, observers came from outside Malawi to be placed under the authority of the JIOG (see note 1), while monitors came from within Malawi and were operating under the aegis of the PAC. These local monitors therefore either could belong to one of the opposition groups, or to the ruling party (MCP), or to one of the churches which were involved in PAC.

5. Particularly for the Central region, where the *Nyau* appeared to have been developing a rather marked symbiosis with one of the three Presbyterian Synods, the so-called Nkhoma Synod, which remained loyal to Dr Banda during the process of democratization, scholarly reflection may lead to further insight on how local political formations react to extraneous processes of intervention. Despite being strange bedfellows, this case (information through personal communication with Prof. Schoffeleers) of a covert alliance between the *Nyau* and members of the Synod may show, although details are yet to be revealed through study and research, how such indigenous political formations forge new and creative alliances to curb external intervention and to preserve internal political supervision.

REFERENCES

Aguilar, L.B. de, 1996. *Inscribing the Mask: Interpretations of Nyau Masks and Ritual Performance among the Chewa of Central Malawi* (Fribourg: Fribourg University Press, Studia Instituti Anthropos 47).

Bayart, J.-F. 1992. 'Introduction', in J.-F. Bayart, A. Mbembe and C. Toulabor, *La Politique par le Bas en Afrique Noire: Contributions a une Problématique de la Démocratie* (Paris: Karthala).

Bjornlund, E., M. Bratton and C. Gibson, 1992. 'Observing Multiparty Elections in Africa: Lessons from Zambia', *African Affairs* 91: 405–31.

Buijtenhuijs, R. and E. Rijnierse, 1993. *Democratization in Sub-Saharan Africa 1989–1992: an Overview of the Literature* (Leiden: African Studies Centre).

Buijtenhuijs, R. and C. Thiriot, 1995. *Democratization in Sub-Saharan Africa: an Overview of Literature, 1992–1995* (Leiden: African Studies Centre / Bordeaux: CEAN).

Carothers, Th. 1997. 'The Observers Observed', *Journal of Democracy* 8(3): 17–32.

Chirwa, C.W. 1994. 'The Politics of Ethnicity and Regionalism in Contemporary Malawi', *African Rural and Urban Studies* 1(2): 93–118.

Cullen, T. 1994. *Malawi: a Turning Point* (Edinburgh: Pentland Press).

Davidson, B.G. 1992. *The Black Man's Burden: Africa and the Curse of the Nation State* (London: James Currey).

Diamond, L. 1993. 'Introduction: Political Culture and Democracy', in L. Diamond (ed.), *Political Culture and Democracy in Developing Countries* (Boulder: Westview Press), pp. 1–33.

Englund, H. 1996. 'Between God and Kamuzu: the Transition to Multiparty Politics in Central Malawi', in R. Werbner and T. Ranger (eds), *Postcolonial Identities in Africa* (London: Zed Books), pp. 107–35.

fiedler, K. 1995. 'The "Smaller" Churches and Big Government', in M.S. Nzunda and K.R. Ross (eds), *Church, Law and Political Transition in Malawi, 1992–1994.* (Gweru: Mambo Press), pp. 154–70.

Forster, P.G. 1994. 'Culture, Nationalism, and the Invention of Tradition in Malawi', *The Journal of Modern African Studies*, 32(3): 477–97.

Geisler, G. 1993. 'Fair? What has Fairness got to do with it? Vagaries of Election Observations and Democratic Standards',*The Journal of Modern African Studies* 31(4): 613–37.

Geschiere, P. 1995. *Sorcellerie et Politique en Afrique: la Viande des Autres* (Paris: Karthala).

Hyden, G. 1996. 'The Role of the Electoral System in Combining Civic Peace with Freedom', *East African Journal of Peace and Human Rights* 2(2): 209–17.

Kaunda, J.M. 1995. 'Malawi: the Post-Colonial State, Development, and Democracy', *Africa* 50(3): 305–24.

Kaspin, D. 1993. 'Chewa Visions and Revisions of Power: Transformations of the *Nyau* Dance in Central Malawi', in J. and J. Comaroff (eds), *Modernity and its Malcontents: Ritual and Power in Postcolonial Africa* (Chicago: Chicago University Press), pp. 34–57.

——. 1995. 'The Politics of Ethnicity in Malawi's Democratic Transition', *The Journal of Modern African Studies* 33(4): 595–620.

Linden, I. and J. Linden, 1974. *Catholics, Peasants and Chewa Resistance in Nyasaland* (London: Heinemann).

Lwanda, J.L. 1993. *Kamuzu Banda of Malawi: a Study in Promise, Power and Paralysis* (Glasgow: Dudu Nsomba Publications).

——. 1996. *Promises, Power, Politics and Poverty: Democratic Transition in Malawi*(Glasgow: Dudu Nsomba Publications).

Mandala, E.C. 1990. *Work and Control in a Peasant Economy: a History of the Lower Tchire Valley in Malawi, 1859–1960* (Madison: University of Wisconsin Press).

Martin, D.C. 1993. 'La Tanzanie et le Multipartisme', *Afrique Contemporaine* 167(3): 3–13.

McCracken, W. 1977. *Politics and Christianity in Malawi, 1875–1940: the Impact of the Livingstonia Mission in the Northern Province* (Cambridge: Cambridge University Press).

Médard, J.-F. 1991. 'Autoritarismes et Démocraties en Afrique Noire', *Politique Africaine*, 43: 92-105.

Meyns, P. 1995. 'Grenzen der Internationalen Wahlbeobachtung. Amerkungen eines Wahlbeobachters in Mosambik', *Afrika Spectrum* 30(1): 35–47.

Nevitte, N. and Canton, S.A. 1997. 'The Role of Domestic Observers', *Journal of Democracy* 8(3): 47–62.

Newell, J. 1995. '"A Moment of Truth"? The Church and Political Change in Malawi, 1992', *The Journal of Modern African Studies* 33(2): 243–62.

Nzunda, M.S. and Ross, K.R. (eds) 1995. *Church, Law and Political Transition in Malawi, 1992–1994* (Gweru: Mambo Press).

Ranger, T.O. 1972. 'Mchape and the Study of Witchcraft Eradication'. Paper presented at the Conference on the History of Central African Religious Systems, 31 Aug.–8 Sept. 1972, Lusaka, Zambia.

Robinson, P.T. 1994. 'Democratization: Understanding the Relationship between Regime Change and the Culture of Politics', *African Studies Review* 37(1): 39–68.

Ross, A.C. 1969. 'The Political Role of the Witchfinder in Southern Malawi during the Crisis of October 1964 to May 1965', in R.G. Willis (ed.), *Witchcraft and Healing* (Edinburgh: University of Edinburgh Press), pp. 55–71.

Ross, K. 1995, 'The Renewal of the State by the Church: the Case of the PAC', *Religion in Malawi* 5: 31–5.

Schatzberg, M.G. 1993. 'Power, Legitimacy and "Democratisation" in Africa', *Africa* 63(4): 445–61.

Schoffeleers, J.M. 1976. 'The Nyau Societies: Our Present Understanding', *The Society of Malawi Journal* 29(1): 59–68.

Schoffeleers, J.M. and I. Linden, 1972. 'The Resistance of the *Nyau* Cult to the Catholic Missions in Malawi', in T. Ranger and I. Kimambo (eds), *The Historical Study of African Religion* (London: Heinemann).

Tall, E.K. 1995. 'De la Démocratie et des Cultes Voduns au Bénin', *Cahiers d'Etudes Africaines* 25(1): 195–208.

Thorold, A. 1997. 'The Politics of Mysticism: Sufism and Yao Identity in Southern Malawi', *Journal of Contemporary African Studies* 15(1): 107–17.

Vail, L. and L. White, 1989. 'Tribalism in the Political History of Malawi', in L. Vail (ed.), *The Creation of Tribalism in Southern Africa* (London: James Currey), pp. 151–93.

Van Dijk, R.A. 1992a. *Young Malawian Puritans: Young Puritan Preachers in a Present-day African Urban Environment* (Utrecht: ISOR, Ph.D. thesis).

——. 1992b. 'Young Puritan Preachers in Post-Independence Malawi', *Africa* 62(2): 159–81.

——. 1993. 'Young Born-Again Preachers in Malawi. the Significance of an Extraneous Identity', in P. Gifford (ed.), *New Dimensions in African Christianity* (Ibadan: AACC – Sefer Books), pp. 66–97.

——. 1994. 'La guérisseuse du docteur Banda au Malawi', *Politique Africaine* 52: 145–50.

——. 1995. 'Fundamentalism and its Moral Geography in Malawi: the Representation of the Diasporic and the Diabolical', *Critique of Anthropology* 15(2): 171–91.

——. 1998a. 'Fundamentalism, Cultural Memory and the State: Contested Representations of Time in Postcolonial Malawi', in R. Werbner (ed.), *Memory in the Postcolony* (London: Zed Books).

——. 1998b. 'Pentecostalism, Gerontocratic Rule and Democratisation in Malawi: the Changing Position of the Young in Political Culture', in J. Haynes (ed.), *Religion, Globalisation and Political Culture in the Third World* (London: Macmillan).

—— and P. Pels, 1996. 'Contested Authorities and the Politics of Perception: Deconstructing the Study of Religion in Africa', in R. Werbner and T. Ranger (eds), *Postcolonial Identities in Africa* (London: Zed Books), pp. 245–71.

Van Donge, J.K. 1995. 'Kamuzu's Legacy: the Democratization of Malawi. Or Searching for the Rules of the Game in African Politics', *African Affairs* 94: 227–57.

Williams, T.D. 1978. *Malawi, the Politics of Despair* (Cornell: Cornell University Press).

Witte, J., Jr., 1993. 'Introduction', in J. Witte, Jr. (ed.), *Christianity and Democracy in a Global Context* (Boulder: Westview), pp. 1–23.

9 The 1996–7 Elections in Chad: the Role of the International Observers

R. Buijtenhuijs

INTRODUCTION

The observation of African elections by international teams, which has, in some sense, become a genuine industry in the 1990s, has given rise to a number of interesting publications. They can be classified in two different categories. The first consists of the *'manual of the perfect observer'*, a phrase used here in a positive sense. A good example is the work edited by U. Engel et al. (1994), although it has the drawback of only being available in German. The authors review problems which observers may encounter in the field and list the conditions which should be met if an observation mission is to be considered serious and valid. They also discuss the criteria an election in Africa has to satisfy to be recognized as a 'free and fair election'. The work contains sixteen mission reports compiled by German observers on particular cases; these cover Namibia, Niger, Lesotho, Eritrea, Malawi, Burundi, Togo and the Central African Republic.

The booklet *Conférence Internationale sur les Élections en Afrique de l'Ouest* (1994) is another example of the same kind. It contains twelve contributions, mainly by African authors, on numerous practical questions: the electoral code, the problem of voter registration, the techniques of manipulation and distortion of results during voting, the scrutiny, collection and centralization of the results, questions of security (the problem of the army and the police force, the role of the administration in the elections). This is also a genuine handbook.

A second category of publications is that of critical studies. The article by G. Geisler is the best example of this kind. This author, who was an observer during the Kenyan elections at the end of 1992, seriously questions the reliability of the observation missions organized to date, listing their numerous imperfections: in most cases, the international observers arrive late on the scene and only observe the voting in the strict sense of the word, without being able to take into account the registration of voters and the electoral campaign, stages during which many irregularities may be committed; too many international missions depend on a particular foreign government and tend to tailor their conclusions to suit the diplomatic interests of their own country instead of adopting a genuinely independent position; sometimes international observers adopt an attitude of paternalism and disdain with regard to the national observers whose work is often much more serious; and so on (Geisler 1993). T. von Trotha (1993) and M. Pilon (1994), drawing their conclusions from the controversial presidential elections in Togo in August 1993, confirm the negative views stated by G. Geisler.

The 1997 Report of the *Observatoire Permanent de la Coopération Française* (1997) belongs to the same category of critical studies. It contains two general chapters on electoral observation by M. Pilon and A. Bourgi, and three case studies on elections in Togo, Niger and Chad. Pursuing this critical vein, I will study in the present article the international observation of the 1996–7 Chadian elections (the Constitutional Referendum of 31 March 1996, the June–July 1996 presidential elections, and the January–February 1997 parliamentary elections),[1] with special emphasis on the presidential elections during which the deficiencies of the international (and national) observation team came to light most blatantly and were severely criticized by Chadian political leaders, and representatives of civil society associations.

The case of Chad is an interesting one, because this country was the last of the ex-French African colonies to organize democratic, or at least multi-party elections, at a time when there were already persistent doubts about the commitment of the international donor community (in particular, France) to the cause of genuine democratization in Africa south of the Sahara. An analysis of the international observation of the Chadian elections may therefore be of some help in evaluating the pertinence of these doubts.

DEMOCRATIZATION IN CHAD

Since Chad gained its independence in August 1960, the country's history has first and foremost been marked by a civil war that began in 1965 and went on for about 25 years. Admittedly, the horrors and destruction wreaked by this internal war were not on the scale of what Liberia, Mozambique, Rwanda or Somalia have known; however, armed struggle has seriously affected all the domains of Chadian life, be it political, economic or social.[2]

It is against this background that one should see the recent democratization process in Chad that started on 1 December 1990, when Idriss Déby took over power, driving away his predecessor Hissein Habré by military means. At that time he was no more than merely one warlord amongst the many others of his kind who had dominated and plagued the Chadian political scene since independence. His victory had been obtained by force of arms, without any popular support whatsoever, but with some covert assistance from France, or rather the French secret service (see Silberzahn 1995). Very soon, however, Déby made it clear that he did not have the intention to respect the 'rules' of the warlord game in the future. Already on 4 December, he set the tone in his first *Message à la Nation*:

> Nous n'aurons définitivement extirpé les démons de la dictature ... qu'après l'établissement d'une démocratie vraie, totale, une démocratie pluraliste ... Le plaisir est immense pour tous les combattants des forces patriotiques d'avoir contribué à l'éclosion du cadeau le plus cher que vous espériez. Ce cadeau n'est ni or ni argent: c'est la liberté.[3]

> [Only after the establishment of a real and total democracy, a pluralist democracy, ... will we definitively have eradicated the demons of the dictatorship. ... For all the fighters of the patriotic forces the joy of having contributed to the blossoming of the most cherished present that you have hoped for is immense. This present is neither gold nor money: it is freedom.]

Not quite the words one would expect from a warlord, and it has to be said that they were received by many of his compatriots with a healthy dose of scepticism. However, this declaration marked the beginning of a democratization process of some kind that has proceeded since, although fitfully and with many hesitations (and sometimes protracted blockages).

During the early days of this process, a little progress was indeed made. From December 1990 onwards, independent newspapers began to sprout and they expressed their opinions very freely. Although some harassment against individual journalist or papers occurred, including in one case the destruction of part of the printing and other equipment of the weekly *N'Djaména Hebdo*, the Déby regime did not interfere with the editorial policies of these newspapers, and refrained from taking legal action, although in some cases Chadian journalists published articles that might have justified such action. Of course, as some of Déby's opponents were quick to point out, this flourishing of independent newspapers is used by the government as a showcase to demonstrate the sincerity of its democratic intentions, a showcase moreover it can easily afford, as Chadian newspapers have a very limited circulation and have great difficulties in distributing their products outside the capital city of N'Djaména.[4] Yet, about four or five rather lively weeklies do exist, one of them (*Le Progrès*) being considered as near to the Déby regime (although it sometimes contains rather critical comments), while the others are outspoken anti-governmental in tone, without propagating the views of only one specific opposition party.

In January 1992, political parties were allowed, which led to the formation of over 65 different groups. From 15 January to 7 April 1993, a *Conférence Nationale Souveraine* (National Sovereign Conference) met which led, among other things, to the adoption of a provisional constitution and the election of a new Prime Minister. Up until that point, it could be said that while slow, the democratization process did make progress. It is mainly after the CNS that the '*démocratisation à la tchadienne*' started to drag along. The period of transition which was supposed to lead up to the first free elections since independence, was only meant to last a year, but the delaying tactics of the government (and even occasionally of the opposition parties) had the result of putting the elections back from one year to the next. It was finally only at the beginning of 1996 that the air was sufficiently cleared for electoral consultations to start in earnest.

First came a constitutional referendum which allowed the Chadian electorate to voice its opinions on the new constitution that was to introduce Chad definitively into the camp of democratic countries. This referendum took place on 31 March 1996, and resulted in the adoption of the new constitution with 63.5 per cent of the vote. A rather low score that can only be explained by the fact that the government, during the election campaign, tried to transform the constitutional referendum into a referendum in favour of the Déby regime, which led part of the political opposition to answer this challenge and recommend a negative vote. International observers were present during the referendum, but they were few in number: 7 French parliamentarians, who officiated with the help of some 20 foreign diplomats posted in Chad, as well as about a hundred national observers. As the constitutional referendum, during which I was myself present in Chad, was on its main points, a really free and fair electoral consultation, the near absence of international observers was not all that important, and it is therefore not very useful to elaborate upon this first round of the Chadian electoral process. One point, however, should be stressed: the eagerness to please in which the international observers indulged, as is shown in the following passages from an *Agence France Press* report:

> Les observateurs internationaux présent au Tchad lors du référendum constitutionnel se sont déclarés satisfaits du bon déroulement du scrutin, en dépit de quelques insufficiencies. Pour le président de la Commission des lois de l'Assemblée nationale française, M. Pierre Mazeaud, 'le scrutin s'est déroulé dans la sérénité et la transparence' … 'Le Tchad rentre dans le processus démocratique de la meilleure façon que nous souhaitons' a-t-il ajouté.[5]

> [Despite some imperfections, the international observers present in Chad during the constitutional referendum have declared themselves to be satisfied with the proceedings of the voting. For Mr Pierre Mazeaud, the president of the Law Commision of the French National Assembly, 'the vote has been conducted in a serene and transparent manner'. … He added that 'Chad returns to the democratic process in the best way that we can wish.']

Quite a few Chadians thought that this was just a little bit too much and expressed their fears that the same obliging attitudes would be adopted by the international observers at the occasion of the presidential elections, a much more important event that, it was feared, might lead the incumbent regime to indulge in electoral fraud.

THE JUNE–JULY 1996 PRESIDENTIAL ELECTIONS

During these elections, which were disputed by no less than 15 candidates, Idriss Déby obtained a comfortable victory, with 69 per cent of the vote in the second round, against 31 per cent for his remaining opponent, General Kamougué. In the first round, Déby already secured 43.8 per cent of the vote, against 12.4 per cent for Kamougué.

Although it is impossible to provide concrete and waterproof evidence, it is almost certain that the government had influenced the result of the elections by fraud, during both rounds; but, as far as one can be sure today, the cheating that was indulged in probably did not alter the final result.

As for the first round of the elections, it is rather doubtful that Idriss Déby really obtained the 43.8 per cent of the vote he has been credited with. Most of his opponents, and especially the more dangerous ones amongst them, have probably been cheated, and knowledgeable experts estimate that Déby's score did not exceed 20 per cent of the vote, or 25 per cent at the utmost, a result that, anyway, would have been sufficient to qualify him for the second round. General Kamougué, on the other hand, is probably the one candidate who was curtailed most by the electoral fraud, and with a probable result of at least 20 per cent of the vote, he too would have been sure to participate in the second round. As for this second round, it is highly probable that Déby would have defeated Kamougué even under normal circumstances, but with a less exuberant result: the high percentages he scored in the Northern provinces (over 95 per cent of the vote) have an almost Stalinist flavour, while the excessively high voter turn-out in the same provinces seems also rather incredible.

If the electoral fraud did not really alter the final result of the elections, why then was the incumbent government nevertheless tempted to use dishonest methods? There were probably two reasons for this:

1. The incumbent head of state refused to take the slightest risk. As there had been no free and fair elections in Chad since 1959, and as opinion polls are an unknown phenomenon in the country, it was almost impossible, before the first round of the elections, to have any reliable idea about the popularity of the respective candidates. Some were thought to constitute a real menace for president Déby, and this was particularly the case of two of his Northern competitors, who might have been able to topple him in the second round. It was therefore imperative to clip the wings of these candidates, a measure that, in the end, would not have been necessary, as their alleged popularity turned out to be partly based on erroneous estimations.

2. Local branches of Déby's party did their utmost to humiliate his opponents at the regional level, in order to compromise their political career for the future. This 'rage de vaincre' (rage to win), as some Chadians called it, certainly played a role in the final result.

One can only regret the Chadian electoral fraud, because, even if it did not alter the result of the elections, it made a very bad impression on part of the electorate. During the first round, voters participated in large numbers and enthusiastically, while four weeks later, for the second round, one could only conclude that the political climate was one of disillusionment and discouragement. The consequences of this doubtful electoral operation are that President Déby, for part of the voters, and especially for important segments of the Southern electorate, still lacks final legitimacy, which will negatively reflect on his coming five-year period of office.

THE ORGANIZATION OF THE INTERNATIONAL ELECTION OBSERVATION

International observers were present during both rounds of the presidential elections. They were officially invited by the Chadian government and worked in liaison with a – theoretically – independent body, the *Commission Électorale Nationale Indépendante* (CENI), in charge of the technical aspects of the electoral exercise. The CENI counted 21 members who were independent in so far as they were not members of any political party. Seven of them were appointed by the government, 7 by the provisional parliament and 7 by the political parties. As the government disposed of a majority within parliament, while quite a few of the parties were in reality government sponsored, the majority of the CENI members, although officially independent, could be supposed to be at least not hostile towards the incumbent government. CENI's role has been severely criticized after the elections and, in my opinion, the main body of these criticisms was entirely justified. CENI, after consultations with the donor community, delegated the supervision of the national and international electoral observation to the UNDP, which in turn subcontracted the practical side of the operation to GERDDES-Afrique, a pan-African group of consultants.[6]

As for the national observers, GERDDES-Afrique called upon its local branch, GERDDES-Tchad, but also on a dozen other associations belonging to the universe of what is called 'civil society'. For the presidential elections the national observers totalled slightly less than 300, who were joined by about 150 international observers of different origins: some of them were diplomats posted in Chad, others were French parliamentarians, while others still represented the 'francophonie' (the ACCT delegated observers from Bénin, Canada, France, Mauritania, Senegal and Togo). There were also present some African and Afro-American labour unionists. Divided into about a hundred teams, these national and international observers were supposed to cover the Chadian presidential elections nation-wide, and they did at least make an effort to do so.

WHAT THE OBSERVERS *DID NOT* SEE

Right from the beginning, the international observers were the object of sharp criticism. One of the reproaches addressed more particularly the limited mandate of the observers and their excessively short stay in Chad. Most of them, indeed, arrived in N'Djaména just four days before the election and left on the third day after the polls. As a result, their observation, including the national observers, was restricted to what happened on election day: the actual voting and, for those observers who accepted to work extra hours, the counting of the vote. Quite often, Chadians as well as foreign journalists, treated the international observers as mere 'tourists', a qualification that has also been used for their counterparts in other African countries (see Geisler 1993).

One-day international electoral observations of this kind are indeed open to criticism because their short duration does not allow the participants to take into account many electoral operations that may heavily weigh on the final results. The following points deserve to be mentioned:

The Voters' Registration

In Chad, this operation was first launched, without any previous consultation, by the Ministry of the Interior. After loud and prolonged protests by the opposition parties (and, it seems, a more discreet reminder by the French minister of Development Cooperation), the government finally returned to square one, and confided this delicate task to an independent commission in which the political parties were represented, together with delegates representing the government. With a few exceptions, the results of the activities of this commission have not been the subject of fundamental criticism, and yet on some points questions do come up. According to the results of the April 1993 national population census, the inhabitants of the nine Northern provinces (*préfectures*) represent 46.65 per cent of Chad's total population, while the inhabitants of the five Southern provinces make up 45.80 per cent of the total, with 8.54 per cent for the capital city of N'Djaména. However, the voters' registers convey a slightly divergent image: 47.79 per cent of the registered voters reside in the Northern provinces, 41.54 per cent in the Southern provinces, and 10.35 per cent in N'Djaména. How to account for these differences? It is, of course, possible that the potential voters in the Northern provinces were more eager to get their names on the electoral lists than their Southern counterparts, but one can imagine also that the agents in charge of the registration executed their mission more zealously in the Northern regions that were supposedly more inclined to come out massively in favour of President Déby and his incumbent party. Whatever the case, nobody was present in the field at the time, and certainly not the international observers.

Media Coverage of the Electoral Campaign

By law, all presidential candidates were allowed an equal amount of time on radio and television for their official campaign, and thanks to the *Haut Conseil de la Communication* this legal provision was duly respected. However, the same HCC has not been able to impose the same treatment of candidates in the state-controlled radio and TV news bulletins that were largely in favour of the candidate Idriss Déby. During the first round of the presidential elections, Déby got at least 45 per cent of the 'electoral pages' of the news bulletins, while his 14 opponents had to share the rest. During the second round, the situation was a little more in equilibrium, but, as was suggested before, at that point Déby was certain to win, and it was easy for the government to show some magnanimity. As the international observers arrived in Chad on the last day of the electoral campaign, they were not aware of what was happening in the media field. The national observers must certainly have seen a lot of things, but, officially, their opinion was not asked for.

The Use of State Assets During the Electoral Campaign
During the presidential elections, the government, Idriss Déby, and his political party freely used state assets for their political campaign. Ministers and other government agents toured the country on state funds, administrative vehicles were used frequently (according to some of my Chadian informants, these vehicles sometimes were provided with false number plates), and so on. Admittedly, this is also the case in European countries, including the Netherlands, but in Chad, where quite a few party leaders do not even dispose of their own private car, this discrepancy is all the more difficult to support. Here too, the international observers were not able to observe anything at all.

The Role of the Chadian Diaspora
Over the last fifty or more years, hundreds of thousands of Chadians have left their country and are now resident in foreign countries, more particularly Sudan, Libya and the RCA. At the end of the *Conférence Nationale Souveraine* (January–April 1993), it was decided that these emigrants would not be allowed to participate in the national elections, at least not in the first post-CNS consultations. The opposition, indeed, suspected that the diaspora vote would be canalized and cornered by the Chadian embassies without any possibility of democratic control. In 1995, however, the government overruled this deci-

sion and re-established the vote of the Chadian diaspora, in spite of vigorous protests by the opposition parties. In the end, this decision could eventually be considered as respectable ('They are Chadians as we are, and the history of the civil war has shown us that the diaspora has to be reckoned with, especially in Sudan'), but in the short run it highlighted the problems of control and observation. Note that the number of diaspora voters is relatively important. Over 300,000 of them were registered (two-thirds of them in Sudan) in a total electorate of 3,500,000. In the not altogether hypothetical case of a tight vote, the diaspora could therefore easily tip the scales. However, the donor community and more particularly the UN made it clear right from the beginning that they would not be able to take charge of the electoral observation in neighbouring countries. Officially because of a lack of financial means, but maybe also because this kind of exercise might have resulted in delicate diplomatic problems. Anyway: no national or international observer stuck his nose into the diaspora vote, which means that about 9 per cent of the electorate escaped any control whatsoever.

The Centralization and the Publication of the Electoral Results
As we have seen, the mission of the international observers did not go beyond polling day, including only the counting of the votes at the local level. Moreover, the observers made public their findings within two days of the elections: before even the publication of the provisional results by the CENI, not to mention the official results that were to be proclaimed by the Court of Appeal. In other words, the observers did not take into account the centralization of the count at the provincial level and even less the final treatment of the results in the N'Djaména electoral headquarters. At these levels, by all evidence, the possibilities of fraud are legion and, as far as we know, the Chadian authorities did not deny themselves these opportunities. Here too, the international observers were totally absent, as most of them had already returned home.

These are the weak points of the short-term mission of the national and international observers at the Chadian presidential elections. It should also be stated that the GERDDES action was criticized right from the beginning. As for its Chadian branch, local journalists strongly doubted its neutral-

ity, claiming that some of its leading members were 'in the
ante-room of the Presidency'.[7] As for GERDDES-Afrique,
several international experts claim that this organization, an
idealistic and disinterested body at the start (that is, around
1990), has gradually turned into a consultancy office in search
of juicy contracts, and is therefore obliged to deal tactfully with
incumbent governments.[8] Right from the start, therefore,
knowledgeable people put some question-marks on the usefulness of electoral observation as it had been conceived by the
CENI and its subcontractors.

WHAT THE OBSERVERS *DID* SEE

What, then, did the observers really see? Their findings for the
first round of the presidential elections, presented at a press
conference on 4 June, by Mr Driss, an UN electoral expert,
were largely positive. About 400 observers had scrutinized the
electoral operation (amongst them slightly less than 150 foreigners), working in about a hundred teams, who had visited
nearly 50 per cent of the polling stations.[9] Their findings were
that in almost all polling stations the electoral materials were
at the disposal of the voters, but that the indelible ink or its
substitute did not really give satisfaction. The observers had not
found cases of pressure on the electorate by officials, with the
exception of some polling stations in military barracks.
Representatives of the different candidates were present at the
polling stations, and the counting of the votes had been satisfactory. Conclusion: the Chadian electorate had given proof of
its maturity and shown a genuine desire for national unity. It is
true, in fact, that on election day everything went smoothly; one
has to admit also that Mr Driss, in his report, kept himself
strictly to what the observers had really seen, without commenting on the eventual 'fairness' of a process of which the
final results were not yet known. His restraint was laudable, but
as we will see below, this did not prevent the Chadian authorities, later on, from using his declaration out of context for
their own purposes. It has to be said also that, on 19 June
Mr Diawara, the UNDP representative in N'Djaména, was less
careful. After an audience with President Déby, he claimed,
indeed, in an interview broadcast by radio and television, that

the elections had been held under quite satisfactory circumstances, as his colleague Mr Driss had stated during his press conference; of course, there had been a few problems, but nothing is perfect in this world, and one had to remember that this was the first democratic experience in Chad since independence. At that moment, the results of the first round of the presidential elections had been made public, results that were surprising, to say the least!

As for the second round of the presidential elections, again, the findings of the international observers were largely positive. Mr Diawara, their spokesman, declared on July 5 (again before the publication of the final results) that the operation had been globally satisfactory. He did mention a few minor weak spots, but praised the CENI for the technical organization of the polling process, without, it has to be added, commenting on the fairness of the electoral exercise globally.

In the end, the international observers thus validated the presidential elections, in spite of a few criticisms on matters of detail, while stressing the fact that they only gave an opinion on those things they had really seen. Unfortunately, one has to admit that their findings had not much to do with reality. As we have seen in the introduction of this paper, it is impossible to say, in the present state of our knowledge, to what extent the elections were rigged, but it is almost certain that the results of the first round (43.8 per cent of the vote for Idriss Déby) do not reflect Chadian political reality. They have been challenged unanimously by all Déby's opponents, even by those who, between the first and the second round, ended up by rallying to his cause, and they created deep feelings of uneasiness amongst the Chadian public. The national and international observers, prisoners of their restricted and short-term mandate, therefore missed the main point of the presidential elections.

Some of the Chadian national observers soon became aware of the discrepancy between their findings and the electoral results, and, in a way, went back on their statement. On 12 June, GERDDES-Tchad stated that the provisional CENI results of the first round of the presidential elections were challenged by the majority of the contestants, and asked the Court of Appeal to carry out its responsibilities by carefully scrutinizing the records of all the polling stations. The next day, GERDDES-Afrique endorsed this statement. About the same time, the association *Tchad Non-Violence* asked the court to proclaim 'the real results' of the election, while the *Association des Femmes Juristes du Tchad* denounced the 'manipulation' of the electoral results by the CENI. Two weeks later, on 28 June, the *Ligue Tchadienne des Droits de l'Homme*, announced that it withdrew its collaboration with CENI and that there would be no LTDH observers available for the second round of the elections. Quite a few national observers thus made it be known that they regretted their 4 June statement on the satisfactory nature of the first round of the elections. At least one international observer, too, later on took the same stand.[10]

As for the parliamentary elections, we can be rather brief. During this consultation, too, electoral fraud occurred on a quite extensive scale, and President Déby's present majority in the National Assembly owes as much to blatant irregularities as to his popularity amongst the Chadian voters. At this occasion also, the international observers were present and obliged. According to their press release, nothing abnormal occurred and '*il y a eu un net progrès dans l'organisation et la maîtrise des opérations électorales*' (There has been net progress in the organization and control of the electoral operations).[11] The two French parliamentary observers were even more benevolent when they pointed out 'the exemplary character for Africa' of these elections which took place in 'peace and fairness'.[12] In this case, however, the national observers disagreed with them and made it known: according to them there had been incidents and irregularities which had escaped the attention of their international colleagues, who had concentrated their efforts too much on the larger cities while abandoning outlying districts.[13]

CONCLUSION

Our final question has to be: what has been the usefulness of national and international election observation during the Chadian 1996 presidential elections? On the one hand, it should be stated that the observers, in spite of the cautions expressed by some of them later on, published hasty and imprudent reports that were used out of context by the Chadian authorities to serve their own ends. One example: in answer to a critical article on the presidential elections in the French weekly *Jeune Afrique*, the Chadian ambassador in France, Mr Mahammat-Ali Abdallah Nassour, published the following statement:

> Quant à l'élection du président Idriss Déby, il s'agit là d'un acte de souveraineté que personne n'a le droit de mettre en question. La régularité et la transparance de ce premier scrutin présidentiel pluraliste de l'histoire du Tchad ont été constatées par les observateurs internationaux présents sur le terrain durant toutes les opérations. L'impartialité de leur témoignage ne saurait être mise en doute.[14]

[As far as the election of President Idriss Déby is concerned, that has been an act of sovereignty that no one has the right to doubt. The regularity and transparency of this first pluralist presidential vote in the history of Chad have been attested by international observers, who were present in the field during all operations. The impartiality of their testimony cannot be called into question.]

The observers have also been used at several times in the internal Chadian political debates by officials near to President Déby in order to refute the accusations of representatives of the opposition to the effect that the presidential elections had been rigged. For example, during a press conference on 11 June 1996, Mr Nagoum Yamoussoum, in charge of Déby's presidential campaign, claimed that the electoral process had been 'transparent', as had been stated by the international observers. Other examples could be quoted to show that the observers, unwillingly, have been used to obsure electoral abuses.

However, according to others, the international observers nevertheless played a positive role. At his press conference on 5 July, after the second round of the presidential elections, Mr Diawara, the local UNDP representative, claimed for example that: 'By our presence, we have to a great extent limited the damage.' This may, of course, be quite true: one can imagine that, without the observer teams, the Chadian authorities in favour of Idriss Déby would also have indulged in fraud on polling day itself, a practice they had to refrain from at least in the areas where the observers were massively present.

It is open to question whether this relatively modest aim of 'limiting the damage' is sufficient to justify the rather costly international observation exercise, and whether this positive side of the operation outweighs the dishonest 'hijacking' of their efforts.

Finally, it can be said that the international observation of the 1996–7 Chadian elections justifies the doubts voiced by more and more experts about the genuine interest of the donor community in democratization in Africa south of the Sahara. As we have seen, in Chad the international observers did a rather lousy job, and yet neither France nor the United Nations nor other donors expressed any dissatisfaction about their work. On the contrary, their local representatives, in private, did not hide their contentment.[15] Undoubtedly Idriss Déby's electoral victories were what they had been hoping for, and the manner in which these had been obtained was of much lesser importance. They too were inclined to deny accusations of electoral fraud by referring to the international observers' reports, a strong indication that such reports may be useful for a lot of people, except for African democrats who, theoretically, should be the first, if not the sole, beneficiaries of these costly exercises.

NOTES

1. For a detailed analysis of the 1996–7 Chadian elections, cf. Buijtenhuijs 1999.
2. For a short overview of the Chadian civil war, see Buijtenhuijs 1998.
3. *Actualités Tchadiennes*, no. 1, March 1991.
4. In 1996–7, *N'Djaména Hebdo*, Chad's most influential weekly (there are no daily newspapers) had a circulation of only 5,000 copies.
5. *AFP Afrique*, no. 14674, 3 April 1996.
6. Groupe d'Etudes et de Recherches sur la Démocratie et le Développement Economique et Social en Afrique.
7. Source: Interviews in N'Djaména, May–June 1996.
8. Source: Interviews in N'Djaména, May–June 1996. As for GERDDES' first idealistic phase, see Bakary 1991.
9. As a journalist of the French daily *Libération* remarked to me, this meant that their visits had been rather short: each team must have covered at least 20 stations between 7 a.m. and 6 p.m.
10. See B. Decq, 'Elections Présidentielles: Trucages ... et Commentaires', *T.S.F. Info*, no. 6, July 1996.
11. *AFP Afrique*, no. 14898, 26 Feb. 1997.
12. *AFP Afrique*, no. 14990, 28 Feb. 1997.
13. See B. Moussa, 'Législatives: Malentendus entre les Observateurs', *Le Progrès*, no. 177, 4 March 1997.
14. *Jeune Afrique*, no. 1856 (31 July–6 Aug. 1996).
15. Source: Interviews in N'Djaména, May–June 1996.

REFERENCES

Bakary, T. 1991. 'Au Bénin, les Premiers Pas d'un Groupe Panafricain "d'Observation"', *Géopolitique Africaine* 14(4): 53–60.

Buijtenhuijs, R. 1998. 'Chad in the Age of the Warlords', in D. Birmingham and P.M. Martin (eds), *History of Central Africa: the Contemporary Years since 1960* (London–New York: Longman), pp. 21–42.

———. 1999. *Transition et Élections Démocratiques au Tchad, 1993–1997: Restauration Autoritaire et Récomposition Politique* (Leiden/Paris: African Studies Centre/Karthala).

Engel, U., et al. (eds) 1996.*Wahlbeobachtung in Afrika: Erfahrungen deutscher Wahlbeobachter. Analysen und Lehren für die Zukunft* (Hamburg: Institut für Afrika-Kunde; 2nd rev. edn).

Geisler, G. 1993. 'Fair? What has Fairness got to do with it? Vagaries of Election Observations and Democratic Standards', *The Journal of Modern African Studies* 31(4): 613–37.

Mouvement Burkinabé pour les Droits de l'Homme et des Peuples, 1994. *Conférence Internationale sur les Élections en Afrique de l'Ouest: Bilan et Perspectives* (Ouagadougou: MBDHP).

Observatoire Permanent de la Coopération Française, Rapport 1997, Paris: Karthala.

Pilon, M. 1994. 'L'Observation des Processus Electoraux: Enseignements de l'Élection Présidentielle du Togo', *Politique Africaine* 56: 137–43.

Silberzahn, C. (with J. Guisnel), 1995. *Au Coeur du Secret: 1500 Jours aux Commandes de la DGSE (1989–1993)* (Paris: Fayard).

Von Trotha, T. 1994. '"C'est la Pagaille": Remarques sur l'Election Présidentielle au Togo', *Politique Africaine* 52: 152–9.

10 Elections in Mali (1992–7): Civil Society Confronted with the Rule of Democracy

M.-F. Lange

INTRODUCTION[1]

The Sahelian country of Mali, considered as one of the poorest countries in the world, today appears as one of the African states that has successfully made a transition to democracy. Following the popular revolts of 1991, elections were held in 1992 and subsequently in 1997. Mali thus seems to anchor itself in a Western electoral system. Nevertheless, the rules of democracy collide with representations and practices of power in Mali that are sometimes at variance with the notions of a consensual society which every democratic system presupposes. The influence of the political culture inherited from earlier African empires and from the colonial period remains a recognizable factor in the evolution of new political relations introduced by democracy, but the latter's dynamics have been shaped mainly in interaction with domestic agents such as organized youth and civil society groups and with donor-country policy.

After presenting a survey of the political systems prevalent up to the revolts of 1991, I will describe the essential characteristics of the electoral process that has been taking its course from 1992 up to 1997.

THE POLITICAL SYSTEMS PRECEDING THE FREE ELECTIONS OF 1992

The Precolonial Period

The precolonial period was marked by a succession of big African empires (of Ghana, Mali, and Songhai), subsequently by the Moroccan invasion and destruction of the Songhai empire (sixteenth century). The big invasions occurring from the seventeenth to the nineteenth centuries (for example, Bamanan, Fulani, Touareg migrations) ultimately led to the formation of feudal states (Gaudio 1992: 29–76). As Gaudio notes:

> La destruction de l'empire songhai avait ainsi permis la formation et le développement d'Etats à l'économie incertaine, fondés sur l'armée et, selon les cas, sur l'Islam et l'animisme, avec la religion et une forte hiérarchie sociale pour points communs. Ils se définirent à travers les guerres féodales.
> (Gaudio, 1992: 69)

> [Thus, the destruction of the Songhai empire led to the formation and development of states with precarious economies, based on the army and on either Islam or animism, with religion and a strong social hierarchy as common traits. They defined themselves as a result of the feudal wars.]

The empires then followed upon each other (the Segou empire, the Fulani empire of Macina, the Toucouleur empire) until the arrival of the French. The 'political culture' in this precolonial period was largely one of a feudalist power structure which installed itself by the force of arms and rested on rent-seeking and tribute collection.[2] The payment of the tributes marked the acceptance of vassal status; refusing to pay it was paramount to insurrection. Political relationships were established, maintained and redefined by force. Recourse to violence to change the existing political order and to substitute it with another (though often retaining existing hierarchies and positions of inferiority) also constituted much of the dynamics of alternating state power structures. The impact of the pre-colonial period has waned and has been decisively transformed by the subsequent colonial experience in Mali.

The Colonial Period

The colonial conquest by the French followed a similar scheme of establishing a political order, as it was imposed by the force of arms, establishing alliances, levying taxes, imposing corvées, and recruiting contingents of soldiers in case of war.[3] Clientelistic relationships prevalent during the pre-colonial period were mostly redefined but continued to form the underlying network of political relations. It is only on the eve of the Second World War that – on the basis of the gains of the Conference of Brazzaville (30 Jan. to 8 Feb. 1944) – a process of democratization was gradually initiated. The elections of 1945 allowed for the participation of Africans in the electoral process. In the first months of 1946 one witnessed the creation of three parties: the *Parti Progressiste Soudanais* (PSP),[4] the *Parti SFIO du Soudan*, and the *Parti Démocratique du Soudan* (PDS), which in fact constituted French–Sudanese sections of French parties.

In October 1946 the Constituent Congress of the *Rassemblement Démocratique Africain* (RDA) was held in Bamako and brought together a large part of the political elite of Francophone Africa. For Félix Houphouët-Boigny, elected president of the RDA, the issue was to establish the unity of Africans in view of the legislative elections of 10 November 1946. Concerning this, article 2 of the statutes of the RDA stipulated that: 'Il ne pourra être formé par Territoire qu'un seul parti politique se réclamant du RDA' (Per 'Territory' only one political party could be formed, making use of the name of the RDA). Under pressure from Houphouët-Boigny, the Sudanese delegates decided to dissolve the three existing parties (PSP, PDS and *Parti SFIO du Soudan*) in favour of their fusion into one, the *Union Soudanaise du RDA* (US-RDA) on 22 October 1946. But after 22 October a break occurred and the PSP asserted its autonomy *vis-à-vis* the RDA, from which a political polarization resulted, lasting up to March 1959 when the electoral collapse of the PSP (which had become the *Parti du Regroupement*

Soudanais) led in fact to a situation of mono-partyism in the French Sudan (Gaudio 1992: 98).

The end of the colonial period (1945–60) was thus marked by a 'learning process' of the rules of the electoral game[5] and of democracy: freedom of association, inauguration of multi-party-ism, freedom of the press and development of trade unionism. The role of the city of Bamako would be a determining factor in the process of decolonization of Africa,[6] in spite of a much-reduced Sudanese elite when compared to the much more nu-merous and much more ancient coastal elites (in Dahomey, Togo, Senegal). The various meetings that took place in Bamako, as well as the participation of certain French Sudanese elected in the French administration, permitted the Sudanese leaders to assert themselves in political dialogue and governance.

In fact, unlike the majority of Francophone Black African countries, Mali benefited much more from an independence ac-corded by the old colonial power than countries that obtained their independence in armed struggle. For the first time in the history of this African region the redefinition of political power was obtained both by the ballot box and by a consensual process: the transfer of political power was carried out without recourse to war. After the failure of the Mali Federation,[7] the old French Sudan (which became the République Soudanaise) took the name of 'Republic of Mali' on 22 September 1960.

From Independence to the Revolts

The events around the arrival to power of Modibo Keïta at the head of the First Republic thus signified a rupture with the tra-ditional political dynamics, where a change of power was real-ized by the use of force. Nevertheless, the regime of Modibo Keïta quickly lost its popularity and the RDA in fact imposed itself as the single party.

In 1968, a military *coup d'état* ended the First Republic and put in place Lieutenant Moussa Traoré at the head of a Comité Militaire de Libération Nationale (CMLN). Following the con-stitutional void produced by the military take-over, a new con-stitution was prepared in 1974; it announced (with a delay of five years before its application) the election of a head of state by universal suffrage, a national assembly and a single party

(Gaudio 1992: 111). On 2 June 1974, the Constitution was approved by referendum with a 99.71 per cent majority, but this was qualified as *farce électorale* by certain opponents (De Benoist 1989: 133). The single party, the Union Démocratique du Peuple Malien (UDPM), was created in 1979 with the aim of filling the political void which followed the military dictatorship. The Second Republic was thus characterized by the conquest of power through the force of arms and the control of this power by a military dictatorship, which did not hesitate to use force to maintain itself. The creation of the single party – and of mass organizations like the National Union of Malian Women (UNFM) and the National Union of Malian Youth (UNJM) – was aimed at keeping a large part of civil society at bay by dividing the country into separate 'compartments'.[8]

However, the military regime never succeeded in rooting out the opposition coming from political trade unionists and educational circles.[9] The school-year 1976–7 was marked by strikes by secondary school pupils and university students, the closure of schools the expulsion of a large number of students, and, following the funeral ceremony of Modibo Keïta on 18 May 1977, the regime proceeded to arrest many persons who had come to participate in the ceremony. During the school-year 1979–80 the students tried to organize the third congress of the National Union of Pupils and Students of Mali (UNEEM). The elected secretary of the UNEEM, Abdoul Karim Camara, nicknamed 'Cabral', was arrested, tortured and assassinated (De Benoist 1989; Diarrah 1996). Since that moment he has incarnated the symbol of school resistance to the dictatorship. But during the years 1970 to 1980, the opposition movements never succeeded in organizing themselves, nor in threatening the dictatorship.

From the Opposition to the Moussa Traoré Regime to the Transition Period

During the 1990s different movements formed opposing the military dictatorship (Bertrand 1992; CERDES n.d.; Fay 1995; Sidibé and Kester 1994). In March 1990 the single party celebrated its eleventh anniversary. On this occasion a conference on democracy was organized within the party during which militants opposed to the dictatorship could make their voices heard. The majority of the participants then spoke out in favour of multi-partyism (Diarrah 1996: 34). Following this, the Union Nationale des Travailleurs du Mali (UNTM), the central trade union that since the arrests of 1970 had collaborated with the regime,[10] opened the way for opposition to the military regime when during its central extraordinary meeting of 28 and 29 May 1990 it declared that:

> Considérant que le parti unique constitutionnel et institutionnel ne répond plus aux aspirations démocratiques du peuple malien ... le Conseil Central Extraordinaire rejette en bloc le dirigisme politique qui entrave le développement de la démocratie au Mali ... opte pour l'instauration du multipartisme et du pluralisme démocratique ...
>
> (CERDES n.d.: 33)

> [Considering that the single constitutional and institutional party no longer answers to the democratic aspirations of the Malian people ... the Extraordinary Central Council categorically rejects the political dirigism that thwarts the development of democracy in Mali ... and opts for the introduction of multiparty politics and democratic pluralism ...]

Thus a break was produced, as a result of which different groups representing civil society went into action: for instance, the Malian Bar (4 Aug. 1990) and a group of citizens who wrote an open letter to the President, which was published in the bi-monthly independent magazine *Les Echos* (7 Aug. 1997).[11]

Following these initiatives, the opposition movement was reinforced and started to organize itself through the creation of democratic associations. On 15 October 1990 the Association de la Jeunesse pour la Démocratie et le Progrès (AJDP) was set up, followed by the Comité National d'Initiative Démocratique (CNID) and the Alliance pour la Démocratie et le Progrès (ADEMA). Youths formed their own associations, like the Association des Elèves et des Etudiants du Mali, l'Association des Diplomés Initiateurs et Demandeurs d'Emploi (ADIDE), and the Jeunesse Libre et Démocratique (JLD). These youth associations would succeed in mobilizing Malian youth, which would form the large majority of the masses of demonstrators against the dictatorship.

From January to March 1991, peaceful gatherings and demonstrations followed one upon the other. During a peaceful march organized on 22 March that year, the army fired on the demonstrators, which then led to five days of violent disturbances. On 26 March 1991, the regime of President Moussa Traoré was overthrown by a group of military led by Lt.-Col. Amadou Toumani Touré. The military installed a Committee of National Reconciliation (CRN) and subsequently, after discussions between the CNR and the Comité de Coordination des Associations et des Organizations Démocratiques (CCAOD), a *Comité Transitoire de Salut du Peuple* (CTSP) was formed, composed of ten representatives of the armed and security forces and of fifteen representatives of the CCAOD. Among the representatives of the CCAOD one notes the prime place accorded to the youth associations (four out of fifteen),[12] which indicates the recognition given to those that rebelled against the dictatorship. One also notes the place occupied by two representatives of resistance movements, which also indicates the importance of armed movements that struggled against the regime of Moussa Traoré.[13] The CTSP then formed a provisional government, led by Mamadou Toumani Touré.

The Transition

From 26 March 1991 to 8 June 1992 the Transitional Government took charge of preparing elections and of managing current affairs. For many authors this period is characterized by a rather slack treatment of existing national problems (CERDES n.d.: 120). Nevertheless, the transitional authorities showed good sense in their refusal – or inability – to effect a systematic witch-hunt, for example, on the political leaders of the old regime and their associates. On the other hand, they were confronted with many claims, often stated in an aggressive or violent manner. Indeed, as Sidibé and Kester noted (1994: 70):

> Sur le plan social, la montée extraordinaire des revendications catégorielles et le développement sans précédent de la violence comme moyen de revendication sont devenus un phénomène majeur, curieusement au moment même où le dialogue politique et social est devenu possible. Ainsi, dès les lendemains de l'installation des autorités de la transition, des mouvements violents s'enclenchent dans le pays.

[In the social domain, the extraordinary increase of categorial demands and the unprecedented development of violence as a means to make demands have become a major phenomenon, strangely enough at the very moment that political and social dialogue became possible. Therefore, only days after the installation of the transitional authorities, violent movements have thrown themselves into gear in the country.]

This attitude may appear all the more paradoxical, as the first demonstrations of opponents to the dictatorship were peaceful and as this opposition was also directed against corruption as well as in favour of the establishment of a new kind of political relations. With the arrival of the CTSP (and later of the Third Republic), violence emanating from civil society in fact replaces that of the state. This appropriation of violence by civil society as a mode of expression of relations of power but also as a force regulating social order[14] imposed itself very quickly and has remained a significant problem until today.

THE 1992 ELECTIONS

Conditions of the Electoral Process

As was the case in a majority of Francophone African countries, a National Conference was organized (held from 29 July to 12 August 1991).[15] In this framework, the setting up of political structures of the new regime, the choice of election procedures, and the establishment of an election calendar were prepared. It was also during this national conference that a new Constitution inaugurating the Third Republic was prepared. This Constitution accords an important place to human rights, as indicated by the substantial number of articles relating to the rights of the human person.[16] The Constitution also defines the attributes of the eight institutions of the republic.[17]

Then a period of intense electoral activity followed which permitted the consolidation of these new institutions. During this period the Mali electorate also had to go to the ballot boxes no less than six times between 12 January 1992 and 26 April 1992, be it for the constitutional referendum of 12 January, the municipal election of 19 January, the legislative elections (in one or two rounds) on 23 February and on 9 March, and the presidential elections in two rounds on 12 April and 26 April 1992 (CERDES n.d.: 52). These elections were organized by the Secretariat of State for Institutional Reforms.[18] A commission for 'equal access to state media' was also created (CERDES n.d.: 53), and several radio and television transmissions allowed candidates to present their programmes and to engage in political debate.

The entire electoral process was supervised or witnessed by about forty *foreign observers* (originating from different countries or belonging to different organizations) 'qui ont unanimement reconnu que les élections maliennes ont été honnêtes et transparantes' (who have unanimously admitted that the Malian elections have been honest and transparent) (CERDES n.d.: 53). However, a reading of Malian press articles that appeared during the elections seems to point only to a feeble role played by these foreign observers. The press gave much more attention to things like the costs of the organization of the elections and the lack of financial independence that was related to it.

Indeed, without the financial aid of donor-countries or international organizations the Malian elections could not have been held.[19] The fear of too much dependence on the goodwill of foreign countries or of being victim of too much interference in political matters is not without grounds. How indeed can a democratic state invent and acquire its own values in such a framework of external assistance?

The Political Parties

The first political parties emerged in the process of transformation of democratic associations created in 1990 (e.g., the ADEMA Association turned itself into a political party and became the ADEMA-Parti Africain pour la Solidarité et la Justice (ADEMA-PASJ)) during its extraordinary general assembly of 26–7 April 1991).

From a situation of institutionalized mono-partyism Mali has quickly become familiar with a situation where the high number of new parties renders political debate near impossible. As Monique Bertrand writes (1992: 13):

Dès l'instauration du multipartisme par l'ordonnance no. 2 du CTSP, la création et la réapparition inflationniste de 3 partis devenus 4 en un mois, puis 45 à l'issue de la Conférence nationale, montre le risque réel de voir le jeu politique s'embourber dans des dérapages personnels et des coalitions précaires.

[Since the installation of multiparty politics under Ordinance no. 2 of the CTSP, the creation and inflationary reappearance of parties becoming 4 within one month, and then 45 in the wake of the National Conference, shows the real risk of seeing the political game being bogged down by personal lapses and precarious coalitions.]

At the time of the elections of 1992 there were 48 parties. Of these 48 official parties, 24 participated in the municipal elections, 22 in the first round of the legislative elections, 9 in the second round, while 10 were represented in the National Assembly.

The creation of parties was done on the basis of recuperating part of the former cadres of the former single party on the one hand, and on systematic subdividing of the first parties created on the other. The high number of political parties as well as the conditions of their creation reinforced the perception of an absence of criteria of demarcation between these different parties: far from being constituted on the basis of societal projects, their foundation seems to be tied to personal interests which the arrival of democracy has permitted to be expressed.[20] The return of one-quarter of the deputies from the old National Assembly, presenting themselves in the first round of the legislative elections in seven parties that were prepared to field them, reveals old, non-transparent patterns of patronage or clienteles, and induced a lack of interest among a large part of the voters, who therefore refrained from casting their vote.

The Weak Participation of Voters

The weak participation is explained by various factors, like difficulty of the organization of the elections themselves or the war situation in the North of Mali (where the Touareg rebellion did not permit voters to go to the ballot box either for reasons of lack of security or because of the fact that a part of the Touareg population had left the area to seek refuge in camps in Mauritania, Algeria and Burkina Faso). However, the disaffection of the voters, which rapidly increased from one election to the next, cannot simply be explained by lack of security or by the large number of elections. The decrease of participation in the elections also reveals deep scepticism among the voters towards a political class that seemed to continue embroiling itself in personal quarrels.

Indeed, only the elections of the referendum saw a rate of participation higher than 40 per cent (see Table 10.1). This 'abstract election' (a vote in favour of a text and not in favour of an individual), the purpose of which seemed clear and consensual, presented a project which concerned the 'common good', in contrast to those which followed and where the personal ambitions of politicians were so exacerbated. In addition, one should recall that the popular uprising against the military dictatorship in the first place expressed a wide consensus against corruption. This unity of purpose was primarily constructed in the name of *kokaje*. This Bambara term *kokaje* has been translated as 'transparency': in the sense that the demonstrators demanded that the judicial authorities would persecute politicians in power for 'economic crimes' (graft, incompetence, and the like) or 'blood crimes' (assassinations) that they had committed while in office. The term *kokaje* is a relatively strong one because it includes implicit references to the idea of 'pollution', of 'dirt'

Table 10.1   Participation of voters in the elections of 1992 (%)

Elections	Date of elections	Percentage of participation
Referendum	12 January 1992	43.58
Municipal elections	19 January 1992	32.10
Legislative elections (1st round)	23 February 1992	22.31
Legislative elections (2nd round)	9 March 1992	20.50
Presidential elections (1st round)	12 April 1992	23.59
Presidential elections (1st round)	26 April 1992	20.87

Source: CERDES n.d.; Diarrah 1996.

which has to be eliminated. Literally it means 'to wash in order to clean', and is thus linked to the idea of 'purification'.

During and after these elections, the feeling of having been deceived among a large part of the Malian people was great. One reason was that of the big delays in the judicial process for judging these crimes committed, another was the resentment to the practices of opportunism and personal enrichment by the new politicians.

Results

Results of the elections for the referendum gave 98.35 per cent yes to the Constitution against 0.78 per cent no. The Constitution of the Third Republic has thus been accepted unequivocally, all the more so since the rate of participation, although low, remains one of the best that the Third Republic has seen until today.

The municipal elections were the first where the parties entered the contest. Nevertheless, more than half of the newly declared parties did not participate in these elections. In addition, the results of these municipal elections seem to indicate that only three parties (ADEMA-PASJ, US-RDA and CNID-FYT) had a measure of support across the entire country, while the other parties did not really succeed in asserting themselves on the national level. A total of 751 municipal councillors were elected (for a period of four years) in 21 *communes* (see Table 10.2).

In the first round of the legislative elections, 15 deputies were elected (of which 10 from ADEMA). Overall, 116 deputies (76 from ADEMA) were elected for a period of five years. ADEMA thus disposed of the absolute majority in the National Assembly.

In the presidential elections, nine candidates emerging from the principal representative parties (with the exception of one independent candidate) were on the list (see Table 10.3). After the first round, only two candidates remained in the race: Alpha Oumar Konaré of ADEMA and Tiéloulé Konaté of US-RDA. It has to be noted that the divisions within the US-RDA led to their presentation of two candidates, which permitted Alpha Oumar Konaré to impose himself very easily after the first round. In the second round he was elected President of the

Table 10.2   Results of the municipal and legislative elections of 1992 according to number of elected candidates

Political parties	Municipal	Legislative 1st round	Legislative 2nd round	Total of Legislative
ADEMA-PASJ*	214	10	66	76
US-RDA	130	1	7	8
CNID	96	1	8	9
UDD	63	0	0	4
RDP	61	0	4	4
UFD	50			
PDP	40	2	0	2
PSP	29			
UFDP	24	0	3	3
RDT	11	0	3	3
PMD	09	0	6	6
PEI	06			
PUDP	05			
PDJ	04			
PDT	04			
RJP	02			
PPS	01			
PMPS	01			
UDS	01			
UMADD	00	1	0	1
TOTAL	751	15	101	116

* In **bold**: parties represented in the National Assembly.
Source: CERDES, n.d.: 60, 81, 84.

Table 10.3   Results obtained in the presidential elections (first and second rounds) of 1992 (%)

Names of candidates and parties	Presidential (1st round)	Presidential (2nd round)
Alpha O. KONARÉ (ADEMA-PASJ)	44.95 per cent	69.01 per cent
Tiéloulé KONATÉ (US-RDA)	14.51 per cent	30.99 per cent
Mountaga TALL (CNID-FYT)	11.41 per cent	
Almamy SYLLA	9.44 per cent	
Baba Akhib HAÏDARA (US-RDA)	7.37 per cent	
Idrissa TRAORÉ (PDP)	4.10 per cent	
Amadou NIAGANDOU (RDT)	4.01 per cent	
Mamadou DIABY (PUDP)	2.16 per cent	
Demba DIALLO (UFD)	2.04 per cent	

Source: CERDES, n.d.: 100–1.

Republic (for five years), with a very high score of 69.01 per cent.

However, even if the predominance of ADEMA tended to be confirmed from the municipal up to the presidential elections, the popular adhesion thus expressed did not lead to or allow for a post-electoral 'social peace' in the country.

THE YEARS 1992–7: DIFFICULTIES IN THE SOCIAL MANAGEMENT OF DEMOCRACY

Instead of renouncing violent means and practices in order to realize their aims, the different opposition movements that had fought together against the military dictatorship (and to which various new corporate groups had aligned themselves) have pursued their struggle with the aim of getting – often extraordinary – advantages and benefits from the state.

The demands of various sectors in society, the conflict in northern Mali and the school crisis tended to relentlessly destabilize the newly elected regime (Bertrand 1992; CERDES n.d.; Fay 1995; Sidibé and Kester 1994) and create a sense of the absence of any state power. This had a very harmful effect on representations of 'democracy' that Malian society was trying to develop. The impossibility of managing all the social demands and the failure of the governmental coalitions created a structural political crisis. Between 8 June 1992 and 15 February 1994 Mali saw three prime ministers, supported by different alliances (like that of the coalition of the US-RDA, the UFD, the RDT, and after the crisis of 1993 a new and enlarged coalition – from April 1993 to February 1994 – with six parties, among which the CNID-FYT, which had until then been in opposition).

Finally, these different coalitions would neither have permitted a social peace nor a restoration of state authority: the relations between state and the different social groups that had emerged from civil society continued to be marked by violence. The arrival of Ibrahim Boubacar Keïta as Prime Minister on 4 February 1994, however, began a new period of government stability. From that date, the ADEMA-PASJ ruled alone, while the other parties joined the opposition. The I.B. Keïta government also succeeded in dealing with certain issues (for example, the conflict in the North, the school crisis, and economic recovery). Nevertheless, the *political* crisis persisted, and on 3 March 1997 the President of the Republic, faced with the difficulties that had emerged in the course of preparations for the legislative, presidential and municipal elections of 1997, dissolved the National Assembly.

The Elections of 1997

The vote in the National Assembly for the Electoral Law (8 January 1997) was to reinforce the judicial framework for elections. This law replaced the decree of the CTSP (Comité Transitoire de Salut du Peuple, see above) of 10 October 1991 which had contained the electoral code. The organization and the management of referendums and elections were from then on to be in the hands of a Commission Électorale Nationale Indépendante (CENI),[21] composed of 30 members, 8 of whom were appointed by the government, 7 by the parties of the parliamentary majority, 7 by the opposition parties and 8 by the various associations.[22]

However, despite the judicial structure put in place, the 1997 elections took place in a sphere of utmost confusion and in a tense climate where fears of a violent outbreaks were often expressed. The first and principal problem that came up during the preparation of the elections was that of the establishment of an electoral register. The problems connected to the registration of voters[23] can be explained by the embryonic civil registration in Mali – the population census data were unreliable and a part of the archives of the civil register was burned during the revolts of 1991. The difficulties of setting up an automated electoral register in poor material conditions (no qualified personnel, numerous electricity cuts) remind us that Malian democracy had to construct itself in a very unfavourable economic and financial environment. At the same time, the establishment of an electoral register was entrusted to a *private* company that proved itself incapable of correctly carrying out that task, which suggests that a state 'retreating' from public life is not really compatible with a process of democracy.

The difficulties coming up in the preparation of these elections led to several delays in fixing the election date. The results of the first round of the legislative elections (13 April 1997), which had proceeded in a most confusing manner, were annulled by the Constitutional Court. These elections were rescheduled to 3 July 1997 for the first round and to 20 July for the second round. The first round of the presidential elections, initially foreseen for 4 May 1997, was delayed until 11 May 1997.

The conduct of the electoral campaigns was marked by utter disregard of chapter VIII of the 1997 Electoral Law (called '*De la Campagne Électorale*'). At least four articles of the twelve in this chapter were violated with impunity, especially by the ADEMA-PASJ. The means used by the three principal parties to 'persuade' the voters also consolidated both clientelistic relations as well as the existing negative image of politicians among the populace. The organization of concerts and demonstrations, the funding of theatre groups (*L'Observateur*, 1997), the distribution of presents and gifts (kola nuts, money for the men, cloths for the women, tea, sugar, T-shirts, balloons for children) went to reinforce the image that power was to be seen in terms 'dividing the cake', because nobody was fooled as to the source of this ostentatious funding, especially the considerable sums that benefited the ADEMA-PASJ. The lack of respect for the Electoral Law of January 1997 as well as the absence of regulations for the funding of parties did not leave any real chance for the opposition. This partly explains their choice in favour of boycott and the reluctance to resort to violent means in order to ensure a political turn-around.

As in the elections of 1992, voter participation remained low: 21.6 per cent of the voters came to the first round of the legislative elections and 28.41 per cent to the presidential elections (see *La Lanterne*, 26 May 1997). Following the boycott by all the opposition parties, Alpha Oumar Konaré was re-elected President of the Republic right in the first round. In the first round of the legislative elections, 123 candidates were elected on a total of 147 seats. The second round, held on 3 August 1997, sealed the massive victory of the ADEMA-PASJ but against the background of the indifference of the majority of Malians, who no longer felt involved in elections which for them seemed to be linked more than ever to the interests of the people in power. The municipal elections, originally foreseen for June 1997 but delayed several times due to disagreements between the government and the opposition, were scheduled for April 1998. Special 'delegations', whose mandate had to be extended several times, were installed to replace the mayors and the municipal councillors. The last such extension was to be valid up to 31 March 1998, just before the upcoming municipal elections.[24]

ELECTIONS AND DEMOCRACY ARE CONFRONTED WITH THE 'POLITICAL CULTURE' OF MALI

On Elections without the Support of Western Codes

In a country where more than 80 per cent of the population is illiterate, the weak mastery of Western-derived socio-cultural 'codes' (for example, the 'literacy code', or the 'bureaucratic code': an attitude and a state of mind implying a different way of dealing with other people) emerges as a certain handicap, if one assumes, as Western donor-countries usually do, that 'democracy' should proceed always in terms of models and conditions known from the Western experience (this is an unrealistic assumption). Indeed every electoral process in this sense seems to rest on a bureaucratic infrastructure that presupposes – at least – statistical knowledge of the population (for the establishment of voters' lists and voting cards), productive capacities (the actual production of the electoral material: indelible ink, ballot papers, envelopes, boxes for secret voting), organizational capacities (distribution of the material, transport of the ballot boxes, control of the voting procedure itself, the counting), as well as adequate financial means.

In Mali, the problem posed by, for instance, the establishing of voters' lists is tied to a situation of a weakly performing and partly corrupt administration on the one hand, and to the popular perceptions of administrative paper-work and documents in general on the other. In an article on the difficulties encountered by the cadres of the Ministry of Secondary and Higher Education in deciding the allocation of allowances and scholarships to students, Diawara (1997) has shown the problems of making the administration properly function in a situation where false civil registration papers[25] – obtained by patronage and protection or by bribing – proliferate. These systematic administrative forgeries reveal that subverting the 'bureaucratic code' (however understandable perhaps against background factors like the national scarcity of places, jobs and opportunities), still remains the norm in Mali. The official paper (identity card, diploma, civil register file) has no intrinsic value: it is at best seen as a necessity, or more often as a means to obtain some advantage. This means or instrument can therefore be fabricated, transformed, sold or lent.

Connections with State Power, or 'Dividing the Cake'

As Sidibé and Kester (1994: 72–3) have said:

La grande masse des personnes qui descendaient dans la rue l'ont fait en réaction à la mauvaise gestion, au népotisme, aux détournements des deniers publics. En un mot, ils se battaient pour la moralisation de la vie publique ... Or loin de disparaître, la corruption, le népotisme et le gaspillage se développent comme par le passé.

[The great mass of persons that went out into the streets did so in response to bad governance, nepotism, and embezzlement of public funds. In one word, they fought for improving the morality of public life ... Well, far from disappearing, corruption, nepotism and squandering developed into what they were like in the past.]

Indeed, one could say that following the unsuccessful imposition of *kokaje* (see above), that is, of combating corruption and idleness and incompetence, and faced with the failure of countervailing forces asserting themselves to guarantee political integrity, there has been a quick turn toward the general demand that 'everybody should have the right to such idleness and profiteering'. From then on, the connection to political power has indeed been perceived, as President Alpha Oumar Konaré said in an interview with *Le Malien* (cited in Diawara 1994: 22), as 'getting a slice of the cake'.

In such conditions, democracy is not seen as a system which permits the free choice of representatives, or the possibility to check them and hold them accountable, but simply as a system that can offer access to state benefits or to profits from the yields of international aid. This is an often diagnosed trait in African 'neo-patrimonial' systems.

The democratic process thus is being perceived primarily as a *process of the democratization of access to the financial resources* either of

the state or of foreign aid. Hence one could ask if the proliferation of civic associations (the number of which has grown from
some 300 to more than 4,000 in a spate of four years), as re-
peatedly testified by international observers,[26] is not in fact in
the majority of cases merely a practical expression of the desire
to appropriate and control the ongoing flow of international aid.
Under the guise of a 'pseudo-culture' of community concern,
and profiting from the lack of interest of the donor-countries
for the *state institutions*, members of the new civic organizations
capture a large part of the funding that used to be accorded to
the state bureaucracy, although in many cases their practices
are not so much different from that of idling and incompetent
state administration. Democracy has thus become a tool for
making deals, either with the West or with the Malian masses.[27]
It is a source of income and has turned into an instrument for
the generation of money, as in the past was the case with 'rural
development' or the big droughts, and today with dominant
themes like AIDS, decentralization or the condition of women.

But this tenacious struggle centred on the obtaining of resources chiefly coming from international aid ultimately cannot
take place without recourse to the use of force (or at least the
threat thereof). In fact, as the 'school crisis' has shown (see
above), resorting to the use of force in order to be able to appropriate the funds is being *legitimized*: among the different corporate groups that were able to express their demands in the
years 1991 to 1994, the higher education students and secondary school pupils seem to have succeeded best in maintaining pressure on the government. Since the political transition,
the 'school crisis', as it is known in Mali, has not ceased to
disturb the social and political scene of the country. The struggles of the pupils and students had thus led to a circa 50 per
cent increase of the money for student allowances in 1991 and
of 75 per cent in 1994, resulting in a rise from 180,000 francs
CFA per year in 1978 to 250,000 per year in 1991 and to 315,000
in 1992. Today, almost 50 per cent of the state budget for higher
education goes to allowances and scholarships. The standard of
living of students thus supported is in fact higher than that of
an average manual labourer or worker. If one interprets the
struggle of the secondary school pupils and students as a means
to capture part of the state's resources or the yields of international aid, this fact is not in any way seen as scandalous by the

parties involved, because indeed the allowance does not permit them an ostentatious life-style or even an accumulation of money. Also, under their noses the big villas or 'castles'[28] continue to be constructed, those built in the 1990s for projects on AIDS (and others funded from outside) following the ones built in the time of the great drought of the 1970s and 1980s. Obviously, the impact of foreign funding derives mainly from the present relationship between countries in the 'North' and 'South', not always with positive effects. The inauguration of a more democratic system in Mali did not stimulate any substantial increase in the flow of aid funds, despite the promises of Western countries. Such funding often remains conditioned by traditional geopolitical interests, and is not much influenced by new democratic credentials gained by those countries.[29]

PROSPECTS

Since the events of 1991, elections have been organized in Mali in 1992 and in 1997. The balance is far from wholly negative, even considering that the participation in the elections has remained low (about one-quarter of the electorate having voted), and even if the opposition boycott has called into question the consensual and regulating function of the electoral process.

The appeal from certain members of the opposition to violence or to revolt has not resonated at all among the larger part of the Malian population, which for the time being prefers an imperfect kind of democracy to a situation of civil war. Also, the armed forces have not tried to intervene and 'settle' the political crisis. But is all this sufficient to assume that the democratic process is consolidating itself?

First of all, it is clear that certain gains are inalienable – such as press freedom and private radio (Keïta 1992, 1995), or the laying of the foundations, however small, for judicial and administrative reform – even if the expected overhaul of the public administration has yet hardly begun. The commitment of the various authorities in the Malian Third Republic to the development of education (despite the discouraging influence of donor-countries) shows the desire to reconstitute ideological foundations for the birth of a new nation-state. Success of the Third Republic in this respect is clearly visible in the 'educational explosion' witnessed since the early 1990s (see Lange and Gisselbrecht 1998). It is certainly one of the rare domains where a consensus between the state and the population has been able to assert itself. This strong demand for education as seen today in fact shows the effectiveness of appealing to the right to education to 'get part of the cake' (see above). But it may also have the social effect of a wider acceptance of the 'literacy code' (and a prelude to integration into the bureaucratic code). If one considers the refusal to attend school was often the expression of opposition to the state, then the active involvement in or commitment to education might be interpreted as a renaissance of a certain commitment from the side of (civil) society to the nation-state (Lange 1987, 1991). However, opposition to the state is also expressed without reserve and without ambiguity in the rather obstinate refusal of people to pay taxes (according to certain experts the actual rate of recovery of taxes has not been more than 10 per cent). Civil disobedience of this kind has often been highlighted without the causes always clearly identified. A weak administrative structure giving people the opportunity to duck payments is one of them, but perhaps more important is the perception that 'everybody' is subverting the law in this respect, including the country's leaders. This contributes to disobedience becoming the norm.

In the economic domain, the results achieved since the beginning of democratization are undeniable. Three sectors of the economy – gold, cotton and livestock – have seen an unprecedented expansion that has permitted Mali to become one of the prime exporting countries of these goods in Africa (see *Jeune Afrique*, 1–7 Oct. 1997) and to dispose of its own resources – certainly insufficient, but making it less dependent on foreign donors. The repair and development of infrastructure (roads, schools) is also noticeable, after several decades of neglect. But the inauguration of a system of democracy has, above all, allowed the well-to-do classes – those who have wealth and possessions, and the entrepreneurs – to make themselves even more comfortable. One may cite the example of the land problem in the capital Bamako, where the only guaranteed real-estate operations are those by private firms and are only destined for the most well-off classes, thus leaving the less fortunate mass of the population in the care of (often corrupt) civil administrators when buying property, and then with often highly contested legal title. Finally, the problem of unemployment (especially among youth) has hardly been solved either.

The essential problems that remain are either of bureaucratic or political origin, and are found today in the practices of corruption and clientelism, obscure party funding, and in what can be seen as their corollary: the recourse of violence by certain groups in society. In addition, the absence of independence or autonomy in public administration contributes to articulate relations of clientelism. Before the start of democratization, corruption was considered as bound up with the political system of the dictatorship – the right of the 'strong' to privileges and favours from the dominated. Between 1991 and 1997, these relationships, however, have far from disappeared. As President Alpha Oumar Konaré himself concluded, the absence of a class of politically responsible people proposing a real societal project creates a problem. The point is, how can the emergence of such a new political class be realized in a clientelistic context which is maintained by both the government (by giving administrative positions to loyalists) and by the ADEMA-PASJ Party (by distributing 'favours' and gifts)?

In this respect, when people perceive the relations with those in power as allowing a 'sharing of the cake' (a zero-sum game), this can only breed violent protest, because, on the one hand, the resources essentially come from international aid and are less and less controlled directly by the state apparatus, and, on the other, their distribution will always be a source of conflict in the absence of clear rules of appropriation. It is here that the question as to the relation between the democratic system and the role of the state comes in.

Two phenomena are conjoined to accelerate the 'retreat of the state' (or *désétatisation*): first, the continued incompetence and corruption of the administrative services inherited from the dictatorship; second, the ultra-liberalism of the donor-countries which, instead of aiding the restoration of a public service and a bureaucracy necessary to institute a state with a rule of law (the *Rechtstaat*), prefer to fund the private sector – about which nothing assures us that it will function on relationships any different or any better that those decried in the state administration. The deficit of state institutionalization, that centrifugal tendencies could reinforce, constitutes a real risk of re-emergence of social crises and national or local revolts. One may ask: can social, economic and political development indeed be realized in the absence of state regulation? In the transition period after the fall of the Traoré dictatorship, the Comité Transitoire de Salut du Peuple (CTSP), in its statement of 5 April 1991, mentioned among its first aims: 'la restauration du crédit et de l'autorité de l'État' (the restoration of the credibility and authority of the state) (CERDES n.d.: 44); but without the state having been *rethought* or redefined, either in its foundations or in its relations with civil society. Until now, the relationships between power and the ensemble of institutions (familial, traditional or of the state) have too often remained under the governance of the bonds of clientelism, whereby the one who 'possesses power' can only retain it by buying allegiance from those s/he dominates.

How to pass from a clientelistic state with systematic privileging (where 'legitimacy' is acquired, on the one hand, by the issuing of favours that can be distributed by the grace of the yields of corruption or of fringe benefits, and on the other hand, by tolerating transgressions of the law), to a bureaucratic rule-of-law state? The distribution of favours and the tolerating of transgressions (as a payment for allegiance to the existing power structure) form the basis of the reproduction of the clientelistic state and ensure the continued domination of the elites in place. For numerous Malians the ADEMA-PASJ today constitutes the central agent whereby this type of relationship is being forged and acted out. In today's conditions also, the electoral process, far from having facilitated the transition of a clientelistic state to a rule-of-law state, has rather opened up a *new* domain of clientelistic enterprise. One may be justified in thinking that at least as long as the Electoral Law of January 1997 is not applied and the funding of political parties is not strictly regulated by the law, the electoral process will never be able to really influence existing power relations nor strengthen the process of democratization in Mali.

It is in this sense that the role of external, foreign observers, which up to now was largely limited to monitoring/evaluating the conditions of exercise of the right to vote, can appear as without any real influence on the democratization process in the country. It is also true that certain observers from Western countries (like those from France), where members of the political class are allegedly involved in affairs of illicit funding of political parties, are hardly in a position either to condemn the above-mentioned practices or to propose solutions for them – which they have not been able to find in order to sanitize political life in their own countries. Is not a kind of consensus – based on common interests – being constructed between African leaders and Western leaders, ready to accommodate regular and 'free' elections which have no real political stakes, lack financial transparency on party finances and electoral campaigns, and which also are increasingly held in the absence of voters?

NOTES

1. Translation from French by J. Abbink.
2. Concerning Macina, see Fay 1997.
3. On the basis of functional characteristics, the colonial empire was hardly different from the African empires.
4. 'Soudanais' referred to the French West Africa region, called the French Sudan.
5. The principal elections have been: the legislative elections of 1945, the referendum of 1946, the legislative elections of 1946, a new referendum of 1946, the legislative elections of 1951, the territorial elections of 1952, the legislative elections of 1956, the territorial elections of 1957, and the referendum of 1958. This was a period of intense political activity of the Sudanese elite, all the more so because of the fact that certain elected French-Sudanese occupied positions in different French administrations (in particular Hamadoun Dicko and Modibo Keïta), and remains unique in the history of Mali up to the elections of 1992. In that year, a new process of democratization began.
6. After having hosted the Constituent Congress of the RDA, the city of Bamako would frequently be the meeting place of African politicians.
7. Which originally included Dahomey, Upper Volta, Senegal and the Sudan and subsequently, after the seceding of Dahomey and Upper Volta, only Senegal and the Sudan. Less than two months after the transfer of administrative power from the French *communauté* to the federation, the two countries split. On the Mali federation, see Ndiaye 1980.
8. According to Fay (1995: 20): 'Le parti est représenté aux niveaux des villages (comités), de l'arrondissement (sous-section), du cercle (section) et au niveau national (Bureau exécutif central, BEC). (La région, le cercle et l'arrondissement sont des découpages administratifs emboîtés, partiellement repris de l'administration coloniale. Ils sont dirigés respectivement par un gouverneur, un commandant de cercle et un chef d'arrondissement).' [The party is represented on the level of

villages (committees), of civil districts (subsection), of 'cercle' (section), and on the national level (the Executive Central Bureau, BEC). (The region, the 'cercle' and the civil districts are 'encased' administrative divisions, partly taken over from the colonial administration. They are led by, respectively, a governor, a commander of the 'cercle' and a district chief.]

9. After the arrest of numerous politicians since 1968 the military proceeded to detain elected members of the bureau of the National Union of Malian Workers (UNTM) in 1970. On the opposition movements to the military regime and the repression to which they fell victim, see Diarrah 1996: 11–29.

10. As noted by O.O. Sidibé in 1997, this collaboration, called 'responsible participation' and adopted by the UNTM during its 1974 congress, encountered opposition from the workers. In fact, after this congress the trade union became co-opted by the single party.

11. The creation of the bi-monthly *Les Echos* on 17 March 1989 permitted the critical discussion of the state monopoly of the press. Its creation followed the foundation of the cultural magazine *Jamana* in 1983 and subsequently the cooperative of the same name set up by Alpha Oumar Konaré. In December 1989 a new publication called *La Roue* saw the light, followed in 1990 by two others, *Cauris* and *L'Aurore*. In contrast with many other African countries the emergence of the free press in Mali has *preceded* the revolts and the written press has been able to play an important role in the struggle against the dictatorship.

12. On a total of 15 representatives, 3 were of the UNTN, 2 of the ADEMA, 2 of the CNID, 2 of the Malian Human Rights Association (AMDH), one of the AEEN, one of the EJDP, one of the ADEIDE, one of the JLD, one of the Mouvement Populaire de l'Azaouad (MPA) and one of the Front Islamique Arabe de l'Azaouad (FIAA) (CERDES n.d.: 38–9).

13. Even if this fact is today systematically obscured by Malian authors, as if the clear role of the Touareg rebellion in the process of weakening the military dictatorship should be effaced from official history.

14. On the subject of lynching of petty criminals and of the 'right of plunder' and the like, see Fay 1995.

15. See *Le Messager Africain*, no. 001, April/May/June 1996.

16. That is, 20 articles out of the 24 of the first section 'Des Droits et des Devoirs de Personne humaine' of the Constitution (République du Mali 1997: 2).

17. These institutions are: the President of the Republic, the Government, the National Assembly, the Supreme Court, the Constitutional Court, the High Court of Justice, the High Council of Territorial Collectivities, and the Economic, Social and Cultural Council. The Malian Constitution thus strongly resembles the French one.

18. This secretariat was created by the CTSP on 26 Aug. 1991.

19. The total sum of international aid towards financing the elections amounted to 1,901,736,320 francs CFA. Among the most important donors one finds the Federal Republic of Germany (300 million francs CFA), the United States (297 million francs CFA), France (250 million francs CFA), and the UNDP (160 million francs CFA) (CERDES n.d.: 53).

20. In view of this multiplication, the state relinquished any funding of parties, among other reasons suspecting that these new creations were considered to be only motivated by the prospect of state funding (*L'Aurore*, 3 Dec. 1991).
21. Article 3 of the Law no. 97-001-/AN-RM.
22. See article 4 of the above law.
23. The number of voters registered on the voters' lists has varied: for the referendum of 12 Jan. 1992 there were 5,233,432 voters; for the legislative elections (first round) of 23 Jan. 1992: 4,780,476; for the first round of presidential elections of 12 March 1992: 5,106,466, for the second round of presidential elections of 26 April 1992: 4,902,603, and for the presidential elections of 11 May 1997: 5,428,256 voters.
24. The municipal elections in the urban regions were planned for 21 June 1998; those in the rural regions for 19 Nov. 1998.
25. For example, the practice of forging civil register papers like a death certificate for one's father (while he is still among the living) by a student: this permits him/her to get a state allowance.
26. See the special section on Mali in *Le Monde Diplomatique* of May 1997.
27. In a survey carried out among teachers in the whole of Mali, the majority of the respondents, when asked about the level of financial support they received, answered that they could not make ends meet with their salary. They noted that most other functionaries (for instance, customs officials, policemen, various administrators) could guarantee themselves their means of existence thanks to their 'additional income'. Far from condemning what we could consider as corruption or embezzlement of public funds, some of the respondents demanded that the teachers get premiums in view of their being handicapped in obtaining additional funds.
28. 'Chateaux': the term designates the luxurious villas constructed by politicians or development project people, either legally (thanks to high *per diem*s or consultancies where foreign currency is earned), or illegally (people appropriating money or material means from state funds meant for the population as a whole). This is not unique to Mali.
29. See, on French assistance, the report of the Observatoire Permanent de la Coopération Française (1997).

REFERENCES

Assemblée Nationale, 1996. *L'Assemblée Nationale. 1ère Législature de la IIIème République* (Bamako: Société Malienne d'Edition).

Benoist, J.R. de, 1989. *Le Mali* (Paris: L'Harmattan).

Bertrand, M. 1992. 'Un An de Transition Politique: de la Révolte à la Troisième République', *Politique Africaine* 47: 9–22.

CERDES, Coalition mondiale pour l'Afrique and Africa Leadership Forum, n.d. *Le Processus Démocratique Malien de 1960 à nos Jours* (Bamako: Editions Donniya).

Diarrah S.M.T. 1996. *Le Mouvement Démocratique Malien. L'Itinéraire de l'ADEMA-PASJ. Origine et Parcours* (Bamako: Graphique Industrie SA).

Diawara, C. 1997. 'Rentrée 97. Bourses: la Foire aux Faussaires', *L'Essor* (weekly) no. 2048, Sat. 18 and Sun. 19 Oct.

Diawara, D. (texts and documents collected and edited by), 1994. *Les Grands Textes de la Pratique Institutionnelle de la IIIème République* (Bamako: Société Malienne d'Edition).

Fay, C., 1995. 'La Démocratie au Mali, ou le Pouvoir en Pâture', *Cahiers d'Etudes Africaines* 35(1), no. 137: 19–53.

——. 1997. 'Les Derniers seront les Premiers: Peuplements et Pouvoirs Mandingues et Peuls au Maasina (Mali)', in M. de Bruijn and H. van Dijk (eds), *Peuls et Mandingues. Dialectique des Constructions Identitaires* (Paris: Karthala), pp. 165–91.

Gaudio, A. 1992. *Le Mali* (Paris: Karthala, 2nd edn).

Keïta, M.K. 1992. 'Réflexion sur la Presse Ecrite', *Politique Africaine* 47: 79–90.

——. 1995. *La Presse Écrite au Mali* (Bamako: Institut Panos-Bamako).

Lange, M.-F. 1987. 'Le Refus de l'Ecole: Pouvoir d'une Société Civile Bloquée?', *Politique Africaine* 27: 74–86.

——. 1991. 'Systèmes Scolaires et Développement: Discours et Pratiques', *Politique Africaine* 43: 105–21.

—— and O. Gisselbrecht, 1998. 'L'Evolution de la Scolarisation', in P. Bocquier and T. Diarra (eds), *La Population au Mali* (Paris: l'Harmattan).

Ndiaye, G. 1980. *L'Echec de la Fédération du Mali* (Dakar: NEA).

Observatoire de la Coopération Française, 1997. *La Coopération Judiciaire. L'Observation Internationale des Élections. Suivi de la Coopération Militaire* (Paris: Karthala).

Republique du Mali, Primature, Mission de Décentralisation, 1997. *Lois et Décrets de la Décentralisation* (Bamako).

Sidibé, O.O. 1997. 'Syndicat et Processus Démocratique au Mali', *Revue du Citoyen*, no. 4, June, pp. 25–30.

—— and G. Kester (eds), 1994. *Démocratie et Concertation Nationale. La Mise en œuvre du Conseil Économique, Social et Culturel du Mali* (Paris: PADEP-L'Harmattan).

Cited Issues of Press Publications:

Aurore (Malian publication), no. 93, 30 Dec. 1991.
Le Courrier du Soir (Malian publication), 7 April 1997 and 16 May 1997.
Les Échos (Malian publication), 7 Aug. 1990.
Jeune Afrique, no. 1917, 1–7 Oct. 1997.
La Lanterne (Malian publication), 26 May 1997.
Le Malien (Malian publication), 3 Jan. 1994.
Le Messager Africain, Pan-Africain trimester publication (Douala), no. 001, April–May–June 1996.
Le Monde Diplomatique, French monthly, May 1997.
L'Observateur, Malian bi-weekly, no. 250, 3 April 1997.

Part III

New Perspectives? Policy Issues and Electoral Observation in Africa

11 International Election Observation: a Discussion on Policy and Practice

W. van Binsbergen and J. Abbink

INTRODUCTION

The Netherlands is one of the donor-countries that has shown a strong commitment to democratization efforts and to participation in electoral observation missions in Africa. This chapter is a reflection on discussions held between observers, academics and policy-makers at the Netherlands Ministry of Foreign Affairs in February 1997 during a seminar organized by the Ministry and the African Studies Centre, Leiden. As the seminar brought together the three main parties in the electoral observation effort and debated on the core issues involved, a summary of the discussions is presented here which in its turn is useful to introduce the two subsequent chapters on the development of policy and practice.

Assessing the potential and impact of election observation on democratization processes in Africa must be based on a continuous dialogue and exchange of views between host governments, countries sending observers, actors on the local political scene of the country holding elections, and domestic and foreign observers themselves. This chapter is an attempt to contribute to such dialogue and is based on discussions and conversations with field observers (active in recent years in African elections), policy-makers and researchers (see also Von Meijenfeldt 1995).

Bringing together these three groups revealed both common concerns as well as differences in perspective on the perceived ideal, context and practice of election observation in Africa. Two central issues in these discussions were: a) the role, status and mandate of foreign election observers in Africa and b) the organization and execution of election observation. From the accounts of the actual field observers, whose experiences and criticisms are not always reflected in the final statements and reports issued after an election is concluded, it often appeared that these two issues are never entirely resolved and need continuous reassessment (see Geisler 1993, Boneo 1996, Engel 1996 and Carothers 1997).

I. THE MANDATE AND ROLE OF ELECTION OBSERVATION

In the Introduction and in Chapter 1, the possibilities and constraints of election observation – as a predominantly Western or donor-country technique of democracy support – has been mentioned. A sustained commitment on the part of the country sending observers as well as of the observers themselves to the ideal of democratic and fair elections as well as long-term democratization of the country in question is a requirement (cf. Goodwin-Gill 1994). A reflection on the mandate and role of election observation relates to some of the ideological justifications of observation and to the personal motives of observers involved in it. Election observation for many observers must be informed and guided by a commitment to and practical implementation of ideals of equality, freedom of political expression, democratic decision-making and equitable justice, of which people in democratizing countries in Africa and elsewhere were, and often still are, long deprived.

When discussing the mandate and role of election observation, at least three issues should be taken into account: 1) the formal and legal mission of the observers. What is their job, what can be expected from them? Related to this the question of the criteria of evaluation of the observers, 2) issues of legitimacy, for example, the *local perception* of the mandate and role of observers, and 3) the relation between foreign and local observers in the country.

1. On what basis are observers invited and sent to an election? The dominant idea behind sending election observers from countries where democratic structures are well-entrenched and non-controversial is that the presence and activities of observers can help to promote an atmosphere of 'freedom and fairness' of the electoral process: free in allowing the unencumbered expression of political and party preferences of the electorate and fair in allowing for reliable procedures of actual voting and counting. Ideally this exercise is supposed to cover the preparatory stage of the election as well: registration of all eligible voters, party formation and campaigning, acceptance of candidates, media access and exposure, and the like. The activity of foreign observers could thus contribute to political stability and orderly procedures, assuming that in the face of their critical presence, illegal practices would be inhibited. In situations of civil unrest or the end of an long armed conflict, the international community often tends to pressure for speedy elections. Such a decision may be an act of self-delusion, because no one's legitimacy, let alone democracy, will be established by it.

This limited role and mandate is being differently interpreted by observers, the host government, the voting public and the donor government providing them. Apart from the fact that the status and position of observers differ according to country of origin and membership in an overarching unit (from the EU or the UN, for instance), the international observer is always in a quandary: s/he has to respect the local 'rules of the game', made by others, which may be at variance with those valid in his/her own country and even be unfair from the start (for example, party registration, campaigning opportunities, voting procedures which easily allow count-rigging afterwards). An evaluation can and should be made by them on whether the 'playing field is level': this requires more attention to context and background than is possible or allowed on election day (for example, on the 'different weight' that certain votes have in certain districts, on gerrymandering practices, on limited opposition party activity). Among many observers, the idea has now emerged that election observation can only gain legitimacy – and thus better fulfil its mandate – if the period of observing is extended before and after the elections. (This idea has now been put into practice in Kenya, in the December 1997 elections; see Rutten in this volume.)

It is not feasible for international observers to harshly criticize the problems of the election or government policy on the basis of their own standards *while* on observation duty. What falls definitely within the role of observers, however, is to give a factual and business-like evaluation afterwards, in the framework of the observation unit in which they operate. In this respect it often appears that many such statements are written in such a way as to see primarily positive aspects of the electoral process, while the mandate of observation is primarily to give a *critical assessment* of it. This is in fact the general advice that the observers received from the governments that send out to Africa: if in any way possible, the process of democratization should be encouraged, and be seen in the light of a probably long process of 'building democracy'. In this context, a mildly worded statement on the elections, even if these did not live up to expectations, should function as a political signal. This practice (recently again demonstrated in the rather lame European Union observer report on the Kenyan elections of 1997) is conditioned by diplomatic convention, UN middle-of-the-road policy, and by *Realpolitik* and rivalry between the larger donor-countries themselves, wishing to keep or extend their local influence. But it ultimately subverts the mandate of observation, encourages complacency with the incumbent regime which 'got away with it', and leads to a loss of confidence among the wider public and civil society organizations.

2. This brings us to the second point: issues of legitimacy and the local perceptions of the mandate and role of observers (by both the government and the wider population). first it should be remembered that around 1990, the initial stimulus to processes of political liberalization and democratization often came from the mass protests and rebellions of the African populations (for example in Benin, Togo, Nigeria, Malawi, Mali, Kenya, Zambia, Zaire). This element tends to be forgotten in many discussions, but points to the fact that demands for democratization protests were formulated in the idiom of social reform, equitable justice, accountability, ending graft and corruption, and political rights for the masses. Hence, this movement has set part of the criteria which define the legitimacy of the subsequent process of democratization, including the institution of rule of law instead of (arbitrary) rule of persons and the electoral process.

While it is true that the international observers come to a sovereign country the laws and customs of which they should respect, they have the offical 'mission' to mediate and to be an agent of communication in the political process, however carefully they should fulfil this role. The local electorate often welcomes the arrival of international observers. The example of Chad was mentioned, where the presence of the observers at least initially signalled to many Chadians that their country was writing history and that they were becoming part of the global movement of democratization.

The performance of observers is also judged from what they say in their reports about the long-term prospects of democratization and the nature of their attitude toward the local government, especially if the latter has doubtful legitimacy. It is here that local observers and the electorate are often disappointed (compare Buijtenhuijs 1996). The opinions of the African voters on international observers, though not extensively investigated, are mixed, but what is clear is that in many cases they expected a lot from them, based on their own democratic norms. While many voters may be illiterate and have little formal education, they have their own norms and conceptions of democracy and political decency (see the Introduction, above) which they expect to be honoured in elections announced as free and fair, and they also expect these to be judged fairly by those international observers. The last point is by no means a sure thing. From cases in Chad, Zanzibar, Togo, Ethiopia or Kenya it is crystal clear that observers fell far short of their expected role, and some were even insulted by voters for not doing what they were supposed to do: expose fraud and complain about dishonesty and manipulation. While not all complaints are credible – as losing opposition groups may try, in their turn, to capture foreign opinion on the election process for their own purposes – it is incumbent on the observers not to dismiss such domestic criticism out of hand.

The observer, however, cannot decisively interfere, only observe and make statements on the rather limited technical procedures of voting. However, even in this last respect, observers frequently note that they are powerless to criticize observed wrongs with the authorities. When they do so emphatically, they can end up having to wind up their activities and leave the country.

3. Closely related to the foregoing is that of the *relation between foreign and local observers* in the country. As part of the democratization programmes supported by donor-country embassies, civic education projects and local NGOs are funded to enhance local capacity and create local stakes in the democratic institution-building process. These efforts are commendable. Up to now, however, the relation between the international and the local observers is not well-investigated or even well-defined. The impression among many Western observers is that the experiences of domestic observation are not sufficiently taken into account (cf. Nevitte & Canton 1997). Perhaps this is due to the perception among donor-embassies that domestic observers are not independent enough (the same argument would apply, with much more force, to the government in the country). But the fact is that in the years of political liberalization since 1989, a significant – though embattled – private or independent press has been emerging in many African countries. Many of these journals, magazines and radio stations have gone through a period of remarkable growth also in the quality and range of their reporting. Next to that, a whole new array of local NGOs, often with development purposes, has emerged, no doubt many jumping on the bandwagon of funding opportunities. A critical assessment of the best of them would, however, yield a significant pool of dependable local observers, in addition to people from the local churches which have often been involved. Hence in this domain, there is scope for much improvement, and dependable observers in the country will be found by building long-term associations with these local NGOs and media, provided their aims are within the sphere of interest of donor-country policy and are *not* political, sectarian, ethno-nationalist, and the like. A moot point is whether party agents (for instance, from the opposition) could be used as observers – the local situation my often not allow it, and it may possibly be putting them in a unpredictable or dangerous position after the elections.

There is, however, no doubt that a measured building and use of local capacity of really independent observers will enhance the democratization process, especially when models of cooperation with the international observers are implemented.

II. THE ORGANIZATION AND EXECUTION OF ELECTION OBSERVATION IN THE LIGHT OF OBSERVERS' FIELD EXPERIENCES

The Wider Context of Electoral Observation

The International Context
Regarding the assessment of existing *practices* of electoral observation and the formulation of specific recommendations for improvement, it might be useful to distinguish between local, regional, national, bilateral-interstatal, and multilateral-interstatal objectives and constraints.

A conspicuous set of constraints exists at the multilateral-interstatal level. Here the room for manoeuvre for any one observer country in defining its relationship *vis-à-vis* the *host country* where elections are to be observed is largely determined by international relations such as exist between the observer country and other countries (for example, fellow member states of the European Union) with which the observer countries entertain rather closer ties than with the host country itself. Thus international observational practices which in terms of organization, recruitment, training, funding, have all the appearance of being predominantly bilateral (they are conducted by or under the aegis of a national Ministry of Foreign Affairs in close association with the host country), in fact are expected to yield to international conventions, priorities, pressures, in a *de facto* multilateral context.

The Conditions for Electoral Observation
Should electoral observation exclusively be staged in response to a specific request from the field (that is, from the country where national elections are being held)?

The alternative is that the initiative for electoral observation is taken in the North, in a situation of conditionality, where the host country's (re-)admission to the international community of democratic states is at stake, or where specific donor support is made conditional to the implementation of specific democratic measures including fair and free elections.

Obviously, such conditionality poses ethical, political and international-legal problems. Is it not a manifest sign of hegemonic relations imposed by the North onto the South? Does it not infringe on national sovereignty? Is it not objectionable for these very reasons? Or are we justified in claiming that democracy is sufficiently sacred a value so as to override considerations of national sovereignty? Beyond such considerations in the field of international law, it is only realistic to admit – from a political rather than legal perspective – that the North is intervening in many aspects of South societies and polities, and will continue to do so in the foreseeable future; from such a perspective the question is not so much *whether* the North should engage in electoral observation and in other forms of intervention, but *on which grounds* the North should be entitled to do so, and on the basis of which principles and procedures.

The Wider Social Context
A wider field of questions opens up here. A commonly accepted point by now is that elections may be a necessary condition for the democratic process, but they are far from a sufficient condition. The peaceful transition of power by means of elections – such as electoral observation means to articulate – can only succeed if all relevant *extra*-electoral conditions are fulfilled. What are these conditions? They differ from country to country and from historical moment to historical moment. Electoral observation (sometimes described as 'a bunch of UN officials isolated in some hotel') may not offer the best possible perspective on these extra-electoral conditions. Instead, the extra-electoral conditions might be better assessed by the local embassies, if they have good lines of communication and information with local organizations such as civic groups, independent press and local NGOs, and national councils of churches.

However, it is important to preserve the independence and neutrality of the mandate of foreign electoral observers. This is a major reason why, from the Netherlands, electoral observation is organized from the Ministry of Foreign Affairs in The Hague, rather than at a local level in the host country, and why the local Netherlands Embassy is not too much involved. (An important change has, however, subsequently been introduced during the Kenyan elections of December 1997, where EU diplomats stationed in Nairobi were actively involved in a new model of observation.) In such a way it is ensured that the electoral observation is perceived as truly multilateral, rather than as a bilateral intervention between the Netherlands and the host country. In practice, however, bilateral and multilateral aspects are intertwined, as we shall see below.

With regard to the many variables that directly or indirectly bear on electoral performance, countries have different profiles, and it is here that specialized academic knowledge can come to the assistance of policy-makers and electoral observers.

At this point an element of cultural specificity needs to be appreciated for which perhaps a comparison with assessment techniques in industry is illuminating. In industry, especially in the context of multinational corporations, the visiting inspection is a usual form of intervention. It is remarkable that citizens of the various European countries differ considerably in their reaction to visiting inspection. From observers' reports and personal communications it appears that, for instance, the British let themselves be guided by the conventional wisdom that under no circumstances should the inspector be met with manifest signs of distrust. The French and the Swiss tend to insist on a flexible response to visiting inspection. This field offers opportunity to study the variety of ways in which codes of international hospitality are implemented locally. In general, Europeans tend to take offence at being inspected; Africans, on the other hand, tend to respond more positively to this idea, since for them the international inspection corroborates the global importance of their national institutions.

Definitions

Electoral observation is a complex field composed of interrelated roles. Therefore it is imperative that one maps out the entire field within which such observation has to take place. We may distinguish between the following roles:

- *the electoral supervisor*: this is a member of the agency organizing the elections, in the specific case that the elections are organized not by the national authorities but by an international agency, or by the European Union or a United Nations division (for example, UNDP).
- *the electoral observer*: this is exclusively an observer, without anything to do with the organization of the elections, and without any right to intervention.

- *the electoral monitor*: this is a local person, usually from the field of non-governmental organizations (NGOs), who functions as an impartial local observer in the case of multi-party elections; the electoral monitor has a limited right to intervention.
- *the party agent*: this is a local person who represents any of the contesting parties within the polling office.

We note that the supervisor's role is to assist in the organization of the elections. By definition a supervisor cannot be an observer since the roles, while complementary, are fundamentally different.

Ideally, any electoral observer should display the following characteristics. She or he should be a person

- with some experience concerning national elections;
- with a certain social status (here a dilemma arises: although the ideal electoral observer should have a certain social status, it stands to reason that this requirement is difficult to meet in the case of *long-term* electoral observers: such social status as they may have would usually mean that they have pressing duties which preclude their availability for long-term observer status);
- with ample social abilities;
- with the ability to report both orally and in writing;
- with the ability to work in a team;
- with a fit physical condition;
- with adequate mastery of at least 1) the international language which is the language of communication within the team; 2) the international language which is the language of communication between the team and the international agency to which the team belongs; and 3) the international language which is the language of communication between the team and the local election officers; in practice these three languages may be one and the same, but this is not always the case;
- with adequate inter-cultural experience.

The electoral observation mission starts with the recruitment of electoral observers. Ideally such recruitment should proceed along uniform criteria implemented throughout the European Union. In practice, however, no such uniformity is achieved. As a result there tend to be great differences in social, educational, economic and professional status among electoral observers recruited for the same mission, which results in considerable problems of communication and leadership within the observation team.

Several speakers during the session insisted that at present the selection criteria of electoral observers are far from transparent, and often rather arbitrary (for example, the fact that one has once worked for the former Dutch Directorate General for International Cooperation, under the Netherlands Ministry of Foreign Affairs section for development cooperation). Certain social positions would seem to be particularly suitable to recruit electoral observers from, for example members of national parliaments, members of the European parliament, and journalists.

Short-term electoral observation is as a rule not remunerated, nor supported by any specific training. There is a general feeling that this state of affairs is undesirable since it may be conducive to amateurism on the part of the short-term observers. Since long-term observers tend to be both remunerated and specifically trained, the current situation also tends to lead to unnecessary estrangement between long-term and short-term electoral observers.

Ideally, the training of electoral observers should at least highlight the following topics:

- the terms of reference under which the specific electoral observation in question takes place;
- the distinction between the various roles in the field of electoral observation (observer, monitor, supervisor, party agent);
- the authority of the electoral observer;
- the scope of the mandate under which electoral observation takes place;
- the relationship between electoral observers and the local election officers;
- the relationship between electoral observers and local monitors;
- the difference between *observation* and *supervision*;
- the relation with the local population;
- the techniques and limitations of eye-witnessing.

On the last point, it is important that the electoral observers realize the weaknesses of eye-witnessing as an assessment technique. It is useful to distinguish between types of observation according to the three phases of the electoral process:

* the observation of procedural mechanisms in the polling office;
* the observation of the processing of the electoral results after the completed voting materials have left the polling office;
* the observation of the electoral results as reported after the processing of all the votes.

Often the role of the electoral observer is conceived as being restricted to the first phase, that of the polling office. This is naive, also in view of the defects of eye-witness observation, as amply demonstrated by observational psychology.

As far as the relation with the local population is concerned, it is important that the electoral observers have ample previous inter-cultural experience, as well as an intensive introduction to the local culture, religions, and social conventions. They should be prepared for a situation where the local perception of electoral observers may show considerable discrepancy with the observers' self-perception as unremunerated, self-sacrificing representatives of lofty democratic ideals. In some cases (as observers from Zanzibar (1995) and Chad (1996) reported), electoral observers were met with signs of hatred from the local population, as if the electoral observers were locally considered to be in league with the national political elite, perceived as corrupt and inimical to popular interests.

Just as we found on the point of selection criteria, there turn out to be marked differences in local preparation and training between electoral observers from the various European countries. In recent times we have seen the emergence of formal training institutions for electoral observation, often in a certain competitive relationship. Such institutions include:

* the International Institute for Democracy and Electoral Assistance (IDEA), a Stockholm-based organization which over the years has built up considerable experience in the field of electoral observation;

- the Association of West European Parliamentarians for Africa (AWEPA), involved in the organization, sponsoring and management of election observation;
- the European Centre for Development Policy Management (or ECDPM, in Maastricht, the Netherlands), which in 1996 initiated a pilot project with EU funding in which 15 member states participate;
- in the Netherlands also, the foundation *Kontakt der Kontinenten* (based in Zeist) is active in the field.

Issues such as training and remuneration raise questions as to the desired level of professionalization of electoral observers. We shall come back to this point in the conclusion.

Debriefing

What is done with the electoral observers' experiences after their return from the host country? Debriefing offers the opportunity of sharing their anxiety and frustration and indignation, if any. The problem, however, is that such debriefing tends to take place at the local level (within the national framework, for example of the Netherlands Ministry of Foreign Affairs), whereas the organization of electoral observation, and such frustrations as the observers may have experienced, normally take place at the international level: that of the European Union, or the United Nations. Even so, there seems to be considerable leeway even at the national level. Some of the problems that electoral observers have experienced during their mission may therefore be attended to at this national level. For example, in Sweden the decision to professionalize electoral observation was taken at the national level, and within a very short time.

The composition of the specific team of electoral observers is considered to be of great importance. The electoral observation team should be composed of members who in general meet the ideal characteristics of electoral observers as defined above. The team should have an equitable composition in terms of gender and age. In addition, each team should comprise at least one member who speaks the local language(s), so that the team is at liberty to communicate with the electoral monitors without involving any third party. The ideal team is composed in such a way that there are no very great differences in social, economic, educational and professional status between the members, so that there will be no insurmountable problems of communication and leadership.

The duration of electoral observation is determined by the agency which organizes the electoral observation, and usually this is not the Netherlands Ministry of Foreign Affairs, but an international organization like the European Union or the United Nations.

For short-term electoral observation a period of three weeks has become established. The reasons for this are largely practical: the electoral observers' professional and personal life suffers minimal disturbance in such a short term; medical examinations can be made prior to departure; and so on. However, it has been suggested that if the organizing agency would rely on an established pool of experienced electoral observers, these practical problems would be reduced to a minimum and different time frames could begin to be contemplated.

Given the intricacies of political cultures, political histories and political structures at the national level, and given the practical problems of communication and logistics (among them, scarcity of transport, relatively paucity of electoral observers as compared to the number of polling stations, cultural and linguistic problems of communication), electoral observation which extends over only a few days around the actual moment of the elections is fraught with difficulties. It may at times have only a symbolic and political function instead of a strictly observational and non-biased one. In order to counter this effect, any short-term electoral observation needs to be informed and facilitated by long-term observation in the hands of more specialized observers (including academics) equipped with extensive local knowledge (for more on this, see Mair 1997). The transfer of knowledge between long-term observers and short-term observers deserves special attention. Even so, it is important that a certain preparation precedes the actual electoral observation, not only in the country of origin, but also within the host country. Electoral observers should ideally be in the host country a considerable amount of time before the actual elections.

Too often the mandate and the code of conduct remain merely implicit. Electoral observation involves complex actions in politically and socially sensitive, complex situations. It is important that the rules governing such actions are made explicit in the first place. However, usually this is not the case. Often the electoral observers' mandate is scarcely if at all defined. This creates immense problems: how, by what concrete procedures, and against what criteria should one assess electoral performance? There are likely to be cultural differences in the interpretation of the mandate, both between the various European nations which compose the team of electoral observation, and between the electoral observers and the host country. And beyond such cultural differences, there are the bilateral political and economic self-interests of the Northern countries participating in the electoral observation, which may be conducive to an oblique interpretation of the mandate. It is a first priority that the mandate and the code of conduct attending electoral observation be made explicit and be agreed upon by all parties concerned.

From Electoral Observation to Judicial Intervention in the Field?
It was suggested during the session that the members of an electoral observation team would be in an excellent position to dispense 'instant justice': not only to witness infringement of the electoral laws and procedures of the host country, but also to redress any such infringements on the spot, thus reinforcing the voters' confidence in the elections as a form of political self-expression. However, it is a principle of electoral observation (and an implicit condition of the host country's agreement to admit electoral observation) that it remains just that, *without* developing into intervention on the spot. Therefore, such judicial intervention is simply impossible and would be counter-productive.

The Official Statement at the End of Electoral Observation
The final product of an electoral observation mission is the *assessment statement*, passing a solemn, international verdict on the quality of specific elections. It is indicative of the problems in this field – problems both of an organizational and political nature – that in most cases of electoral observation no explicit procedure has been evolved for the formulation of such an assessment statement. Minority opinions within the team of observers are difficult to accommodate. There is great pressure

towards unanimity, and there may also be pressure, to a lesser extent, towards a positive assessment. All this means that there is no water-tight guarantee that the official assessment statement as produced and publicized is in actual fact supported by all observers, despite its suggestion of unanimity. A major point of concern on the part of individual electoral observers is therefore the way in which their individual report is incorporated in the official overall assessment statement as issued by the international organization of which the individual electoral observer is a member. There is much apprehension that especially critical, potentially explosive individual reports are likely to be swept under the carpet. The dilemma here is: either to articulate one's own individual views, or to allow these views to be submerged in the wider international framework of the agency organizing the electoral observation. Here there are considerable pitfalls. Electoral observers from one country may, for example, come to the conclusion that they are being hijacked by the bilateral interests of another country (for example, some European countries by France in francophone Africa). Only the articulation of explicit, clear and universal rules can prevent such a situation.

THE INTERNATIONAL LEVEL AND THE ELECTORAL OBSERVER'S FREEDOM OF OPERATION

The Multilateral Context of Electoral Observation

Electoral observation today usually takes place in a context where various fellow member states of international bodies or the EU and UN are involved. Also, more than one international body may be involved at the same time. This situation calls for rather greater and consistent coordination than is now common practice in the field of electoral observation. We have already noted the defects of the present situation, making for great discrepancies in such fields as the selection and training of electoral observers.

Who organizes the elections? This is of course neither a foreign donor-country embassy nor a foreign Ministry of Foreign Affairs. Electoral observation may, however, be organized to a large extent by foreign parties like the European

Union, the United Nations, or the OSCE (Organization for Security and Cooperation in Europe), as in Bosnia, or in Namibia and Angola.

But multilateral frameworks often create opaque complexities and entanglements, and it may not be advisable to have a situation where the *same* agency organizes both the elections *and* the electoral observation. Bosnia 1996 is a case in point: both were organized there by the OSCE. Such a situation clearly poses very specific problems from the point of view of electoral observation and its independence.

In general, the crucial question in this connection is: how does one guarantee a maximum of *independence* to the electoral observer? Here again the formal framing of electoral observation in accepted policy and written procedures does not offer the electoral observer much guidance. How is the concept of independent operation formally defined by the policy-makers as part of the mandate and the code of conduct? Are there discrepancies between the various Northern countries, and between them and the host country, in this respect? This remains a point for further analysis.

In addition to such formal procedures, *logistic aspects* of electoral observation (such as the observers' transport, lodging, food) constitute major boundary conditions on which the independence and representativeness of electoral observation depends. Observers who are confined to one place for lack of adequate transport, who are poorly lodged or poorly fed, cannot function optimally, and have difficulty preserving their independence from political actors on the local scene who may provide the transport, shelter and food they are themselves lacking. Here shocking discrepancies can be observed. Electoral observers working in Africa and Europe may be discouraged by the extreme differences (on such points as logistic facilities, military protection, financial resources) between recent situations of electoral observation in these two continents. For example, against 400 troops protecting electoral observers in Angola in 1992, as many as 30,000 troops were available for such an assignment in Bosnia in 1996!

Such discrepancies have an alarming effect on the individual electoral observers and make them wonder whether, after all, they are not merely being used for window-dressing, in order to rubber stamp a political performance in the South which, while falling short of formal requirements, yet serves the interests of states of the North.

CONCLUSION

When considering the *role and mandate* of electoral observation in Africa, it can be said that a clearer definition would be necessary beforehand, both for the observers and for the international organizations involved. The legitimacy and the integrity of the observers in the local setting, especially *vis-à-vis* the emerging local civil society and the wider electorate, should be of prime concern, and not the maintenance at all costs of diplomatic niceties with the host country. Criticism (if necessary) of the actual running of the preparatory stages and the actual voting, of the political contest, of campaigning, of institutional hindrances to political freedom and lack of equitable judicial proceedings, should be communicated in the final reports, next to concrete suggestions to the local government for improvements. A suggested trajectory for future democratization – based on good knowledge of the country, its history and its political system – should be laid out. A point often made is that no rhetorical compromise at the expense of substance should be made, because in the end international elections observation will thereby undermine itself and become irrelevant in the eyes of all parties concerned (cf. Cooper & Stroux 1996).

Concerning the *actual organization* of election observation, the idea of *professionalization* of electoral observation often comes up (for a proposal to this end, see Tostensen et al. 1997). But is it at all acceptable? If so, *what* should be professionalized in the field of electoral observation? Perhaps this should be not so much the role of the electoral observer as such (for elections, however important, are relatively rare events, and the requirements of neutrality and social engagement on the part of the electoral observers would rather point to non-professionals who discharge this specialist role only occasionally). Of course, the selection of observer candidates in the donor-countries could be substantially improved, notably in choosing people who are familiar with other cultures, have a sensitivity to and basic knowledge of history and social context, and do not only focus on elite politics (these minimal criteria have by no means been applied in the past). In addition, one should work towards a professionalization of *the organization of electoral observation procedure itself* (compare Rutten's chapter in this volume). This would have to include agreements on the division of labour, logistical operation, work methods, standards of integrity and honest reporting, and resistance to diplomatic pressure to manipulate final statements.

There is one thing certainly to be said against total professionalization: it reveals scepticism or even, in some cases, despair with regard to the future of democracy in the host countries. For surely, one would hope that electoral observation is, if not a once-and-for-all thing, at least an exercise with a limited time span, i.e., the observers should never have to come back if the democratic structures are being put in place in the country. Assistance by donor-countries with this process can also take other forms.

REFERENCES

Boneo, H. 1996. 'The Future of Election Observation', in *Democracy Forum: Report of the 'Democracy Forum' in Stockholm, June 12–14, 1996* (Stockholm: International Institute for Democracy and Electoral Assistance), pp. 15–21.

Buijtenhuijs, R. 1996. '"On Nous a Volé Nos Voix!": Quelle Démocratie pour le Tchad?' *Politique Africaine* 63: 130–5.

Carothers, T. 1997. 'The Observers Observed: the Rise of Election Monitoring', *Journal of Democracy* 8(3): 17–31

Cooper, L and D. Stroux, 1996. 'International Election Observation in Uganda: Compromise at the Expense of Substance', *Afrika Spectrum* 31(2): 201–9.

Engel, U. et al. 1996. *Deutsche Wahlbeobachtung in Afrika* (Hamburg: Institut für Afrika-Kunde, 2nd rev. edn).

Geisler, G. 1993. ' "Fair? What has fairness got to do with it?" Vagaries of Election Observations and Democratic Standards', *Journal of Modern African Studies* 31(4): 613–37.

Goodwin-Gill, G.S. (ed.) 1994. *Free and Fair Elections: International Law and Practice* (Geneva: Inter-Parliamentary Union).

Mair, S. 1997. *Election Observation: Roles and Responsibilities of Long-term Observers.* (Maastricht: European Centre for Development Policy Management, Working paper no. 22).

Meijenfeldt, R. von, 1995. *Election Observation: Report of an ECDPM Workshop* (Maastricht: European Centre for Development Policy Management).

Nevitte, N. and S.A. Canton, 1997. 'The Role of Domestic Observers'. *Journal of Democracy* 8(3): 47–61.

Tostensen, A., D. Faber and K. de Jong, 1997. *Towards an Integrated Approach to Election Observation? Professionalising European Long-term Election Observation Missions* (Maastricht: European Centre for Development Policy Management).

12 Election Observation: Policies of the Netherlands Government 1992–7

O. van Cranenburgh

INTRODUCTION

Chapter 1 of this volume offered a general description of practices and problems of election observation. These outcomes were not explicitly linked to any conscious or systematic attempts of governments or (international) organizations to achieve certain effects, in other words to policies. The emergence of election observation has prompted many Western governments to formulate such policies for election observation missions. In this chapter I will review Dutch policies on election observation in Africa. Examining policies of Western countries is relevant because African democratization processes are increasingly affected by concepts and policies of Western donor countries. Western governments not only have made economic aid conditional upon democracy and the human rights performance of aid-receiving countries, they have also developed policies aimed at supporting these political reforms.

The chapter is largely descriptive, relying primarily on an analysis of policy documents and a number of reports from African observation missions. Bearing in mind the problems reviewed in Chapter 1 of this volume, I will focus on opportunities for the Dutch government to contribute to improvements in the quality of election observation, while also examining the constraints. Any systematic attempt to link Dutch policies to certain outcomes, however, would require a lengthy and systematic research effort. Moreover such an effort would raise the problem to which or whose policies certain outcomes must be attributed. The Netherlands government is only one of the

277

international actors involved in election observation. Dutch policies for election observation take place in a context affected by the actions of other Western governments, governments of observer-receiving nations and international organizations. In particular, Dutch election observers sent to African countries often operate under the umbrella of the United Nations. Increasingly, the EU is active in the field of observation. The involvement of international organizations creates both opportunities and constraints. Furthermore, election observation is affected by the actions of governments receiving international observers, whether resulting from conscious policy or not. As will be seen, these actions may amount to significant constraints.

The concept of policies may refer to a number of phenomena. first, it may refer to stated policy goals. In this form, policies are primarily intentions. I will speak of 'official policy goals' to cover this meaning of the term. Second, the term 'policies' may refer to actual measures taken to further the goals; measures in the form of allocation of funds, usually in the form of financial or technical assistance. I will call these 'policy outputs'. These concrete measures may be announced in a policy document, or may evolve in practice. It is entirely possible that such concrete measures turn out to be out of line with the stated policy goals or may even be absent. Third, a complete policy analysis would include policy outcomes: the effects of actual measures taken in the field. Given the methods used, this chapter cannot make a systematic analysis of outcomes. I will focus my analysis on the official policy goals and clearly visible policy outputs of the Dutch government.[1]

DUTCH POLICIES FOR ELECTION OBSERVATION

The significance of democratic reforms in developing countries was already addressed in the Dutch government policy paper 'A World of Difference' issued in 1990, shortly after social democrat Jan Pronk reassumed office as Minister for Development Cooperation. The government intended to link human rights and democracy to development cooperation. first, there is the use of political and human rights conditionality (this was coined 'negative linkage'); second, a policy of 'positive linkage' was announced. Through positive linkage, the Dutch government intends to support the democratization process itself. These positive linkage policies cover a wide range of issues, including support to strengthen 'civil society', support to human rights NGOs, various forms of support for elections, and in some cases even support to political parties (South Africa).[2]

Election observation emerged within the framework of these positive linkage policies. The wide scope of these policies shows that at the level of official policy goals the Dutch government does not adhere to the 'minimal approach' to democracy discussed in Chapter 1 of this volume. Election observation policies, however, as an element of these broader policies, focus on one aspect of the democratization process – that is, the introduction of political competition, in other words free and fair elections. However, as discussed in Chapter 1, assessing free and fair elections implies a rather broad scope of things to monitor. In an internal policy memorandum of 1994, the Dutch government adopts an 'integral approach', involving the need to cover the preparatory stages of the electoral cycle. A range of measures is mentioned to address the preparatory phase, and the memorandum states that observers may be sent during the preparatory stages. Despite this intention, this chapter will address below the tendency for concrete policy measures ('policy outputs') to remain heavily focused on the immediate polling period.

In the first phase, the government took initiatives to support elections in the context of country programmes; it was decided to provide financial or technical support to hold elections, or to send observers. In this phase, election observation policy was in its infancy. Decisions were made in an *ad hoc* manner, and little experience existed. Allocations were made either in the context of country programmes or under the budget category for 'emergency assistance and human rights'.[3]

In a second phase, the institutional framework changed. With the formation of a new cabinet in 1994 a major reassessment of Dutch foreign policy was announced, primarily with the view to a better integration of different aspects of foreign policy.[4] As a result of this reassessment, a major reorganization of the foreign affairs bureaucracy took shape. In 1996 a new unit was created, named the Directorate for Human Rights and Democracy. Policies for election observation became institutionally embedded and gained a higher profile.

The first official (public) document explaining the government's approach to election observation was issued in January 1997, in the form of a letter to parliament.[5] However, this official document reproduced part of an internal policy memorandum written in 1994 by the office of the Human Rights Coordinator (then charged with coordinating election observation). Before 1997, parliament had been informed regularly about the countries in which elections were expected and to which observers might be sent, but without a comprehensive description of the government's policy. In such a letter to parliament sent on 18 December 1995, the government stated that it is difficult to predict Dutch involvement in these elections, since governments of countries experiencing democratic reforms often wait a long time before setting precise dates for elections, and often wait a long time before inviting observers.[6] This fact turns out be a significant constraint both for the Dutch government and for the UN in preparing adequately for the sending of observers and for realizing a more long-term presence during elections.

The letter to parliament of 23 January 1997 indicates the goals of sending observers. The official *policy goals* concern (i) expressing solidarity with newly democratizing countries; (ii) strengthening public faith in the electoral process; and (iii) contributing to a free and fair electoral process. The letter states that support to elections is seen as part of a broader policy for human rights and democratization. Elections are not to be seen in isolation, but as part of a broader process of democratization, also including the rule of law (the idea of '*Rechtstaat*').

The Dutch government sends observers upon invitation by the authorities of the country holding elections, and uses the following *criteria*:

a) there must be a favourable prospect in the democratization process (political stability, respect for human rights and reasonable conditions for free and fair elections);
b) there is sufficient support in the country for the elections and for receiving observers;
c) observers are added to an international team with a joint mandate, preferably in the framework of an international organization;

d) the organization is adequately prepared for an effective operation.

The criteria show the importance attached firstly to what may be called an 'enabling environment', and secondly to international cooperation. With regard to observation in African countries, the Netherlands will send observers mostly in the context of the UN or the EU. The Dutch government attaches great value to coordination to prevent fragmentation of the efforts of the numerous international actors involved (for Africa: the UN, EU, Commonwealth, OAU as well as international associations and NGOs). The coordinating agency should be responsible for contacts with the local authorities, formulating the terms of reference of the mission, receiving and guiding the observers and coordinating the reporting.

The letter mentions some problems in coordination and the guidance of observers in the receiving country: insufficient information, communication and transport problems, and insufficient coverage of the entire process. Except when observation is done in the framework of a peace-keeping operation, the coordination by the UN suffers from problems. The letter indicates that sufficient attention should be paid to the adequate organization of election observation, this presumably in view of a number of complaints received from returning observers that logistical support and adequate guidance had been lacking.

The Dutch government further intends to increase the involvement and strengthen the coordination capacities of regional organizations. However, with respect to Africa, it is immediately recognized that the OAU is not very active in the field and does not possess a capacity in this regard. If the coordinating agency is not capable of realizing a long-term presence in the country receiving observers, the policy is to utilize other missions and agencies. The Dutch government wants to learn from observation experience by holding debriefings upon return of mission participants. It is emphasized that international observation is in a stage of development and needs to be guided.

The letter to parliament also states that observers should not be sent in all cases. A deliberate decision must be made to send observers; the letter announces the intention to formulate fundamental preconditions and priorities in the context of the EU. The letter does not give insight into the concrete require-ments to be met before observers are sent. Such requirements are formulated, however, in the internal policy memorandum of 1994. Besides the general criteria discussed above, this memo-randum lists the need for an official request by the country in-volved addressed to a number of countries and/or international organization(s); the request not to imply partiality to any party involved; that there be practical feasibility and sufficient time for decision-making. The internal memorandum further elab-orates in which cases observers may be sent during the prepara-tory phase or the polling phase. For the preparatory phase the number of observers and period of observers must be such that a good insight may be gained into the preparatory activities. For the polling period, the memorandum states that it requires involvement in the preparatory phase. However, this condition is not required if other donor-countries have been involved in the preparatory phase and if there is sufficient insight into the preparatory phase, as well as a favourable prospect.[7] The latter criteria regarding involvement in the preparatory phase are not repeated in the letter to parliament. Perhaps this is due to the fact that the Dutch government has sent observers in many cases where it was not involved in the preparatory stage, and the decision was taken using the criterion of a 'favourable prospect'.

An annex to the letter to parliament provides information on observers sent since 1992. With respect to sub-Saharan Africa, the Dutch government sent observers to ten countries in the period 1992 through 1996 (see Table 12.1).

For the year 1997, elections were planned in Burkina Faso, Congo, the Ivory Coast, Cameroon, Kenya, Liberia, Mali,

Table 12.1   African countries receiving Dutch observers

1992: 3 (Ethiopia, Angola, Kenya)
1993: 1 (Malawi)
1994: 4 (Uganda, South Africa, Malawi, Mozambique)
1995: 1 (Tanzania)
1996: 1 (Uganda)

Source: Ministry of Foreign Affairs, *Notitie inzake Verkiezingswaarneming* (Jan. 1997).

Mozambique, and (then) Zaire. Dutch missions were sent eventually to Liberia and Mali only. In Cameroon and Kenya the government did not send missions due to a lack of democratic perspective; in the Kenyan case a different model for diplomatic observation was tried out, while the government also supported national monitors (see Chapters 6 and 13 of this volume).

The letter to parliament notes that in most instances, elections observed were reported to be conducted relatively well. Usually, the result was accepted by the parties involved. Two exceptions in Africa are mentioned: Tanzania (doubts about the outcome in Zanzibar) and Angola, where UNITA refused to accept the outcome. However, the letter to parliament concludes that even where circumstances do not meet all democratic standards, the observation mission may contribute to political stabilization, allowing further democratization.

DUTCH POLICY GOALS AND CRITERIA

The three policy goals as stated in the letter to parliament are of a different nature: while two concern rather intangible aspects such as expressing solidarity and strengthening confidence, the third goal purports to be a direct contribution to the democratization process, namely contributing to free and fair elections. The latter goal is problematic in view of the fact, discussed in Chapter 1 of this volume, that election observers' mandates still lack a clearly agreed set of criteria for free and fair elections. Both in the pre-assessment whether conditions for free and fair elections are present, and in the judgement of the free and fair nature of the electoral process, such criteria are usually not formulated explicitly. The official policy document formulated an intention to formulate more strict conditions under which to send observers in the context of the EU; however, as of March 1997 this had not yet been achieved.[8] As one of the criteria the internal policy memorandum of 1994 stipulates that an international team should have a clear mandate. For criteria for free and fair elections, the policy memorandum refers in an annex to a number of international documents. At present, however, an operational elaboration of the criteria for free and fair elections is lacking in the decision-making process to send observers or in the mandates of observer missions.

Despite the absence of explicit criteria, the official policy document of 1997 noted that some elections observed were flawed. Apparently in these cases the presence of observers did not contribute to free and fair elections. The argument in the policy paper implies that this does not amount to a failure of policy, however. The document expresses the view that in such cases the sending of observers may help political stabilization. In my view, such situations are more problematic than the government appears to acknowledge. The absence of clear criteria for election observation in observers' mandates implies an overly wide 'grey zone' of imperfect or flawed elections, which are legitimated by observer mission statements. Observer missions tend to report in a generally positive tone about elections observed.[9] Observer missions often avoid the use of the terms 'free and fair' in their election statements and resort to rather vague and impressionistic statements that the elections 'appear to represent the will of the people' or amount to a 'step towards democracy'. The effect of the absence of clear and explicit criteria is that doubtful elections still receive an (increasingly symbolic) legitimation.

The problem of flawed elections must be addressed explicitly. While politicians are likely to strive for a certain room to manoeuvre in view of the political context in which observers are sent, current policies do not show awareness of the possibility that the presence of observers in a severely flawed election may contribute to de-legitimation of the election observation exercise, and by implication may erode the confidence of African citizens which the policy of sending observers intends to strengthen. It points to the need for a clearer pre-election assessment, and the formulation of operational criteria for free and fair elections. There is a gap between the ambitious and laudable policy goals and policy outputs. Without a clear operationalization, the policy goal of contributing to free and fair elections is in danger of being undermined.

The criteria formulated for deciding to send observers do not fill this operational gap. The first two as formulated in the letter to parliament are at a relatively high level of abstraction, concerning what may be called the presence of an 'enabling environment' for both the elections and the observers. As with the policy goal discussed above, these criteria require elaboration. The first criterion regarding a favourable prospect for democracy is rather broadly formulated, and leaves room for completely different assessments. The case of Uganda (1994 and 1996) illustrated that donor-governments differ in opinion as to the question whether free and fair elections require a multiparty system. In the absence of such an indicator of pluralism, there are no explicit criteria which are applied to assess whether effective freedom of organization and opinion are present. This means that policies for election observation will lack in transparency, a principle the international community considers an important aspect of 'good governance'. The criteria formulated in the internal policy memorandum of 1994 appear more practical, but in the end boil down to the same assessment that there is a favourable prospect for democracy.

While political differences between governments will make the agreement on such criteria difficult, it is not impossible. However, it would require a more explicit incorporation of a human rights perspective in election observation policies. The point is to apply the currently available internationally agreed legal norms on free and fair elections and incorporate them into criteria for the pre-assessment (decision to send observers), and in the mandates of observer missions.[10] Election observation policy will gain in transparency and effectiveness if it is more explicitly integrated with the human rights approach. Both the criteria to decide to send observers and the criteria for the conduct of free and fair elections must be elaborated and incorporated, preferably by granting a leading role to the UN Electoral Assistance Division (see below). A next concern, of course, would be that such criteria are applied consistently.

WORKING THROUGH THE UN IN ELECTION OBSERVATION

The last two criteria formulated in the policy paper of 1997 address the working channels and thus come closer to an operational aspect of policy. It concerns working through international organizations and the preparedness of such organizations. The policy creates opportunities for coordination and cooperation. While it is evident that international observation cannot be done without the cooperation of other international actors, working with or through such international actors also implies that outcomes are affected by the weaknesses of such organizations. It also requires a careful assessment of the performance of these organizations and where necessary support to build up their capacity. Because Dutch policy is to work through international organizations, it is necessary to examine briefly the implications of their involvement. I will focus on the role of the UN.[11]

In 1991, in the wake of the new wave of democratic reforms, the UN General Assembly created a Trust Fund for Electoral Observation. In April 1992 the it created a separate bureau for its new electoral activities. The Electoral Assistance Division (EAD) was to be in charge of guiding the UN involvement in elections. The Under-Secretary General for Political Affairs was assigned the role of focal point to whom all requests for assistance had to be directed. The unit is involved in a range of electoral activities, including in some cases the actual conduct, verification or supervision of elections. The UN intends to increase its efforts to strengthen domestic capacity for election monitoring, until now only achieved on a large scale in the Mexican elections of 1994. However, the majority of its activities concern involvement with observation or in an advisory role.[12] Moreover, with respect to observation, the EAD has focused its activities on support and coordination of observation, rather than being involved in observation directly. This section will focus on the latter role in coordination and support of election observation and leave aside grand operations such as those conducted in South Africa, Angola and Mozambique (actual verification) or other missions requiring a special mandate (Western Sahara, Namibia). (See Table 12.2.)

Table 12.2   UN coordination and support of election observation in African countries

---

1992: 4 (Ethiopia, Central African Republic, Djibouti, Kenya)
1993: 6 (Niger, Lesotho, Congo, Djibouti, Burundi, Malawi)
1994: 4 (Uganda, Malawi, Guinea Bissau, Namibia)
1995: 4 (Benin, Equatorial Guinea, Cote d'Ivoire, Tanzania)
1996: 3 (Sierra Leone, Chad, Comoros)

See: UN EAD/DPA 1996, *Types of Electoral Assistance*, pp. 3–5.

Technical coordination of international observation is often done through a joint international observer group. This activity does not require a mandate from the UN Security Council of the General Assembly, and allows the UN to keep a low political profile. In the case of a technical coordination and support role, the UN is not responsible for the content of the final judgement. In technical coordination of election observation, the UN relies on the UNDP as focal point. The unit aims to support election observation through writing guidelines and handbooks.

Before deciding on its role, the Unit conducts a needs assessment, based on a report on the political situation by the regional division of the Department of Political Affairs and an assessment mission. Prior to the sending of observers, the EAD favours a very clear assessment of whether conditions allow the holding of free and fair elections. As to the preceding decision whether conditions for a free and fair election exist, the unit faces pressures from member governments (in the case of Uganda, some donor-governments pressured for the sending of observers, while others were not convinced that fundamental preconditions for free and fair elections were present). The issue of an adequate mandate to be formulated for an international observer group is considered highly important at the EAD, but the unit faces constraints due to political sensitivities. As indicated above, a conscious attempt to incorporate a legal, and in particular a human rights, approach may create more room to manoeuvre and limit the impact of political constraints. Moreover, the formulation of these criteria should be achieved at a general level and should be divorced from decision-making on specific countries. Working through the UN provides an opportunity to arrive at broadly agreed, generally applicable criteria for free and fair elections.

However, the EAD is troubled by a number of constraints. first, the unit suffers from lack of staff. Since the departure of its director, this vacancy has not been filled (at time of writing); another vacancy has remained unfilled. As a consequence, the unit frequently employs consultants to act as coordinators in the field. In 15 of the 21 African countries receiving coordination and support missions, consultants were employed. Second, funds are a continuing constraint, leading the EAD to issue an appeal to replenish the electoral fund in late 1997. The EAD has been forced to reject a number of requests for technical assistance or coordination of observation due to insufficient funds. However, the reason for rejection of such requests which is most often cited is 'insufficient lead time'. Thus, also at the UN, it is clear an important constraint emerges from governments in democratizing countries who frequently wait too long to request observers from governments or coordination and support services from the UN. In a small number of cases, the reason for rejection was the lack of an enabling environment.

The Dutch government decision to work through international organizations implies a need to actively support building up their capacity. Secondly, it implies the need to monitor the performance of international organizations in charge of coordination. In practice systematic monitoring of their performance is not achieved. Working through consultants implies that it is difficult to build up an institutional memory. The performance of consultants charged with coordination in the field varies widely. In my view, the skills required for technical (logistical) coordination in the field and those involving substantive knowledge of elections and democratization processes are hardly ever combined in one person. Consequently, it may be better to separate the two functions. Another issue to monitor is the combination of roles international organizations sometimes assume. It is important to note that international organizations may be involved in both observation and advising for the elections. The EAD, for example, has been involved in advising the electoral authorities in addition to observation in a number of cases. At the EAD there is some uneasiness with this combination of roles. An assessment is necessary of whether the double role threatens the independence and objectivity of the judgement made in the context of observation, or whether an adequate separation of tasks and responsibilities may be achieved.

In the context of technical assistance or involvement in the actual organization of elections, the UN frequently works through the UN Office for Procurement and Services (UNOPS). It is apparent that large contracts are involved for the production of election materials. In many cases, these materials are imported from Western countries (for example, the UK). This may well constitute the greater booming industry behind democratic reforms. The Dutch government should make sure that UN procedures are monitored to see that procurement policies are adequately competitive. Moreover, an assessment should be made to utilize the local capacity in this regard. It is undesirable that newly democratized countries become dependent on external support for elections, in the form of the subsidized importation of election materials from abroad.

COPING WITH PROBLEMS OF ELECTION OBSERVATION

The policy paper of 1997 shows that certain problems in the practice of election observation were known to the Ministry through the information obtained from observers. However, there has been no systematic analysis of these problems, and a result, few concrete measures are found in the document to achieve possible improvements. The internal memorandum of 1994 is somewhat more elaborate. However, concrete measures with respect to the problem of limited coverage of the electoral cycle, the recruitment and training of observers, the need to monitor and evaluate election observation missions, and the inadequate coordination by international agencies involved are not addressed sufficiently.

In Chapter 1 the practice was discussed that most observation activities revolve around polling day. Observers frequently have reported on the need to cover a longer time period. To assess the free and fair nature of elections, Chapter 1 of this volume noted that observers must cover the period preceding polling day, beginning with the formulation of election laws and regulations, the delineation of constituencies, voter registration, and campaigning. After polling day, the counting must be followed until results are announced. Both at the UN and the Institute for Democracy and Electoral Assistance (IDEA) in Stockholm, 'full coverage' has been adopted as an important principle for election observation.[13] The Dutch policy paper expresses an intention to achieve full coverage, but few concrete measures are announced to achieve it. In the policy memorandum of 1994 the possibility is mentioned that observers may be sent in the preparatory phase. However, the conditions under which observers are sent, while stating the desirability of involvement in the preparatory phase, allow the possibility of sending short-term observers without such involvement. In practice, the bulk of election observation still revolved around polling day in the period reviewed here. In several cases the

Dutch government has sent 'long-term observers', but in practice their presence often was too limited in time and their mandate inadequate. The longer-term observers tend to fuse the logistical roles of coordination (preparing for the arrival of short-term observers) and substantive monitoring of the stages in the electoral cycle. The latter activities again are hindered by inadequate training and the lack of clear guidelines (derived from criteria for free and fair elections). The policy paper calls for the involvement of other agencies to cover the entire election cycle. Thus the problem appears to be delegated to other international organizations, who often lack the capacity. In my view, the principle of full coverage necessitates clear choices. Full coverage implies longer-term observation missions. It is necessary to weigh the desirability of allocating funds to short-term missions in view of the requirements of a longer-term presence. The policy goal calls for setting clear funding priorities and clear mandates.

The recruitment and selection of observers is not addressed in the policy document of 1997, but received attention in the internal memorandum of 1994. Observers are to meet a number of general criteria. For short-term observation, the Dutch government primarily relies on volunteers, besides parliamentarians and officials. This implies a limitation in recruitment possibilities. In the case of employed professionals, the employer of the observers must allow their release from normal duties (excepting those observers who are willing to use their vacation time for missions). The sending of politicians, which is also the practice of many other governments, implies some problems. firstly, politicians are usually available for a very limited time period; they rarely cover more than a few days around polling day. Secondly, politicians often lack knowledge of the country they are visiting and are often preoccupied with politics at home. In some cases politicians show insensitivity to the local culture and institutions.

Observers require an adequate preparation before departing to the country concerned. Usually, the country bureau of the Ministry prepares a dossier with background information about the political situation of the country and relevant electoral laws or regulations. In many cases, however, this is done very shortly before departure. This has to do with the decision-making process which is finalized just very shortly before the observers are sent. In some cases, this is due to the lateness of receiving countries' request for election observers. However, the fact that several different bureaux in the Ministry are involved also creates delays and problems of coordination. No extensive training of observers has been done by the Ministry. It is assumed that the coordinating agency in the receiving country will provide sufficient information, but in many cases this agency does not perform this function well. In 1997, the Ministry emphasized training more by providing for the possibility of training of observers, some financed by the EU.

The Ministry organizes debriefing sessions to receive feedback from observers. However, learning from experience cannot be realized simply through the holding of debriefing sessions. Explicit reporting by the participants of an observation mission on the organizational performance of the coordinating agency is required, while periodic evaluation of observation missions by an outside (third) party would be desired. Procedures for follow up are also required. The 1997 decision to use a team leader in observer missions may constitute an improvement if the team leader is charged explicitly with monitoring the performance of the coordinating agency, while also monitoring the performance of observers in the team. Establishing a small pool of experienced observers to fulfil this role may also help to build institutional memory and allow a learning process.

CONCLUSION

Election observation constitutes a relatively new field of international cooperation. The Dutch government has participated actively in this new enterprise and thereby shown solidarity with those Africans aspiring to democratic reforms. Dutch observation policies have moved out of the infant phase, and some lessons have been learnt from early problems. However, these policies still suffer from some childhood diseases. The main policy document of January 1997 primarily lists policy intentions. Besides relatively intangible aspects, these intentions include the concrete objective of furthering free and fair elections. I have argued that the absence of operational criteria for free and fair elections in the decision-making process prior to the sending of observers and in observer missions' mandates contributes to a gap between this policy goal and policy outputs. Policy goals require a translation into concrete measures (policy outputs) which may help to further the goals to be achieved. The criteria formulated in the Dutch policy document do not fill this gap; they are rather abstract, and those criteria addressing which channels to use mostly lack translation into concrete measures (policy outputs).

I have indicated that the absence of such clear operational policies may in some cases undermine the policy goals the government has set and imply a lack of transparency. Furthermore, I have argued that working through international organizations provides opportunities but also implies dealing with constraints. It requires a greater emphasis on strengthening the capacity and monitoring the performance of the UN agencies involved.

Finally, I have noted that several constraints emerge from the actions of the governments of observer-receiving countries, such as late invitations, or inhibiting an 'enabling environment'. A firm commitment to the official policy goals would imply a decision to refuse sending observers if no reasonable 'lead time' is available. Moreover, if the government of the country concerned is not clearly committed to democratic reforms, the sending of observers may end up granting undue legitimation of the elections, which implies that the decision on the preconditions is in fact a crucial one. The government's intention to emphasize the assessment of the situation before sending observers requires an effort to formulate more explicit criteria to assess whether an enabling environment is present.

Lastly, enabling environment for democracy also depends on active citizenship and the mobilization of domestic forces for democracy. The Dutch government must be alert that enough is done to support the development of a domestic capacity for election monitoring. While such activities are funded through other elements of the Dutch government's positive linkage policies (aid to NGOs), it also should receive attention in the context of observation policies. In this respect, the government's policy regarding Kenya in 1997 may prove a significant precedent for those cases which lack a favourable prospect for democracy. The government refrained from sending observers while contributing finances to domestic monitors. The clue to international election observation policies may well be to know when not to get involved.

NOTES

1. Examples of less visible policy outputs, which cannot be covered here, are diplomatic *démarches* and pressures exerted on governing boards of international organizations.

2. For a description of these policies, see the 'Nota Een Wereld van Verschil: nieuwe kaders voor ontwikkelingssamenwerking in de jaren negentig', Netherlands Ministry of Foreign Affairs 1990 (pp. 197–9); Van Cranenburgh 1995.

3. This following a parliamentary motion (known as 'Motie Aarts') addressing the policy to support democratizing countries.

4. This reassessment resulted in a Ministry of Foreign Affairs policy document, 'De Herijking van het Buitenlands Beleid', 1995.

5. See Ministry of Foreign Affairs 1977 ('Notitie inzake verkiezingswaarneming', 23 Jan. 1997, DMD/BC – 012/97).

6. See Letter of the Ministry of Foreign Affairs (DGIS/CM/896/95) to the Dutch Senate dated 18 Dec. 1995.

7. See 'Notitie inzake Nederlandse ondersteuning aan verkiezingen', Internal Memorandum of the Ministry of Foreign Affairs, Office of the Human Rights Coordinator (July 1994), pp. 5–6.

8. See Letter to the Permanent Commission for Foreign Affairs of the Second Chamber of Parliament, dated 12 March 1997 (Ministry of Foreign Affairs DMD/BC – 71/97).

9. Many observers have complained that the final statement about the election does not adequately reflect their observations (information obtained in observer seminars, informal discussions with observers and personal experience).

10. For a good overview of legal norms on free and fair elections see Goodwin-Gill 1994.

11. The European Union has also developed an active role in election observation. In 1994, the EU worked independently in South Africa, in the framework of the common foreign and security policy (this did entail cooperation with the UN). The EU faced some problems due to inexperience. EU missions sometimes worked through the UN (as in the case of Mozambique); in those cases the EU acted as coordinator of the observers sent through the EU. See Rutten's chapter in this volume for an example of 'coordinated observation' in the Kenyan elections of December 1997.

12. For an overview of election activities of the UN see EAD/DPA 'Types of Electoral Assistance' (New York 1996), and UN General Assembly, 'Support by the United Nations System of the Efforts of governments to Promote and Consolidate New or Restored Democracies' (7 Aug. 1995, A/50/332).

13. See IDEA 1995: 7.

REFERENCES

Cranenburgh, O. van, 1995. 'Development Cooperation and Human Rights: Linkage Policies in the Netherlands', in P. Baehr et al. (eds), *Human Rights Yearbook 1995* (The Hague: Kluwer, and Oslo: Nordic Human Rights Publications).

Goodwin-Gill, G.S. 1994. *Free and Fair Elections: International Law and Practice* (Geneva: Inter-Parliamentary Union).

IDEA, 1995. 'International Election Observation' (Stockholm: IDEA).

Netherlands Ministry of Foreign Affairs, 1990. *Nota Een Wereld van Verschil: Nieuwe Kaders voor Ontwikkelingssamenwerking in de Jaren Negentig* (A World of Difference – New Frameworks for Development Cooperation in the Nineties) (The Hague: SDU).

Netherlands Ministry of Foreign Affairs, 1995. *De Herijking van het Buitenlands Beleid* (The Re-evaluation of Foreign Affairs Policy) Sept. 1995 (The Hague: SDU).

Netherlands Ministry of Foreign Affairs, 1997. (DMD/BC – 012/97), 'Notitie inzake Verkiezingswaarneming' (Policy Paper on Election Observation), 23 Jan. 1997 (The Hague).

UN Electoral Assistance Division/Department of Political Affairs, 1996. 'Types of Electoral Assistance' (New York: UN EAD/DPA).

UN General Assembly, 1995. *Support by the United Nations System of the Efforts of Governments to Promote and Consolidate New or Restored Democracies* (7 Aug. 1995) (A/50/332) (New York: UN).

13 The Kenyan General Elections of 1997: Implementing a New Model for International Election Observation in Africa

M. Rutten

INTRODUCTION

In 1992, Kenya held the first multi-party elections since the *de facto* single-party elections of 1969. Church leaders had started campaigning for the return of the multi-party system in the beginning of 1990. Politicians, NGOs and the Kenyan public at large followed their example. Even more important, by November 1991 the international donor community also openly pressed for political as well as economic reforms and threatened to withhold aid. The following month President Daniel arap Moi announced the withdrawal of section 2(A) of the Constitution, making Kenya a *de jure* multi-party state again. New political parties were launched. finally, on 29 December 1992 Kenya followed the footsteps of Zambia, which had, among the English-speaking African countries, heralded the transition from single to multi-party politics in October 1991 (see Andreassen et al. 1992).

The Kenyan 1992 elections were characterized by widespread allegations of irregularities, such as the stuffing of ballot boxes, destroying of opposition votes and count-rigging (see Barkan 1993; Mulei 1996; NEMU 1993; *Weekly Review* 1993; *Africa Confidential* 1993). Local observer groups had united in the National Electoral Monitoring Unit (NEMU). They trained and deployed some 8,000 domestic observers throughout the country.

The international community observed the elections in the usual way: election observers from all over the world were flown in some days before election day (29 December) and left shortly afterwards. The two most important outside teams were the Washington-based International Republican Institute and the Commonwealth team. In addition, national delegations from Denmark, Egypt, Germany, Japan and Switzerland were sent. Still, there were fewer than 200 international observers for 7,000 polling stations. Coordination of efforts by the foreign missions was minimal (see *Africa Confidential* 1992). Also, 'Neither the foreign nor the local observers groups had the capacity or resources to investigate comprehensively rigging allegations. Consequently they reported only the most blatant and easily verifiable irregularities' (*Africa Confidential* 1993).

Accusations of 'election tourism' were also made (see Geisler 1993: 615). In preparation for the observation of the 1997 elections, it was thereupon concluded by the donor community that a more coherent and thorough approach was needed to reach an objective overall judgement concerning the way elections are conducted.

THE CREATION OF THE ELECTION OBSERVATION CENTRE

In the months of May and June 1997, member states of the DDDG (Donors for Development and Democracy Group) – 24 Western donors[1] – held a number of meetings and decided to install an Election Observation Centre (EOC). This small secretariat was to coordinate all activities by and for the DDDG member states' representations in Nairobi.[2] Its major purpose was to provide information to the DDDG missions concerning election rules, constituencies to be visited and what to observe, and to coordinate the travel plans of the DDDG missions.

The Western donors made funds available for a mission to design the EOC and to provide a workplan. The main bottleneck was the uncertainty regarding the date of the election. In principle it should have been held in 1997, five years after the 1992 elections and at the end of President Moi's first term. The elections could be held within a period of some two months after the president decided to dissolve parliament. As a result, the donor group needed to prepare themselves for observing the elections somewhere between August 1997 and April 1998.[3]

The main rationale for collaboration was to avoid a duplication of efforts. Another element was dissatisfaction with the traditional, short-term election observation by hastily prepared teams of international observers. Moreover, it had become more clear in recent years that an election is more than polling day: it includes many phases such as the issuance of ID cards, registration of voters and nomination of candidates. Also, information concerning the election process provided by the relevant authorities and media in Kenya lacked credibility. A need was felt among donor-country representatives to look for *an alternative model for election observation*. The Dutch took the lead and convened a meeting on 28 May to discuss the creation and terms of reference for a 'DDDG Election Observation Secretariat'. Interested parties were Denmark, USA, the EU commission and the UK. Except for the latter, all showed their immediate willingness to combine both funds and personnel in the establishment of a secretariat.[4] It was decided that a next step would be to decide on what resources would be required for the secretariat to function properly and under which precise conditions.

In July, two consultants, Marguerite Garling (EU) and Judith Geist (USAID), provided a proposal for the set up and operation of the Diplomatic Election Observation Secretariat. Three models for election observation were discussed: a) 'Do-it-Yourself'; b) small coordinating Secretariat; c) UN coordinated formal observation.

In the first model the missions would gather information by themselves. At best they would pool their observers and share the information collected. In the third model, observation would be along the traditional lines. A UN-supplied coordinating team would run an independent office and provide a full range of services to the diplomatic community. This option was considered to be a rather inflexible, costly and unsatisfactory one. Thus, in the end, it was recommended to embrace the second model, for two main reasons: 1) some DDDG members had indicated that staff resources were limited and that additional observer capacity would be welcomed, and 2) the UN option would take too much time to establish and fund a well functioning unit, while the elections were near. finally, experience had shown that a UN unit would have difficulties in crafting a joint verdict on the process and outcome of the elections. The structure, functioning and necessary resources of Model 2 were outlined by Garling and Geist as follows: the resources to run it should be acquired from individual diplomatic missions. It was proposed to contract a coordinator with overall supervision, liaison and public relations responsibilities; an information and analysis officer; three or four research assistants; and an office manager. The secretariat should assist in the production of observation forms, news summaries, briefing material, and a deployment strategy as well as with actual field observation. This intermediate model between 'Diplomats Do-It-Yourself and 'UN Stand Alone' was somehow drawn on a model employed in the Ethiopian 1995 elections, but foremost a new experiment.

By early July it became clear that the UN had no intention of setting up a UN electoral Unit during Kenya's 1997 General Elections. This position was explained to the DDDG by a UN representative. He also stressed the need to support local observers. The UN was considering several options in this respect and was pleased to learn that the donors intended to provide financial assistance to domestic groups. That same meeting the donors accepted the consultants' proposal almost in full length except for the hierarchical structure of the Election Observation Centre. Instead they opted to divide responsibilities between at least three to four coordinators. As indicated by the donors in the Terms of Reference to these coordinators, the main tasks of the EOC were to:

- Collect and analyse material concerning election rules and regulations, constituencies and the location of polling stations;
- Monitor local newspapers and journals;
- Liaise with the diplomatic missions of the DDDG;
- Provide advice to the DDDG missions on which constituencies would merit visits and guidance on what to observe;
- Produce checklists for diplomatic observers, for each phase of the election period;
- Coordinate observer travel plans;
- Maintain and distribute records of observer reports;

- Coordinate travel planning of the DDDG missions;
- Maintain close contact with domestic observer organizations, other international observer teams, if any, and with the political parties;
- Maintain close contact with the Electoral Commission.

The EOC was not conceived as a formal entity in its own right, but rather as a tool that the DDDG used to gain a maximum amount of shared information while economizing on diplomatic time spent in official efforts to obtain such. EOC members were to refrain from making public or press statements. At the same time the EOC needed to be transparent about its intentions and working methods to the Electoral Commission of Kenya, the political parties, the domestic observers and the civil society actors at large.

KENYA'S 1997 GENERAL ELECTIONS: THE CONTEXT

The context of the 1997 General Election in Kenya could be characterized as one of rising tension since the beginning of that year. Cabinet reshuffles resulted in the return of certain ministers known to be 'hard-liners' while other, more modest and reform-oriented ministers left. Opposition parties, civil society groups and religious institutions combined efforts and intensified their calls for the abolition of certain repressive laws and for constitutional reforms to create a (more) level playing field before the 1997 General Elections. For this purpose the so-called National Constitutive Assembly was created and had its first Plenary Session in Limuru on 6 April 1997. In the following months its executive arm, the National Convention Executive Committee (NCEC) organized and channelled mass protests to an extent that the government seriously felt threatened. The clashes along the coast which erupted in August and September, whereby especially non-KANU groups became victims of attacks thought to be organized and instigated by (local) KANU-politicians, further deteriorated the situation. It has been claimed that this tragedy was part of an initial phase of a larger state-sponsored plan to undermine the constitutional reform movement.[5] However, international protests and ongoing national pressure finally resulted in the adoption of a minimal reform package through the *Inter-Parties Parliamentary Group* (IPPG). Though criticized by some sections of the opposition, this package enabled the restoration of a more calm environment. For example, freedom of political demonstrations and gatherings was allowed, and Safina (a new opposition party) after a long period of delay and uncertainty, finally registered. It was against this background that Kenyans voted on 29 December 1997 for a new five-year period of local and parliamentary government and for the Presidency.

ACTIVITIES PERFORMED BY THE EOC

By the end of October 1997 the British coordinator arrived and started to prepare the Election Observation Centre (EOC) for operation. He met with a large number of diplomatic missions, Kenyan politicians, domestic observer groups and civil society NGOs, and arranged practical issues such as financing, housing, equipment, collection of election profiles, and relevant documentation from back-issues of newspapers and weekly magazines. By the second half of November the EOC started to become fully operational. All coordinators had arrived and the coordination of election observation by the 24 DDDG missions was fully put into practice. Within the EOC specific tasks were attributed to the coordinators and staff members, as shown in Table 13.1.

The 1997 Kenyan elections can be subdivided into five distinctive phases:

1. Registration of voters (conducted from 22 May to 3 July 1997);
2. Internal political party elections to decide on their candidates ('party primaries') (late November–early December);
3. A two-day period for officially nominating these candidates to the Kenyan Electoral Commission (2–3 December presidential and 8–9 December local and parliamentary candidates);
4. The campaign period (10–28 December); and
5. Election day (including counting of the votes), 29 December and following days.

Table 13.1   Attribution of tasks, DDDG Election Observation Centre[6]

	Co-ordinator for	Political party	In relation with
David Throup	Central	DP	Electoral commission
Judith Geist	Nyanza	FORD-K + FORD-A	Donors
Marcel Rutten	South Rift	SDP + KSC	Media
Palle Svensson	Ukambani	FORD-P	IPPG
Sabitha Raju	Coast	NDP	Gender
Catherine Duhamel	Central Rift	KANU	Human rights NGOs
Jennifer Loten	Nairobi	Ford-P	
EOC	Northern Rift + NEP	Safina	
EOC	North of Eastern		
EOC	Western		

Note: NEP = Northeastern Province.

Registration of Voters

Before the official start of the EOC its coordinators witnessed the voter registration process in some 25 districts. An evaluation of voter registration concluded that up to two million young Kenyans between the ages of 18 and 23 had *not* been issued with their National Identity Cards and thus were denied the right to exercise their franchise.

Registration of voters started on 22 May 1997 and was supposed to last 35 days. The exercise started with controversy over the use of old and new identity cards (*Economic Review* 1997: 30). Allegations were made that in certain areas people were denied registration on the basis of ethnicity (see *Economic Review* 1997a: 20). In other constituencies (for example, Nairobi Westlands) very high rates of registration were recorded or initially wrong voter cards issued (Luo districts of Nyanza Province). Faced with numbers far below the target, the Electoral Commission chairman, Mr Chesoni, extended the voter registration period by a paltry two days and then grudgingly added another few days, with 3 July being the final day. finally slightly over 9 million people registered.

Party Primaries

Deployment plans and checklists for observation of the party primaries were ready by the end of November. Detailed information on each constituency had been collected from newspapers, weekly magazines and knowledgeable individuals. It was used in the analysis for determining which constituencies needed priority in the observation exercise. All of this information was provided to the diplomatic observers in a meeting on 24 November. Representatives of domestic observer groups were also present at this meeting. They shared their knowledge and experiences with the donor community.

Mainly the British, Dutch and Canadian diplomats observed the party primaries. Based on reports for KANU, DP, NDP and Ford-K primaries from some 24 districts, the EOC produced a short report, which was presented to the DDDG. It was concluded that in general the primary process was done fairly similarly to the one in 1992. Some 2 million Kenyans participated in the selection of their parties' candidates. Among the main differences, though, was the less important role played by the Provincial Administration. Problems were greatest in urban areas. Notwithstanding this observation, and despite violence in Likoni, and along the Trans Mara-Kisii border, the November–December 1997 party primaries were conducted in an environment much less constrained by ethnic violence than in 1992.

Nomination of Parliamentary and Civic Candidates

After the party primaries a detailed 'plan of action' was produced by the EOC to streamline the activities and division of labour. Nomination observation forms were produced and handed out, together with constituency profiles, and other relevant information, to the international observers. Certain constituencies had been ear-marked as potential problem areas needing observation. On 8 and 9 December, some 11 Western missions participated in the observations. Over 50 observers visited a similar number of constituencies. Again Dutch, British and Canadian observers provided the bulk of the observers. Observation forms had to be returned to the Centre by 10 December. If serious incidents happened contact was to be made with the EOC. The EOC received complaints by political parties about problems in Siaya and Nandi areas; diplomatic observers and the EOC made checks in those districts. The DDDG Chair contacted the Electoral Commission of Kenya and summarized the international observers' concerns for Nandi, where opposition parliamentary and civic candidates were denied clearance of their nomination papers. In the end, no cases of candidates being barred from the nomination process were reported for this area. In contrast to 1992, the nomination process on 8 and 9 December was more peaceful and conducted in greater accordance with the regulations. Most nomination centres opened on time and were efficiently organized. This time problems seem to have come from interference by party headquarters. Sometimes at the last moment attempts were made to replace the official candidate by another person (such as in the case of KANU in Kajiado Central and South constituencies).

The Campaign Period

On 10 December the Kenyan general elections 1997 campaign period officially started. The EOC informed all missions in preparation for the campaign observation and handed out campaign rally checklists and information packages. Deployment plans for the period up to 21 December were distributed on 15 December. It also indicated areas where the EOC would like to send diplomatic observers.

The EOC collected details on campaign programmes for the political parties. This was hard to obtain, and mainly restricted to the presidential candidates. Likewise, dates, venues and times could easily change. This hampered the observation of the campaign period. Besides, the ability to hold political rallies and access to the media are an important aspect of observation. From July 1997 the Kenya Human Rights Commission (KHRC) in partnership with 'Article 19' (the International Centre Against Censorship, based in London) monitored the (state-owned) Kenya Broadcasting Corporation (KBC) radio and television coverage of political activity in the period leading up to the 1997 General Election. KHRC published monthly reports in both a quantitative (air-time for political parties) as well as qualitative sense (negative/positive) (see KHRC and Article 19).

During the months of July, August and October, coverage of KANU and President Moi took up more than 80 to 90 per cent of KBC television and radio reports. By contrast, its coverage of the opposition was some 5–10 per cent only – and mostly negative. Following the IPPG reforms in early November and the subsequent amendment of the Kenyan Broadcasting Act, requiring KBC to maintain a fair balance in allocating air-time between the different parties, the time allocated to the opposition increased dramatically, rising from 10 to 32 per cent in the last week. However, 96 per cent of opposition coverage in week four was negative. From the start of the official campaign onwards, KBC Television and radio returned to giving a disproportionate amount of time to KANU and President Moi. Coverage of the opposition parties and candidates was much more equal in the print media. Journalists were permitted to record the process and to take photographs. International observers witnessed their presence on the nomination days and during the campaign period.

International observers witnessed bribery and intimidation of minority party supporters in many constituencies throughout the election period. Nevertheless, in general the electoral process was considered more peaceful than in 1992. So-called KANU zones, constituencies declared to be 'no-go' areas by KANU politicians, were more or less absent this time. In opposition areas threats were mainly directed at KANU activists. Few opposition meetings were prohibited or interfered with by the Provincial Administration or police. There were exceptions, however, including the use of tear gas against opposition presidential candidates and life threats to, among others, Mr Kandie, the opponent to President Moi (see Andreassen 1998). Female candidates in particular complained that they were singled out for attacks purely on the basis of their gender.

Voting Day

Towards 19 December, the workload at the centre reached its maximum levels. Because of public holidays in the week before the General Election Day the time-span to finalize the deployment plan, prepare the field Guidance Manual and the 'Observation Kit', and organize an instruction meeting with all observers was minimal.

The *Diplomatic Election Observers field Guidance* contained general guidelines for observers (for example, code of ethics, dealings with the press, security) and gave detailed information concerning the Kenyan electoral process (for example, election rules, voting and counting procedures and irregularities). It also included election observation forms, investigation and reporting guidelines. The EOC had made arrangements for the observers to immediately report to the Centre on 29 December if serious incidents occured. The 'Observation Kit' contained, among others things, constituency profiles, map of the area, lists of returning officers, Electoral Commissioners, district electoral coordinators, polling stations and team deployment details. Also included were the official Electoral Commission of Kenya Election Manual, IED Election Observer (Training) Manual, vehicle posters, an international observers T-shirt and Electoral Commission of Kenya observer badges. Observers also carried a letter of accreditation. On 19 December all international observers were instructed. That same day the DDDG also informed the international press of their plans for the observation of the elections. By 24 December all materials had been handed out to the diplomatic missions.

Most diplomats left one or two days before 29 December, so as to witness the opening of the polling stations, scheduled at 6.00 a.m. However, the distribution of ballot papers was flawed at three stages: first, from the printers in Britain, secondly, from the central stores of the Electoral Commission in Kenya; and finally by returning officers in many constituencies.[7] As a result many polling stations opened late. The Electoral Commission, in an attempt to overcome this problem, extended the poll to Tuesday 30 December. Unfortunately, this announcement came rather late and was contradictory, creating considerable confusion in many areas.

The Count

The count of the Kenya 1997 elections started on 30 December and was done at constituency level in a central counting hall. There were too few counting officials and the count took far too long: in certain areas up to a week. Still, the count was conducted in a fair and transparent manner in most constituencies, and intimidation and/or rigging were witnessed or are suspected to have taken place in about 15 constituencies. Incidents reported include attempts to smuggle filled ballot papers into the counting hall; arrival of ballot boxes after the count had begun, usually without party seals or agents; counting clerks caught attempting to spoil ballot papers; deputy returning officers kidnapped; and the mishandling of empty ballot papers in the possession of Commission officials. The EOC coordinators witnessed in person particular serious irregularities at the count of Westlands constituency. Among the problems observed were interference by State House officials; change of final result in favour of the KANU candidate for parliament; refusal of a recount; attempts by the election officials to remove the ballot boxes without sealing them; and opening all the boxes and intermingling of ballots from different polling stations to reduce the number of ballot boxes. It was claimed that the latter was done on the instruction of the Electoral Commission because of lack of storage capacity.[8] In conclusion, especially with reference to this case, the idea of having a small secretariat with observing capacity worked very well.

Reporting the Observations

While following the Westlands situation closely the EOC staff members entered data from 500 polling stations which had been gathered by more than 150 international observers who had visited 115 constituencies. On 2 January they had all reported back to the EOC for a debriefing session. Experiences were shared in small regional groups and in plenary discussions. This qualitative information was added to the quantitative analysis of the observation forms. By 4 January, the EOC finalized its report on the overall conduct of the elections, including information on serious irregularities. Graphs and tables showing the 107 over 103 victory for KANU were also included.

The final report was forwarded to the DDDG missions. It concluded that the EOC was of the opinion that the win by President Moi of the presidential election was, though at some stages flawed, 'acceptable'. The most important conclusion, however, was that in '5 per cent of the Parliamentary contests, the irregularities in the poll and count were so great as to invalidate the elections in these particular constituencies and, consequently, the legitimacy of the overall KANU majority in the

National Assembly'. According to the EOC in at least three constituencies (Westlands, Kitui West and Changamwe) the count had been rigged in favour of KANU. In other words, the 107–103 majority should have been a 106–104 victory for the opposition. A meeting with all ambassadors was held the next day to discuss the report. It was agreed to follow up on certain issues raised by the meeting, such as collecting information from domestic observers to verify and extend the information on a number of constituencies, which had been earmarked as having suffered from 'serious irregularities'. On 8 January the draft report was discussed with a core group of the DDDG. Adjustments were made along the lines of editing the text to maximize clarity, update or correct information on the outcome of the elections and to rephrase the text along more diplomatic lines. For example, the 'legitimacy' issue was dropped. Among the arguments used was the *sub judice* rule.[9] Publication of the report might interfere with coming petitions by contenders against the outcome of the elections. It was agreed that following the last type of adjustment the internal EOC report would be turned into a DDDG report and should be named as such. The EOC members finalized this version on 9 January and handed it in to the chair of the DDDG for distribution among its members. It was hoped that in one week's time the report could be made public. A small delegation of ambassadors would visit the Electoral Commission for this purpose as well. The political parties were also earmarked as among the likely receivers of the report.

Most members of the EOC left by the middle of January. A few stayed and continued gathering information from domestic observers, journalists and representatives of political parties, churches and civic rights NGOs. A number of constituencies were revisited again to do follow-up research to obtain more detailed knowledge of the elections. One major activity was the screening of events in the Molo and Kilgoris constituencies. fights had started in the Laikipia area, which had at a certain stage an undeniable political character and had spread by 25 January to the Njoro area south of Nakuru in Molo constituency. fights between Kalenjin and Kikuyu groups were witnessed and taped on video. These findings were reported to the international press. finally, by late January a third version of the international observers' report was sent to all missions. This version had been slightly adjusted and the British High Commission acted as chief editor. Except for a few lines with references to the 1992 elections, no essential changes had been made to the version handed in by 9 January. The main change was that recommendations to the ECK for coming elections had become an integral part of the report again. It seemed as if the report had simply been shelved. It took another two weeks until the report was made public and discussed in the Kenyan press on 15 February.

EVALUATION OF PERFORMED ACTIVITIES AND SUGGESTIONS FOR IMPROVEMENT

The main aim of the Election Observation Centre was to facilitate and support the observation of the 1997 Kenya elections by the diplomatic missions. In particular its task was to coordinate the election observation by advising where, when and how to observe the elections.

The EOC performed all of these specific tasks requested by the DDDG. Throughout the observation period the missions were provided with maps and constituency profiles with information on candidates and specifics of their constituencies. Also, practical information was forwarded on accommodation and transport. The EOC frequently contacted (most of) the political parties, individual politicians and domestic observer organizations (the IED, NCCK and Catholic Justice and Peace Commission, Kenya Human Rights Commission, among others). For logistical matters the EOC contacted the Electoral Commission of Kenya (for example on provision of the Kenya Election Manual and the location of polling stations). It is thought that the coordination of the missions' activities resulted in better reporting and more knowledge and understanding of the Kenya 1997 elections as compared to the 1992 observation exercise. The idea to optimize the availability of manpower and financial means and to share information gathered by the individual missions to get detailed and insight on the preparation period for the vote and the voting process on election day itself materialized rather well.

Still, there is room for improvement. Among the main problems experienced during the period of coordination and observation, two should be singled out:

a) problems within the operations of the Election Observation Centre (internal problems);
b) problems outside the operations of the Election Observation Centre (external problems).

It should be kept in mind that there is sometimes no clearcut division between these two types of problems. Also, one should keep in mind that some of the problems experienced are due completely to the experimental character of this project.

Problems in Relation to the Operations of the Election Observation Centre

The mixed professional background of the EOC members (historian, geographer, political scientist, human rights lawyer), their knowledge of the country and its people, and experience in election observation allowed for addressing the broad variety of tasks needed to coordinate the observation activities. Still, some issues need attention:

- The late announcement of election day is considered to be a major factor in frustrating a timely, clear and overall comprehensive start of the Election Observation Centre. The coordinators arrived rather late and at separate moments.
- For a centre without an official overall leader, the Plan of Action proved to be a very useful tool. It showed in detail deadlines to be matched, tasks to be performed and meetings to attend. It assisted also in the communication between the coordinators, who at times themselves were out in the field observing.
- A total of four people is not sufficient to run the EOC. There is, in particular, tension between coordinating tasks and observing duties. In that sense it should be mentioned that the EOC profited very much from staff members that volunteered their services.
- In principle, the tasks within the Centre had been divided between the coordinators on a regional basis. Yet, because of lack of coordinators some areas were not specifically

assigned (for example, Northern Rift and North of Eastern). The initial idea to coordinate all observations in one region under one person did not materialize. In practice, it turned out to be more effective to start from the perspective of linking EOC staff to specific embassies. At certain moments this meant that the logistics workload prohibited a thorough analysis of the elections.

* The political parties of Kenya are not well organized. As a result, the provision of information to the missions by the EOC was seriously hampered and time consuming. Campaign meetings in particular suffered a lack of detailed information for observers because dates and venues were either known very late or changed at the last moment.

Some recommendations on the division of labour within the EOC are the following:

* Timely arrangements should be made for recruitment of co-ordinators and other members of staff;
* Preferably coordinators and staff members should have a mixed professional background;
* Coordinators and staff members should be familiar with Kenya and its politics;
* Coordinators should be stationed at the EOC office; modest travelling is recommended;
* Budget for a personal assistant at the EOC to each coordinator to share the workload. Having a good knowledge of Kenya (its geography) and having a wide network of contacts is an advantage in assuring the collection of up-to-date information (logistics as well as content), especially for the more remote areas. In this respect, a local assistant is very helpful;
* Lists of names and contact addresses of all local coordinators should be made available to the EOC and vice versa. Local observers should play a more profound role in indicating to the international observers certain hot-spot areas.

Problems in Relation to the Deployment of DDDG Missions

First and foremost, note that elthough 22 missions and two international organizations were united in one group of donors, they still showed a broad diversity concerning:

- (extra) financial means available;
- total personnel available;
- flexibility in supplying personnel;
- knowledge of Kenya and its politics;
- understanding of the (particularities of the) constituency representation system (Westminster 'winner-takes-all' system);
- devotion and interest in careful observation;
- willingness to share information;
- involvement (otherwise) in the elections (for example, supporting domestic observers).

The above mix of characteristics results in a continuum where we find, on the one extreme, countries that provide financial means and many flexible, knowledgeable and devoted persons, while on the other extreme, missions that lack in all of these aspects. In some cases, national law or politics apparently prohibits a full participation in the diplomatic observation exercise (for example, France, UK and Germany). In others, it is because these missions are small and/or not so knowledgeable concerning Kenyan politics. With respect to a lack of personnel we should mention that Denmark and Norway were able to overcome the rather limited size of their embassy staff by providing international observers from their countries. However, the Scandinavian observers only arrived some two weeks before the general elections.[10] Finally, some countries were to a larger extent involved in the election observation exercise because they financed most of the costs of the EOC (notably the Danes, Swedes, Finns, Swiss and Dutch missions) or assisted by providing equipment and housing (Japanese and Australians). Likewise, and even more costly, some missions (Denmark, the Netherlands, Sweden and UK) enabled the recruitment and training of the local observers by providing US$1.5 million to three Kenyan NGOs (the National Council of Churches of Kenya, the Catholic Justice and Peace Commission, and the Institute for Education in Democracy). finally, the UK was also involved in the elections by way of British companies providing ballot boxes and ballot papers. It should be noted that this aspect resulted in the British High Commission, in the view of some groups in Kenyan society, being partisan on one side.

The following observations have been made:

Flexibility in deployment of international observers is a necessary precondition in a situation where the full and constant coverage of all constituencies is not possible. In the case of the Kenya 1997 elections approximately 30 observers were available in the period up to election day, 29 December. This means that even if they were able to cover two constituencies at a time, only about 30 per cent of the areas could be visited. By directing observers to 'most-needed' venues the most effective use is made of the manpower available and the quality of the overall observation exercise can be enhanced. Some countries, notably the Dutch, opted for a flexible attitude towards deployment of personnel. However, a flexible set-up of election observation also brings along some disadvantages, for the mission and for the EOC. The short intervals between party primaries, nomination day, campaign period and the actual election day, and the preparations needed to guide the observers, call for a fixed deployment schedule. When this is not possible or not wanted, a disproportionate amount of time has to be devoted to making last-minute enquiries and arrangements in practical matters (transport, accommodation) and also regarding content (up-to-date newspaper cuttings, copies of area profiles, former observation reports, maps). The risk of such late arrangements on the side of the diplomatic missions is that at the crucial last moment transport and manpower are not available. Likewise, for the EOC it means that fulfilling the above requirements leaves less time for analysis of observation reports and getting/keeping in close contact with political parties, media, local groups, and so on.

As a result of this mixture in capabilities, attitudes and interests, especially in the period proceeding 29 December, only a small core group of countries performed most of the observations. For example, campaign and nomination observations were foremost left to UK, Denmark, Sweden, Canada and the Netherlands. The latter country was at one time responsible for one-third of all observers! In some respects this is the result of some missions being rather small. On the other hand, a country like the USA, having a huge observing capacity, opted not to co-operate closely with the EOC.

The mixed background of the DDDG missions also interfered with the final phase of the election observation: reporting.

Regrettably, the final report provided to the DDDG missions took too long to be made public. The delay must have frustrated other missions, because according to information from the *Daily Nation* newspaper, one of the embassies had handed to one of the *Nation*'s reporters the 'serious irregularities' document. In the end, the delay in presenting the full results of the international election observation backfired on the donor community, and on the British in particular (see for example, *Economic Review*, 26 Jan. 1998: 24–6: 'Donor Conspiracy – Western Countries Opt to Hide Election Findings', and 23 Feb. 1998: 25–6: 'The Truth Is Out – Embassies of the Major Western Donor Countries Altered International Observers' Report').

The following recommendations concerning the deployment of DDDG missions could be made:

- Allocate one contact person plus one or two assistants at the embassy.
- Provide in advance, and update constantly, an overview of availability of personnel.
- Preferably locate diplomats in areas they are familiar with, within a set-up that starts from a 'flexibility' approach.
- At mission level, there should be a sharing of information by the diplomatic observers by exchanging copies of observation reports and/or small meetings before and after each phase in the elections. Likewise, observers should contact directly and share information with colleagues who visited a constituency earlier or are very knowledgeable about the area.
- Local observer groups have been of major assistance to the EOC's activities in providing background data on specific areas and people. These groups are capable of playing the role of the memory of election observation. Before the onset of the elections they shared their experiences from the 1992 elections with the ever-rotating diplomats. Still, collaboration between the two groups of observers should be improved.[11] Support to these groups should be part of any observation exercise in Africa. Local capacity-building needs to be among the first priorities.
- Make sure that embassies' means of transport are claimed in advance irrespective of the destination and exact dates of travel.

- Deploy drivers in such a way that they are able to vote on election day in the constituency where they are registered.
- Discuss, check and counter-check the statements made in the final report by the donor community. Be as sober as possible in claiming irregularities. Be careful in using information, including election results from the local newspapers.[12] However, there is no need to use vague formulations out of fear of interfering with possible election petitions. The *sub judice* rule does not apply to the donor's report. Publication of the report should not extend beyond a period of three weeks after election day, and should be made available to the Kenyan public at large.
- In general, it is recommended that missions of former colonial rulers should *not* head the donor community's observations. This, in particular, includes the writing up of the final report. Likewise (private companies of) former colonial rulers should be extremely reluctant to be involved in the provision of ballot boxes and ballot papers. The reason is that, notwithstanding the quality of the services provided (for example, no mistakes on ballot papers), interested groups will always point, rightly or wrongly, to the former close links and potential interests of the former colonizing country.
- It should be realized that in years to come other diplomats will be present at the foreign missions. To prepare these observers, a video was made for the Dutch Embassy showing, among other things, the election and count in Kajiado Central Constituency. This video should be used in training diplomats in coming elections.

CONCLUSION

In conclusion it must be stressed that the experiment of a new model of international election observation in Kenya has largely been successful. The combination of a small group of professional, academic election observation coordinators, most of them Kenya specialist, and of having a large political network built over many years, together with a large group of diplomatic observers stationed in Kenya, having specific political and social networks, was helpful in collecting detailed information on recent political developments there. It is important to realize that no other model is able to provide this unique blend of relevant information-gathering networks.[13]

In short, the main *positive aspects* of the Kenyan 'EOC-diplomats' model are:

- Diplomats are familiar with the area, the population and politics of the country.
- The use of diplomats as international observers is very cost efficient. In some respects it is part of their daily job, while others spend their free time. The EOC running costs are estimated at US$30,000 (excluding salaries/DSA of the coordinators).
- Election observation is done over a long period, allowing for a better understanding of the election process itself as well as further enhancing the diplomats knowledge of Kenya.
- Cooperation and sharing of information between diplomatic missions as well as with Kenyan society at large (political parties, NGOs, clergy) is strengthened and might also contribute to a better knowledge of the country.
- The unified and coordinated observation exercise results in a single donor observation report. This enhances chances of their voice being heard and appropriate action taken by all parties involved.

Negative outcomes of the experiment are:

- Too large a variety in attitudes of embassies towards the observation of the elections. In the end it all comes down to the interest shown and time and energy devoted by the local diplomats in the election observation exercise.
- Too long a delay in publishing the final report. This created irritation between diplomatic missions and, in the end, resulted in two versions circulating in the Kenyan press. This is likely to be (mis)interpreted by the Kenyan public.

Among the main objections made to diplomats is that they are not willing to speak out clearly and loudly if irregularities are observed. One should, however, realize that the group of diplomats is diverse. The Kenyan experiment has shown that as a result it is most unlikely that the final verdict will not be made public. In the group of foreign missions some will not allow this to happen. Moreover, the group of coordinators and the domestic observers also act as a kind of watchdog. finally, some of the negative aspects of the model can be overcome in time, while the advantages far outweigh the possible problems. Therefore, implementation of this model of election observation in other African countries is sincerely recommended. A prerequisite is complementary assistance in the recruitment and training of domestic observers. A nation-wide coverage of polling stations by domestic observer groups is an integral element of the new model.

In summary, the new approach of election observation by diplomats in collaboration with a group of professional coordinators is more cost efficient, sustainable and proficient than the old model of flying in election observers from abroad.[14] first, diplomats remain in the country and continue to meet, discuss and make policies relevant to the host country. This will in the short and middle run strengthen the consistency of the Western donors' reactions to the process of democratization: the donors' 'memory' is more profoundly present for the government of the host country. Second, contacts between the diplomatic community, civil society and political parties (opposition and government alike) will be intensified. Third, support to domestic observer groups allows for the existence and further development of a source of information on local politics and election observation. This local 'memory' is also of major importance in preparations for coming elections.

To some countries (host and observing alike) this might be a less welcome scenario.[15] As a code of conduct for the host country it should allow resident diplomats to observe the elections, while observing countries should likewise refrain from flying in observers from abroad. This scenario should only be employed as a last option if an insufficient number of local diplomats are available to observe the elections in a substantial and profound way. These observers, who should all have a good knowledge of local politics, should follow the instructions and guidelines explained in training sessions set out by the coordinating Election Observation Centre. They should report to the EOC, and refrain from individual statements.

I strongly believe that under the old model chances of legitimizing fraudulent elections are higher. As a result, this approach should be abandoned altogether. The new model should become an essential element of the new code of conduct for election observation, to an extent that failure to implement it renders, at beforehand, any election 'not free and fair'.

NOTES

I am grateful to Mr N. Braakhuis and Dr F. Grignon for information and comments on a draft version of this chapter.

1. DDDG members are Australia, Austria, Belgium, Canada, Czech Republic, Denmark, finland, France, Germany, Greece, Hungary, Italy, Japan, the Netherlands, Norway, Poland, Portugal, Spain, Sweden, Switzerland, United Kingdom, United States, European Union and UNDP.

2. The staff members of the EOC consisted of four coordinators: Dr Judith Geist (USAID), Prof. Palle Svensson (Denmark – Aarhus University), Dr David Throup (British Foreign Office) and Dr Marcel Rutten (Netherlands – ASC). In addition, full-time assistance was provided by Ms. Catherine Duhamel (Canada) and Ms. Sabitha Raju (UK), while Dr François Grignon (France – IFRA), Mr Charles Hornsby (UK – Shell), Mr Peter Njenga (Kenya – SNV) and Mr Ralph Peters (Germany) contributed to the EOC's operations for short periods. Overall logistics and financial management was in the hands of Mrs Laurie Rees (UK).

3. The legal parameters required that parliament be dissolved no later than 25 January 1998 and an election held within 90 days.

4. The British, after some hesitation because of directions from the London office, joined later. They realized that USAID and the EU political counsellors in Nairobi were serious with their ideas of a jointly funded Election Observation Centre, and delegated Mr David Throup, a Foreign Office-employed scholar who specializes on Kenya and elections in Africa, to the secretariat, as well as Ms. Laurie Rees as office manager. No direct British funds were made available, however, as they opted to finance local observer groups only.

5. See, for example, Kenya Human Rights Commission, *Kayas of Deprivation, Kayas of Blood – Violence, Ethnicity and the State in Coastal Kenya* (Nairobi 1997).

6. In addition, Dr François Grignon (France – IFRA) should be mentioned, who assisted Palle Svensson in coordinating efforts in Ukamabani. He also made available detailed maps of the constituencies. Mr Charles Hornsby, a former aide to David Throup in 1992, had come from Ghana to assist the EOC during the last week of December and early days of January 1998. He assisted in analysing election results by the provision of figures showing turn-out, presidential and parliamentary results per province, and the like. David Throup (by

interviewing Paul Muite) and Marcel Rutten (meetings with Richard Leakey) did information-gathering from Safina. Rutten also was in close contact with Ford-K politicians and activists.

7.   These problems were particularly acute in the local government elections but affected some parliamentary and presidential polls as well. In some polling stations ballot books were not delivered, or the names of candidates and symbols of political parties were missing or wrongly printed.

8.   It is also noteworthy that the result announced by the returning officer, 18,590 for KANU against 17,721 for DP, which was also broadcast on radio and appeared in the print media, conflicted with the result endorsed by all opposition parties and observers (17,829 for DP against 17,790 for KANU) as well as with the official result published by the Electoral Commission of Kenya of 17,882 (KANU) to 17,877 (DP).

9.   The term *sub judice* literally means 'under judicial consideration'. Derived from it is the *Sub Judice* Rule: It is undoubted law that, when litigation is pending and actively in suit before the court, no one shall comment on it in such a way that there is a real and substantial danger of prejudice to the trial of the action (see Nowrojee 1997: 1).

10. In many constituencies, indeed, in perhaps two-thirds, the party primary is as, if not even more, important than the general election in selecting Kenya's future Members of Parliament and local councillors. In that respect, we need to conclude that the presence of international observers was very crucial. However, reasoning from the same argument, the number of international observers during these days should be further increased in coming elections.

11. This remark is made notwithstanding the fact that the domestic observers made premature statements on the 'free and fairness' of the elections. At the same moment problems came to a head in Westlands, the domestic observers gave a press conference some 500 metres from the Westlands Counting hall, declaring that 'the results do on the whole reflect the wishes of the Kenyan voters'. This also increased tensions between and within the three participating organizations, the IED, CJPC and NCCK.

12. In the initial analysis based on election results published in the local daily newspapers it seemed as if there were an above 100 per cent turnout in Molo Constituency. Later it became clear that the Molo number of registered voters had been interchanged with the one of Kuresoi. Likewise, the total number of votes cast and the number of valid votes were sometimes mixed up in the daily newspapers. This interferes especially with the analysis of the number of votes cast for the presidency as compared to those cast for the parliamentary election. finally, the official figures of the Electoral Commission of Kenya also have to be checked carefully. For example, in the Presidential Results per Constituency overview published on 14 January the figures for Kipipiri are the ones of Maragwa. These figures now suggest a turn-out of 105.87 per cent. Also, the results for Moi and Ngilu in Yata Constituency have been interchanged to the detriment of the latter.

13. (Political) diplomats have contacts with journalists, politicians, human rights groups, international donors, and the like. This amounts to an

up-to-date package of views and relevant information which aids profound understanding of the politics and main issues at stake, and is
helpful in streamlining the election observation exercise.

14. The call to do away with election tourism and for a large and well-
trained group of international observers can be heard nowadays. Yet it
is my opinion that a group of some 100 professional international observers, moving from one election to another, will not be able to form
detailed and up-to-date local contacts and obtain specific country
knowledge. This model cannot offer the same quality of observation.
Even more importantly, this model will not be able to provide hands for
a follow-up to the strengthening of the democratization process, as the
mix of local diplomats and a small group of country specialist coordinators would.

15. While observing in Narok District a local MP candidate and incumbent
Minister of the Cabinet told two local observers that 'if it was to him
they would not be allowed to observe the elections'. Likewise, the
Kenyan government did not allow resident diplomats to observe the
1992 elections (see Geisler 1993: 614).

REFERENCES

Andreassen, B. 1998. 'Report from a Post-election Visit to Kabarnet Town,
Baringo Central' (Nairobi).
Andreassen, B., G. Geisler and A. Tostensen, 1992. 'Setting a Standard for
Africa? – Lessons from the 1991 Zambian Elections', Report 1992: 5
(Bergen: Chr. Michelsen Institute).
Barkan, J.D. 1993. 'Kenya: Lessons from a Flawed Election', *Journal of
Democracy* 4(3): 85–99.
DDDG, 1998. 'Final Report Kenya General Elections 1997' (Nairobi: the
Donors' Democratic Development Group).
Duhamel, C. 1997. *Diplomatic Election Observers Field Guidance* (Nairobi: Donors'
Democratic Development Group Election Observation Centre, Dec.).
ECK, 1997. Press Conference, 31 Dec., Nairobi.
ECK, 1998. Press Conference, 4 Jan., Nairobi.
ECK, 1998. Parliamentary Election Results per Constituency (Nairobi, 11 Jan.
1998).
Elklit, J. and P. Svensson, 1997. 'The Rise of Election Monitoring: What
Makes Elections Free and Fair?' *Journal of Democracy* 8(3): 32–46.
EOC, 1997. The Party Primaries (Nairobi).
EOC, 1998. 'Kenya General Elections 1997 Final Report – for Donors'
Democratic Development Group' (Nairobi).
Garling, M. and J. Geist, 1997. 'Diplomatic Election Observation Secretariat –
Proposed Structure and Operation' (Nairobi).
Geisler, G. 1993. 'Fair? What has fairness got to do with it? Vagaries of
Election Observations and Democratic Standards', *Journal of Modern African
Studies* 31(4): 613–37.
IED, 1996. *The Electoral Environment in Kenya – a Research Project Report* (Nairobi:
Institute for Education in Democracy).

IED, CJPC and NCCK, 1998. 'Final Statement on Kenya 1997 General Elections', Nairobi, 3 Jan.

KHRC, 1997. *Kayas of Deprivation, Kayas of Blood – Violence, Ethnicity and the State in Coastal Kenya* (Nairobi: KHRC).

KHRC and Article 19, 1997. 'Elections '97: Media Watch – Media Monitoring in Kenya, July–December 1997 Reports' (Nairobi).

Mulei, C. 1996. 'Historical Perspectives of Elections in Kenya', in the Institute for Education and Democracy, *The Electoral Environment in Kenya – A Research Project Report, Institute for Education in Democracy* (Nairobi: IED), pp. 24–39.

NEMU, 1993. *The Multi-Party General Elections in Kenya – 29 December 1992*, the Report of the National Election Monitoring Unit (Nairobi).

Nowrojee, P. 1997. 'The Sub-Judice Rule', paper presented at the workshop on court/legal reporting of the Media Institute, held at the Professional Centre, Nairobi, 21–2 Nov. 1997.

Rutten, M. 1998. 'Kenya General Elections 1997 – Implementing a New Model for International Election Observation in Africa', Draft Report submitted to Royal Netherlands Embassy – Nairobi / African Studies Centre – Leiden, March.

Periodicals Consulted:

Africa Confidential 33(25), 1992, 'Kenya: Democracy Could be the Loser'.

Africa Confidential 34(1), 1993, 'Kenya: Failing the Democracy Test'.

Economic Review (Nairobi), 26 May 1997, p. 30, 'Elections '97: Invalid Cards? – New Voters Cards May Not Comply with the Law'.

Economic Review, 30 June 1997a, p. 20, 'Registration Controversy – Kajiado North Luos Claim Bias'.

Economic Review, 26 Jan. 1998, pp. 24–6, 'Donor Conspiracy – Western Countries Opt to Hide Election Findings'.

Economic Review, 23 Feb. 1998a, pp. 25–6, 'The Truth Is Out – Embassies of the Major Western Donor Countries Altered International Observers' Report'.

Weekly Review (Nairobi), 12 March 1993, 'Nemu's Verdict on the Polls'.

Index

321